# Breakthrough 'Boys

# Breakthrough 'Boys

The Story of the 1971 Super Bowl
Champion Dallas Cowboys

Jaime Aron

MVP
BOOKS

*For Dorita and Hertzel, Marlene and Ron*

First published in 2011 by MVP Books, an imprint of MBI Publishing Company and the Quayside Publishing Group, 400 First Avenue North, Suite 300, Minneapolis, MN 55401 USA

MVP Books titles are also available at discounts in bulk quantity for industrial or sales-promotional use. For details write to Special Sales Manager at Quayside Publishing Group, 400 First Avenue North, Suite 300, Minneapolis, MN 55401 USA.

To find out more about our books, visit us online at www.mvpbooks.com.


ISBN-13: 978-0-7603-4039-4

Library of Congress Cataloging-in-Publication Data

Aron, Jaime.

Breakthrough 'boys : when the Dallas Cowboys went from next year's champions to America's team / Jaime Aron.

p. cm.

ISBN 978-0-7603-4039-4 (hb w/ jkt)

1. Dallas Cowboys (Football team)--History. I. Title.

GV956.D3A75 2011

796.332'64097642812--dc22

2011010553

Editor: Adam Brunner

Design manager: Brenda C. Canales

Book designer: Helena Shimizu

Cover designer: Diana Boger

Front Cover Photo Credit: AP Images


Printed in the U.S.A.

# Contents

# Introduction

**B**OB LILLY COULDN'T TAKE IT ANY MORE. Another season was about to end with a loss, another championship opportunity missed. Only this time the Dallas Cowboys blew it in the final game, the Super Bowl. And they pretty much gave it away.

Lilly's rage and frustration got the best of him after a 32-yard field goal put the Baltimore Colts ahead 16–13 with five seconds left in the deciding game of the 1970 NFL season. In one motion, he pried off his helmet, cranked his left arm, and hurled his headgear high and far—nearly 50 yards by the time it stopped tumbling across the artificial turf, the padding and chin strap unable to last the whole ride.

The game wasn't done, though. The Cowboys downed the kickoff at the 40-yard line and had one last snap.

Understudy Roger Staubach watched from the sideline as he'd done all afternoon—since early October, really—as starting quarterback Craig Morton called out the signals. Morton dropped back and threw deep, hoping for something to finally go his way this afternoon. His pass was caught, all right, but by Baltimore safety Jerry Logan. Super Bowl V was finished now, and the Dallas Cowboys still hadn't won the big one.

What was it about this franchise?

—★—

Nowadays, the Dallas Cowboys are "America's Team," the NFL's flagship franchise. Regardless of how many games they win, the Cowboys remain TV darlings and merchandising mavens. With shimmying cheerleaders who are an international sensation in their own right, this club seems to have been born with a silver-and-blue spoon in its mouth.

Only that's not true. Not even close.

The Cowboys got off to the sorriest start imaginable. Their first offices were inside an auto club. This football team practiced at a condemned baseball stadium with varmints crawling around the locker room. Home games were played at another old stadium, and they shared it with a team from a rival league.

They joined the NFL too late to take part in that season's college draft, so the initial lineup was filled with players other teams didn't want. No surprise then that they didn't win a single game that year. Losing records continued for three, four, five seasons. When fans became restless and wanted a new coach, the owner gave his man a 10-year contract extension. Oh well. It was his money—and he was losing plenty of it.

Progress came in the sixth year. They broke even in the standings and on the financial ledger. They also finally made the postseason, a battle of runners-up called the Playoff Bowl. Giddy just to be there, they lost 35–3.

This pushed the franchise into the next phase of its evolution. The Cowboys were about to become one of the best teams in the NFL.

They just couldn't become *the* best.

In 1966 and '67, they lost the games that would've sent them to the first two Super Bowls. The first time, they were wide-eyed overachievers who showed how far they'd come by taking the venerable Green Bay Packers down to the final minutes. The second time was a rematch known as the Ice Bowl. Primed to knock off the mighty champs, the upstarts faced a kickoff temperature of minus 13, with a wind chill of 40 below. They lost on a quarterback sneak in the final minute.

"You can tell the real Cowboys," Coach Tom Landry said. "They're the ones with the frozen fingers and broken hearts."

No expansion team had become so good, so fast. But after the Cowboys got bounced from the playoffs in the first round the next two seasons, they headed into the 1970s saddled with a reputation as under-achievers. They were no longer a growing power. Other up-and-coming clubs soared right past the Cowboys.

- The Minnesota Vikings began a year after the Cowboys but made it to Super Bowl IV.

- The New York Jets started in the rival American Football League the same year the Cowboys debuted in the NFL and won Super Bowl III.
- The Kansas City Chiefs—who began in 1960 as the Dallas Texans, the club that shared the Cotton Bowl with the start-up Cowboys—played in the first Super Bowl and won Super Bowl IV.

The success of the Chiefs was a huge slap in the face for Cowboys fans, leaving them feeling as if they'd backed the wrong horse. In the stands at Super Bowl IV, someone hung a banner that read, "Come home, Dallas Texans."

In 1970, the Cowboys seemed to be moving in reverse. After all those years of climbing, they were sliding back down.

On the Sunday before Thanksgiving, they were 5–4, stuck in third place in their division. They'd been spanked 54–13 by the Vikings and humiliated 38–0 by the Cardinals—at home, in their debut appearance on *Monday Night Football*, with former quarterback Don Meredith in the broadcast booth and angry fans chanting for him to step back under center.

Landry was so exasperated that he told his players they might as well go play touch football. So they did. Lilly and linebacker Lee Roy Jordan encouraged everyone to understand what was happening: Nobody believed in them any more, not even their coaches, so it was up to them to come together and prove everyone wrong.

The Cowboys won their next seven games to reach the Super Bowl for the first time. And at halftime, they were leading by a touchdown, having already knocked out the other team's starting quarterback.

Yet they still couldn't break through.

—★—

It made no sense.

The Cowboys were built for greatness from the start by a wealthy oil man and a visionary club president. They revolutionized the way talent was gathered in the NFL, from a computer that could find a star in the Ivy League to a network of spies who could look at a basketball player and project him as a starting cornerback. Their coach broke down the game like no one before him, coming up with brilliant new ways to play offense *and* defense. The only thing the Cowboys hadn't figured out was the thing that mattered most: how to win a championship.

Something was missing. Or someone. If only they knew who or what it was.

Sitting on the white plastic benches inside their locker room at the Orange Bowl in Miami, Lilly and his long-suffering teammates took their time peeling off sweaty jerseys and ripping the tape from their wrists and ankles. There were so many emotions to work through: anger, regret, guilt, doubt, jealousy, embarrassment.

All this game showed was that the Cowboys remained nothing but a tease.

"Unbelievable," Lilly said.

Maybe golfer Lee Trevino was right when he said, "If the Cowboys owned all the pumpkins in the world, somebody'd make Halloween illegal." Jim Murray of the *Los Angeles Times* explored similar theories in his column after Super Bowl V, opening with, "Remind me never to get reservations on the same plane as the Dallas Cowboys."

"They would pull strings to get outside staterooms on the *Titanic*. They would have asked Amelia Earhart if she had room for one more," Murray wrote. "They search around for 59 minutes and 51 seconds of every football game to find a way to lose. They know it's there someplace and they never give up 'til they find it. . . . Dallas has found the black cat once again, the dark lining in the silver cloud. The pot at the end of the rainbow doesn't have gold in it."

The game was dubbed the "Blunder Bowl" because it was so sloppy. The next day, the nation's first fan, President Richard Nixon, said, "I sure hope I don't make that many mistakes."

There were 11 turnovers—seven by Baltimore, four by Dallas. While the Cowboys treated the gifts as unwanted charity, the Colts knew what to do with theirs, cashing in on them for the tying touchdown and the winning field goal.

The damndest part for Dallas was that the costliest error wasn't made by a Cowboy. It was by line judge Jack Fette on their first turnover, a fumble by Duane Thomas. The ball squirted through several hands before Dallas center Dave Manders came away with it. The two officials closest to the play didn't signal which team recovered it. The call came from Fette, who'd been behind 6-foot-7 Bubba Smith and 6-foot-3 Charlie Stukes. Fette went along with it when Baltimore's Billy Ray Smith hollered "Our ball! Our ball!" He claimed that cornerback Jim Duncan controlled the ball before the play was whistled dead and that Manders snatched it after the whistle.

"I don't have any complex about this game, and I'm not going to take any lip about it," Jordan said, still in his uniform as if he was ready to go out for a fifth quarter. "We're coming back. I hate to tell 'em, but we are. We've got a great bunch of people, we're playing defense, and all we need is a passing game."

Landry was his usual solemn self. He hated the mocking label "Next Year's Champions," but he couldn't shake it. He was as distraught as Lilly, Jordan, or anyone else—perhaps more. He just reacted differently. More like a statue.

"This game will nullify a lot of fine things we've accomplished this season," he said. "I can only say that I do not believe, nor do any of our players believe anymore that we can't win the big games."

Sure, they'd won some biggies to get to the Super Bowl. But they needed a championship to shed their reputation and validate themselves as an elite franchise.

On the flight back to Dallas, Landry processed it all through his computerlike mind. He thought about plays that weren't made and the players who didn't make them. Should he change the players, or the plays?

Landry got up and went back to the players' section, to the aisle where Roger and Marianne Staubach were sitting.

Staubach had just finished his second season in the NFL, but he was no kid. He would be 29 in a few weeks, with three daughters at home and another on the way. He'd given up a career in the U.S. Navy to become a starting quarterback, not a backup. If the Cowboys weren't going to give him the chance, he wanted them to find a team that would.

He had plenty of reasons to doubt Landry's sincerity about making him a starter.

As a rookie in 1969, his big chance came when Morton hurt his passing shoulder. Morton had just become the starter following Meredith's retirement and he wasn't about to risk giving his backup a chance at stealing the job. So he insisted on playing through the pain, and Landry let him.

Morton developed a new throwing motion to compensate for the shoulder problem, and that messed up his elbow. His arm strength was sapped, his accuracy compromised. Fluid built up inside the elbow, so much that he had to have it drained every week.

Morton was a wreck during the two-week build-up to Super Bowl V. He didn't even practice the first week in Dallas; that was also the week the game plan was installed. When the team got to Miami and it was time for him to play catch-up, he lost his voice. All that, and Staubach still didn't play against the Colts. He was the only healthy player who suited up but didn't get into the game.

Now Landry was encouraging Staubach to work harder than ever in the offseason. Staubach could've taken it the wrong way, considering his dedication and work ethic were beyond reproach. But Landry was working toward his real message.

"You've got to be ready to compete for the starting job," Landry said. "I think you can make your move this coming year—if you're ever going to make it."

— ★ —

The entire club wasn't on that flight back to Dallas. Some guys went to Los Angeles for the Pro Bowl. Linebacker Chuck Howley and his wife went to New York to collect his new car, the reward for being named MVP of the Super Bowl.

The presentation came during a luncheon at Mamma Leone's restaurant. The mood was light. Howley received the keys to his 1971 Dodge Charger and it was immediately dubbed the "Chuck Wagon." Someone suggested giving an Edsel to everyone who played in that clunker of a game. Told that rival coach George Allen once said there's nothing money can buy that a loser could enjoy, Howley was practically jingling his keys as he smiled and said, "That's his philosophy. Not mine."

Then the conversation turned to the future of the Cowboys, and whether they would ever stop being the NFL's ultimate bridesmaids.

Howley was done joking.

"We're not going to roll over and die now," he said.

★

# SECTION I

---

# Setting the Stage

# Tex & Tom: A Foundation for Greatness

CLINT MURCHISON JR. WAS a man of wealth and privilege, the son of an oil billionaire at a time when the world had few millionaires. He owned an airplane, a yacht, and a Caribbean island.

What he really wanted was a pro football team.

Murchison was 29 when the NFL arrived in his hometown in 1952, and he was smitten. No matter how bad the Dallas Texans were, he wanted to buy them anyway just to be part of this intoxicating sport. But the team's owners wanted to cut a deal without letting him look at their books—"They said I'd have to take their word for it"—and daddy Clint Murchison Sr. didn't raise no fool. The MIT graduate backed away.

Deals to buy the San Francisco 49ers and Washington Redskins fell apart. Then, around 1958, Murchison got word the NFL would be expanding. His longtime interest made him an ideal candidate to own one of the new teams. The fact a rival league was starting up—and that its founder was the son of another oil billionaire in Dallas—certainly helped his chances. The NFL wanted a presence in the same market, figuring its more-established product would prevail.

Murchison got his team in January 1960 and decided it would be first-class all the way: the best front-office people, the best coaches, the best players. But he wasn't going to be splashing around his money. So imagine how he felt when the first guy he interviewed to run this prospective team told him to brace for losing around $2.5 million before the franchise would get on its feet.

Tex Schramm got the job anyway. And he turned out to be right.

"We lost something in the neighborhood of three million dollars before we finally began making a profit," Murchison said.

Schramm was the No. 2 guy in the sports department at CBS when Murchison hired him in late 1959. Only 39, Schramm already had put in 10 years in the front office of the Los Angeles Rams. It was a valuable decade, too, as he was part of a club that revolutionized pro football on and off the field—hiring the first full-time scout, creating the first helmet logo, signing and drafting the first black players of the modern era—all of it orchestrated by an owner who had the guts and confidence to move from Cleveland and become the first pro sports team to plant roots west of St. Louis. Owner Daniel Reeves made his share of mistakes, too, and Schramm learned from it all as he rose from publicity director to general manager.

In his three years at CBS, Schramm had turned down chances to run the Detroit Lions, the Detroit Pistons, and the Montreal Alouettes of the Canadian Football League. But when he heard that Dallas might get an NFL team, it seemed too good to be true—creating a team from scratch, and in Texas, no less.

His full name was Texas E. Schramm Jr., named for his dad. The elder Schramm was from San Antonio and had played basketball at the University of Texas in the early 1900s. Tex Jr. grew up in San Gabriel, California, but became a Longhorn, too, and still had many friends in the Lone Star State.

The start-up aspect was what appealed most to Schramm.

While painters, musicians, and writers can have all the blank slates they want, it's rare for sports executives. Schramm had long thought about what he would do with such an opportunity. His dream always ended the same way: building the NFL equivalent of the Yankees in baseball and the Montreal Canadiens in hockey. Pro football never had a club get to the top and stay there for decades, and Schramm wanted to create the first. He also knew the nation was ready for it after seeing the reaction to the 1958 NFL championship game between the Baltimore Colts and New York Giants, which was won in overtime by the Colts and was being called "The

Greatest Game Ever Played." Most of all, he knew he could be the brains behind such an organization because of all the dos and don'ts learned from his tenure with the Rams and his experiences in television.

Living in New York, Schramm knew all about the assistant coach the Giants had running their defense, Tom Landry. He was a Texas native who happened to have been a Longhorn at the same time as Schramm and who happened to already have made Dallas his offseason home. Landry was hired as the upstart franchise's head coach the day after the Giants' 1959 season ended.

Murchison's philosophy toward ownership was to "hire the best possible people you can find to run your business, then step back and let them run it. And unless you have evidence they aren't getting the job done, you leave them alone." That fit with the chain of command Schramm demanded based on his experiences with the Rams: Players would answer only to Landry, Landry would answer only to Schramm, and Schramm would answer only to Murchison.

"This is the way it has to be if you are going to have a chance to win," Schramm said. "If everyone doesn't know that there's a definite line of authority, you have chaos."

—★—

The Schramm-era Rams lived by the philosophy that the only way to do things better than everyone else was to do things differently than everyone else. This was especially true in the vital area of acquiring players.

The Rams had the first full-time scout in the NFL, and he went on the road to personally look at the guys they'd be drafting, something that was unheard of at the time. The club paid college coaches around the country to file reports on their players and those they faced. Schramm eventually realized the small colleges weren't being mined, so he came up with an ingenious plan to get the schools to scout themselves.

His cover story was a Little All-America team. Billed as a way to draw attention to these often-overlooked players, the nomination process was the team's real value to Schramm. Coaches sent the Rams the height, weight, and 100-yard dash times of their best players, uncovering gems like Tank Younger of Grambling, the first player from a historically black college to join an NFL team, and Andy Robustelli, who would become a

Hall of Famer. The Rams also scouted military teams, finding Eugene "Big Daddy" Lipscomb in the marines.

The draft board was another of their creations. The Rams printed the names of all prospective players and hung them in the order they wanted them. As the draft went along, they plucked off the name of each player taken. When it was their turn, they simply picked the top name available on their list.

They pulled a fast one in 1949 by drafting Norm Van Brocklin a year before everyone else thought he was eligible. Their diligent pre-draft research had turned up the fact he could graduate a semester early.

"It's almost laughable how much ahead we were," said Bert Rose, who worked alongside Schramm in Los Angeles and in 1971 was with the Cowboys.

Rams receiver Elroy "Crazy Legs" Hirsch had his own scouting tip for the front office—a kid who lived near him back home in Milwaukee. His name was Gil Brandt and he wasn't much of a player, but he probably knew more about college football players than most NFL front offices.

As a student at the University of Wisconsin, Brandt became the first draftnik in NFL history. He called colleges posing as a high school coach and requested game films, which he used to make his own evaluations of the top prospects. After college, Brandt came up with another slick plan, one that provided a decent salary and left him plenty of time for his hobby of scouting football players. The scam: baby photography. Brandt bought cameras for nurses to take snapshots of newborns, then he developed the prints. The hospital added $3 to the proud parents' bill and Brandt made $2.25 on each transaction.

The Rams used Brandt enough in the 1950s that Schramm thought of him immediately when starting the Cowboys. Schramm ordered Brandt to sign as many free agents as he could and sent him out with a stack of faux NFL contracts; because Dallas didn't actually have an NFL team yet, Schramm created one using a blank russled up from the Rams.

"He sent me thirty contracts in two days and I had to tell him to slow down," Schramm said. "I also had to hire him full time as our personnel director."

Between Schramm's experience, Brandt's wily nature, and Murchison's deep pockets, the Cowboys developed quite the scouting department. They kept it cranking by greasing a lot of palms.

Brandt paid college coaches for information until the NCAA cut that off. The Cowboys instead put that money into an entertainment budget, letting scouts wine and dine coaches and their wives. They also were generous with hats, T-shirts, and anything else with a logo on it to keep their team front and center with players who might have a choice of NFL teams to join and with coaches who might help guys with that decision.

"Dammit Gil, you don't miss a trick," Penn State's Joe Paterno wrote to Brandt. "You sent my son a Cowboy T-shirt and now HE's a big Cowboy fan."

The biggest weapon in Dallas' scouting arsenal needed no bribery. Just punch cards and a wall socket.

The Cowboys moved a quantum leap ahead of the competition by bringing computer technology to scouting in the mid-1960s. The idea stemmed from Schramm's experiences with the Rams and Murchison's willingness to let Schramm work the 1960 Winter Olympics for CBS a few weeks after the NFL approved the Dallas franchise.

The CBS offices at the Olympics were in the same building as IBM, which handled the scoring for all events. Schramm befriended some folks there and talked to them about computerizing the scouting process in pro football. Schramm wanted a way to quickly sift through the overload of information (four years' worth of data on roughly 600 players) and to weed out human biases (for instance, a scout who treasured players from the Big Ten Conference). He figured a machine could do it all, and in 1962 he began working with a software developer named Salam Querishi, a native of India who knew lots about computers and nothing about football.

Querishi was given a list of 300 traits coaches look for in a player. He said the computer could only handle 80. So they developed a scouting question-naire to grade prospects in 16 categories, with a rating from one (terrible) to nine (special). The machine spit out a ranking of all players, regardless of position, and the Cowboys could use it as a checklist on draft day.

With so many ways to procure players, the Cowboys slowly but surely stacked their roster. The nucleus of the 1971 Cowboys ranged from five first-round picks to three guys drafted in the seventh round or later who would become Hall of Famers. There was a starter signed as a free agent from an NAIA school that had never produced an NFL player and another starter who never played college football. Yet another player was signed from Europe without knowing a thing about American football.

Murchison was spending $200,000 on scouting by 1971, but he was getting his money's worth.

Then again, the Cowboys could afford to be lavish with their scouting because they were so stingy with their payroll.

In 1971, most players didn't even know how much their teammates or opponents earned, and the fans had no clue at all. Salary figures were such closely guarded secrets that details were often revealed only through court cases, such as divorces. The flow of this information eventually increased from a trickle to a river with agents bragging about their clients' large contracts. But at this time, only a few guys were using agents.

So it was big news that July when the NFLPA released the results of a league-wide salary survey.

The Colts were revealed as the most generous, paying an average of $31,300. The Cincinnati Bengals were the cheapest, paying $18,600.

The Cowboys were toward the bottom of the wage scale with an average salary of $24,000. It was quite a bargain considering Dallas was the only team to have made the playoffs every year of the Super Bowl era.

Their frugality was no secret—more like a point of pride.

Melvin Durslag of the *Los Angeles Herald-Examiner* described Dallas' contract negotiations as if they were handled by Alfred Hitchcock: "The Cowboy management may descend a creaky staircase to a darkened room. Lighting a candle, it will work the combination deftly and open a safe containing a coin purse. And from it the Cowboys may extract a little something." Running back Dan Reeves warned teammates about the time he tried negotiating with Schramm and came away feeling "lucky to even be playing for the Cowboys." Center Dave Manders said, "When you go in to see Tex Schramm, you start by offering to take a ten percent cut, and he won't let you go until you agree to fifteen."

Brandt usually handled contracts for rookies and made sure to set the bar low, taking advantage of their naivety with the plausible line, "We don't want to set a precedent. If we do it for you, we've got to do it for forty other guys." The Cowboys' network of college coaches were accomplices, telling players Brandt and the Cowboys were good, honest folks who would pay a fair price. A few years into their careers, players would learn better.

Schramm wanted his stars to think they were breaking the bank, so he'd tell them to keep quiet about their salary for fear of making others jealous. This ruse wasn't revealed until later in the 1970s, when Bob Lilly got into a discussion about salaries while at the Pro Bowl. The man known as "Mr. Cowboy" was making around $27,000 when he learned that Merlin Olsen—a distinguished player at the same position, although not as distinguished as Lilly—was hauling in close to $80,000.

Another ploy the Cowboys used to their advantage was playoff bonus money. Considering how good the club was, Schramm didn't see it as a bonus at all. He urged players to expect it. The reward was significant, too. Assuming an annual salary of $24,000, a Super Bowl title would reap an additional bonanza of just under $27,000.

- Playing a first-round game paid an extra game check, or one fourteenth of their full-season salary.
- The league championship game paid $8,500 for winning, $5,500 for losing.
- The Super Bowl paid another $15,000 to the winners, $7,500 to the losers. The winners also would be invited to play against the college all-stars the following summer and would receive another game check for that.

Schramm also encouraged players to do charity work and free promotional appearances. He told them it would boost their image and build relationships, which could pay off once they finish with football. Of course, while they were playing, it helped his team's image.

—★—

With Schramm, it was easy connecting the dots between his decisions in Dallas and his experiences with the Rams.

With Landry, it was his entire upbringing that shaped his outlook on coaching and everything else in his life.

Thomas Wade Landry grew up in Mission, Texas, down in the Rio Grande Valley. As a senior in high school, he was the star quarterback and defensive back on a team that didn't allow a single point the entire season.

He left college after one semester to join the U.S. Air Force. He was deployed to Europe and flew 30 missions in a B-17 bomber. One time, all four engines conked out; this huge aircraft was in a freefall over the Netherlands when Landry managed to get the engines going again. Another time, his crew survived a crash landing in France.

"War had tested me, but I had survived," Landry wrote in his autobiography. "And that experience had given me not only a broader perspective on life, but a confidence in myself I had never known before."

He returned to college in 1946, but couldn't play quarterback because the Longhorns had Bobby Layne. Landry moved to fullback and was part of teams that went to the Sugar Bowl and Orange Bowl. Walking off the field following his last game, he signed with the New York Yankees of the All-America Conference. The league went under after one season and he joined the Giants.

Landry got the most out of his marginal skills as a defensive back and punter. Had he been more gifted physically, he may have never had the great revelation of his playing career—how much easier the game is if you know what the other team is going to do, which he discovered could be figured out based on how they line up. He called it "reading his keys," and it unlocked his future.

Landry not only had a keen grasp on Xs and Os, he also had a knack for explaining it. That skill was revealed in 1950, when Giants coach Steve Owen came up with a new scheme to slow the Cleveland Browns but struggled to teach it to his players. It was essentially the birth of the 4–3 defense and Landry understood it right away. He went to the chalkboard and took over the lesson to his teammates. The Giants beat the Browns 6–0.

In 1954, Landry became a player-coach. The Giants became much stingier on defense, and Landry made All-Pro for the only time in his career. He became strictly an assistant coach in 1956. Staffs were much smaller then. There weren't even coordinators, just an assistant on each side of the ball. He was the defensive guy; the offensive guy was Vince Lombardi. No wonder the Giants won it all that season. They played for the championship again in 1958 and '59.

Landry's dad was a mechanic, and his own college degree was in industrial engineering. Maybe that's why he loved tinkering with his playbook.

In the early 1960s, when many teams were running his 4–3 defense, Landry came up with the multiple offense to counter it. The idea was to move around backs and receivers before the snap, with linemen standing up to make it tougher for the defense to reconcile all the changes and process what was going to happen. Next came the "Flex" defensive front, a picket-fence type of alignment. Landry also liked to experiment with players' positions; sometimes it worked, sometimes it didn't.

As a person, Landry came across as exciting as Xs and Os on a chalkboard. It stemmed from his attitude that football was serious stuff, not fun and games. To Landry, nothing worth laughing about ever happened on a football field. He posted this quote from Lombardi in the locker room: "The quality of a man's life is in direct proportion to his commitment to excellence."

Landry wasn't much of a screamer. A stare known as The Look was enough to let anyone know they'd done or said something he didn't like. In a conversation, an "Okay?!" meant he was done talking.

Landry avoided personal relationships with players. He knew he would eventually have to cut or trade them, and he didn't want anything beyond their ability as football players influencing his decision. That doesn't mean he was without feelings. It just means he learned to hide them behind a face seemingly made of stone. The emotional distance Landry kept from players worked to his advantage. Guys craved his approval, which came in the form of him using their first name. Many remember the first time they heard it.

Fans mostly saw him as the stoic guy on the sideline, looking sharp in his fedora hat.

He taught himself to become unemotional during games. Of course, he had been born with an extra helping of calm. A guy who jerked a bomber out of a nosedive when everyone else in the cockpit was ready to hit eject clearly knew how to perform under pressure. In football, Landry realized that celebrating or lamenting a play that's finished merely gets in the way of preparing for the next play. Being dispassionate allowed him to process whatever happened and to react accordingly. Since he was calling all the defensive plays and, by 1970, all of the offensive plays, there was little time for anything else anyway.

The robo-coach persona was further fueled by Landry's attitude toward motivating his team. He just didn't believe in it. Shouldn't players give it everything they've got simply because a game is going to have a winner and a loser, and it's better to be the winner? The only words he could imagine bringing out someone's best was advice and instruction. And that was supposed to come during the week, not in a pre-game or halftime speech. To Landry, players should draw confidence from being properly prepared.

"Emotion can cover up a lot of inadequacies, but in the end it also gets in the way of performance," Landry said. "An emotional team cannot stay that way consistently over a full season or even a few games."

Landry also emphasized fitness. He kept himself from looking like an old, pot-bellied coach by lifting weights and running regularly—up to three miles a day in the offseason, about one mile as often as he could during the season. People meeting him for the first time often came away saying he was fitter and stronger than they thought from seeing him on TV.

Landry's disciplined, structured ways knew no bounds. He told a college girlfriend he wouldn't kiss her until she stopped smoking. Alicia Wiggs did, and they married a few weeks after he signed his first pro contract.

They made Dallas their family home in the '50s, with Landry selling insurance during the offseasons as a start toward a career after football. By 1959, Landry realized he had everything he'd ever wanted: a great marriage, three kids (Tom Jr., Kitty, and Lisa), and more than a decade playing and coaching pro football. But he also felt "an emptiness" in his life. Then a friend invited him to a prayer breakfast. Landry had been a regular churchgoer, but he had never really studied the Bible. The passages he read that morning led him to realize the missing piece in his life was a devotion to Christ.

Landry was soon telling players his priorities were God, family, then football. He began holding chapel services on Sunday mornings. Alicia started a weekly prayer group among the wives of Cowboys players and coaches. In 1970, Landry allowed the Reverend Billy Zeoli of Gospel Films Inc. to make a behind-the-scenes movie called *A Man & His Men* about Landry's faith and its impact on the club; cameras rolled all the way through the Super Bowl.

By 1971, Landry was on the board at Highland Park United Methodist Church and regularly attended a men's study group at 7:30 a.m. on Thursdays. He was the national vice president of the Fellowship of Christian Athletes and a member of the group's national board of directors. He also took on his biggest non-football role yet, becoming general chairman for the Billy Graham Greater Southwest Crusades that were scheduled to be held in September at the new stadium being built for the Cowboys.

Sports are littered with people who talk about their faith more than they practice it. Landry was true as can be. He wrote an article published in March 1971 that provided insight into how Christianity steered his life.

Landry described his nighttime ritual of making a spiritual assessment of his day: "Was my criticism of the quarterback handled right? Did I get across to the squad my moral convictions without preaching? Was I too stern with my daughter Kitty over her report card? The main evaluation concerns whether I had brought the Lord into these situations or whether I was barging ahead on my own."

He recalled making his nightly assessment following a particularly devastating loss.

"As almost always happens during these sessions with Him, I soon found perspective," Landry wrote. "A crushing setback today, yes, but I've learned that something constructive comes from every defeat. I thought over my relationships that day, with the players, coaches, officials, friends, family. Nothing wrong here. No bad injuries either. 'Thank you Lord for being with me out there,' I said. And with that prayer the bitter sting of defeat drained away."

There were many sides to Landry, but few that he revealed to his players. All they were supposed to do was listen and follow orders. Their attitude toward him was summed up by Manders while speaking at a high school banquet in the spring of '71.

"Not all of the forty players on the team like him," Manders said, "but they sure respect him."

# The NFL in 1971: Year Two of the Merger

PRO FOOTBALL FAILED IN Dallas the first time around because folks weren't ready to devote their entire weekends to the sport. Friday nights were based around high school teams and Saturdays were all about college games. Sundays were reserved for family time.

That was 1952. The Dallas Texans of the NFL started with much fanfare in September and left for good in November, run off by a lack of interest.

By 1960, Dallas had grown, television had entered more homes and Sunday afternoon football had worked its way into the routine. So many folks were convinced the area was ready for pro football that two teams started, the Cowboys and the Dallas Texans of the AFL.

By 1971, pro football on Sundays was a Dallas fixture, and the Cowboys had the local sports scene pretty much to themselves. MLB's Washington Senators wouldn't land in Arlington and become the Texas Rangers until 1972. The Dallas Mavericks of the NBA didn't begin until 1980, and the NHL was more than a decade from joining the picture. There were other minor diversions, but nothing that drew like the NFL.

As for the NFL, the just-completed 1970 season was the start of an entirely new way of doing business.

It was the first year of the merger and the "new" National Football League. The old NFL had become the NFC, and the rival AFL became the

AFC. Each conference featured 13 teams split into three divisions. The team with the best record among non-division winners got a "wild card" spot in the playoffs. The winners of each conference met in a championship game that—for the first time—officially carried the name Super Bowl. The winner received a sterling silver trophy made by Tiffany's that had been given out since the first AFL-NFL championship game in January 1967, but was now called the Vince Lombardi Trophy in honor of the coach who died suddenly shortly before the 1970 season.

Television powered football's rise in popularity. But the networks went into the 1970s still not convinced of the NFL's drawing power. NBC and CBS were offered the chance to show a regular-season game every Monday night but didn't want to interrupt their prime-time lineups. So Commissioner Pete Rozelle took his idea to the lowest-rated network, ABC. *Monday Night Football* was a hit from the start. The program drew nearly 31 percent of the audience, with more than 30 million people watching at least some of the weekly broadcast. College football play-by-play man Keith Jackson helped viewers keep pace with down, distance, and score, but audiences turned up the volume to hear the bombastic comments of New York loudmouth Howard Cosell and the homespun reflections of former Cowboys quarterback "Dandy" Don Meredith. Viewers knew they might as well get ready for bed when Dandy started crooning, "Turn out the lights, the party's over."

The Cowboys had a fateful appearance on *Monday Night Football* during the show's inaugural season. It was bad enough that they lost 38–0 to St. Louis at the Cotton Bowl. Worse still, fans chanted, "We want Meredith!"

"I ain't going back down there, I tell you that, folks," Dandy told the national audience.

The Cowboys made the Super Bowl without him. The championship game against the Colts provided the best indication yet that pro football was a national sensation. An estimated 46 million people watched it, more than any regularly scheduled program in four years and the most for a sports event. Three of every four televisions turned on that afternoon were tuned to the Super Bowl. Imagine how many more might have watched had it been a *good* game.

Rozelle and team owners knew they were onto something. In only five years, the Super Bowl had gone from a game that filled only about two-thirds of the L.A. Coliseum to the nation's most anticipated game.

Regardless of who played or where, everyone wanted to see for themselves which team was the best in all of pro football.

A Gallup poll released the week of Super Bowl VI provided further proof: Asked to name their favorite sport to watch, 36 percent of Americans said football, while only 21 percent picked baseball. A decade earlier, the numbers were almost reversed, 34 percent for baseball and 21 percent for football.

New stadiums were another indication of the NFL's runaway success.

The Cowboys, Eagles, 49ers, and Patriots were moving into new stadiums in 1971. The Bears left Wrigley Field for Soldier Field. More new parks were on the horizon: Kansas City in 1972, Buffalo in '73, New Orleans in '75, and the Giants in 1976.

# The Birth of Texas Stadium

THE COTTON BOWL WAS built in the 1930s in the heart of Fair Park, home to the State Fair of Texas. It was a useful, venerable place. But once the Cowboys had the local scene to themselves, team owner Clint Murchison Jr. was ready for an upgrade.

Murchison asked the city to fix up the place in 1965. Attendance had just spiked, and he suggested that half of the extra revenue be spent on adding water fountains and decent toilets for the fans, and better dressing rooms for the clubs. Maybe they could get rid of the splintery wooden benches and put in chairback seats. Adding parking lots would cut down on the robberies, assaults, and vandalism that came from fans leaving their cars on the streets of the surrounding neighborhood.

City leaders resisted, figuring they held all the cards. Where else would the Cowboys play?

Murchison knew that's what they were thinking, so he offered up a few more ideas. Rather than refurbish the Cotton Bowl, how about bull-dozing the fairgrounds, selling the land and using that money to start over somewhere else? When folks shuddered at the thought of walking away from the tradition and the money long since spent on the place, Murchison proposed a downtown stadium paid for by revenue bonds. The parking lots could be used by businessmen during the week, and games would help bring life to the area on the weekends. They could even connect an art museum and a music hall to share the lots to keep the area lively year-round.

Anything Murchison wanted, Dallas Mayor J. Erik Jonsson opposed.

The son of Swedish immigrants, Jonsson came to Dallas in the 1930s because of his business career. He became cofounder of Texas Instruments and a very rich man after the company invented the computer chip. He also became passionate about his adopted hometown. Elected mayor following the assassination of President John F. Kennedy, Jonsson helped restore the city's reputation. He gave much of his fortune to support city projects, and it irked him that the Murchison family was among the richest in the world, yet hardly cut any checks to improve their city.

So the battle lines were clearly drawn: new money versus old, ours versus mine. They were headed toward a showdown.

A smart guy like Jonsson should've known better.

In late 1966, Murchison spent $1 million on a tear-shaped, 90-acre plot surrounded by three major highways. The area was known as Turkey Knob, and it was located in the suburb of Irving—outside the domain of Jonsson and other city of Dallas poobahs. On an icy day early in 1967, Murchison invited about a dozen Irving leaders to the Dallas Gun Club to unveil a model of the partially domed stadium he wanted to build. Similar meetings were held—in secret—over the following months to make sure the right people were behind the project. Shortly before Christmas, a chamber of commerce official became the first to spill the beans, talking it up during a speech to the Lions Club.

Some Dallas leaders thought Murchison was bluffing. Still, they offered $12 million in improvements for Fair Park, with a portion for the Cotton Bowl. It was too late. The formal announcement of Texas Stadium came a few days later.

Murchison had detailed artists' renderings and a unique financing plan—the fans would help pick up the $25 million tab. In order to buy season tickets, they had to first purchase a bond that cost $1,000 per seat between the 30-yard lines, $250 per seat anywhere else.

"What could be fairer? The people who like football games are putting up the money," Murchison told his critics. "I'd say we lost a whole group [of fans] in the $12,000 to $20,000-a-year salary range who could afford season tickets at the Cotton Bowl but couldn't afford to buy bonds. If we discriminated against them, we discriminated against them. But no more than all America discriminates against people who don't have enough money to buy everything they want."

His building wouldn't be enclosed like the Astrodome in Houston. He wanted the best of both worlds, indoor and outdoor. So he tapped into the engineering and math skills he learned at Duke and MIT and came up with a roof that would cover the fans while leaving the field exposed to the elements. At least, that's how he spun a concept that was really designed to avoid heating and cooling costs.

His plans called for many more bells and whistles—escalators, luxury suites, and an abundance of water fountains and restrooms. A football-only stadium like this was unprecedented.

"I've researched this for three years, and I'm convinced this will be the world's finest football stadium," Murchison said.

In December 1968, the Texas Stadium Corporation and the City of Irving put their deal in writing. The dirt began turning in February 1969, with plans to open for business in the fall of 1971. When Jonsson asked Murchison what the city should do with a stadium lacking a primary tenant, the oil man said, "What about an electronics plant?"

(Dallas officials got some measure of revenge by chopping the team's cut of concessions from 50 percent to 25 percent for 1968 to 1970.)

The Cowboys were scheduled to play at Texas Stadium for the first time on August 14, an exhibition game against the New Orleans Saints.

"Of course, there is always the possibility of a labor problem coming up," stadium manager Bert Rose said during a February tour of the construction site. "But that sort of thing is out of our hands. It looks like everything will be on schedule."

Tex Schramm came up with another idea to make the place sizzle—having some lovely young ladies serve as usherettes.

The Cowboys' cheerleaders at this time were the Belles & Beaux, a troupe of local teenagers, high school girls and boys who did college style "sis-boom-bah" kind of cheers. So Schramm figured he'd go for sex appeal in the aisles.

By July, there were newspaper ads seeking 125 attractive girls to become "a fabulous 'Texette' at the new Texas Stadium and other Dallas–Fort Worth entertainment events." Qualifications: 18 to 32 years old, at least 5-foot-1 and a resident of the DFW area. The ad showed a girl in a hat, skirt, and cowboy-themed attire. Applicants were asked to "please wear shorts or minis. Bring heels."

"We have no precise standards," said L. D. Lewis Jr., president of the company coordinating the girls. "We only want them to be attractive;

representative of warm, gracious Texas hospitality; and, perhaps most important, eager to make every attraction at which they serve a pleasure from beginning to end."

—★—

Though his stadium was not even built, Murchison declared it worthy of hosting the Super Bowl. Since NFL owners had yet to select a site for the upcoming game, the Cowboys decided to go for it.

There was plenty of competition: Miami, which hosted three of the five Super Bowls, had folks lobbying to make it a permanent site; Los Angeles, site of Super Bowl I; New Orleans, which was getting artificial turf in Tulane Stadium to prevent another soggy mess like Super Bowl IV; and also in the running were Jacksonville, Florida, and the domed stadium in Houston.

Murchison dismissed the Astrodome as being too small and mentioned the problems rain might cause anywhere else. He and Schramm pushed hard to extol the virtues of their semi-domed stadium.

"It would be somewhat of a tragedy if you played a game like the Super Bowl, televised to all parts of the U.S. and Europe, and had empty stands because of bad weather," Schramm said. "Texas Stadium can insure against that with all covered stands and the playing of the game would not be affected because of the artificial turf."

That is, provided Texas Stadium would beat the elements like the hucksters said it would.

The Cowboys continued to try stacking the deck in their favor. They headed to the league meetings at the Breakers Hotel in Palm Beach with a high-powered bid team—including the lieutenant governor of Texas and the president of American Airlines—and a full-color brochure put together by the TracyLocke ad agency. The theme was "Dallas Is a Football Town." There were details about weather (mean temperature of 55 on Jan. 16, the date of the upcoming game) and boasts of having a centralized location (a three-hour flight from practically every NFL city), plenty of hotel rooms, a "United Nations list" of fine restaurants, a national reputation as a shopping destination and an "intriguing" night life.

Murchison had at least one vote beyond his own: Kansas City Chiefs owner Lamar Hunt, who lived in Dallas. Hunt brought up the notion of the game rotating between AFC and NFC cities. Since the last game was in Miami, home to the Dolphins of the AFC, that made it the NFC's turn.

"Mainly, I just think the game should be played at a new and different site," he said.

Hunt was an influential owner. Better still, Rozelle was in favor of the idea. And, said Raiders boss Al Davis, "Whatever Mr. Rozelle wants, Mr. Rozelle gets."

The candidates quickly narrowed to Dallas and Miami. Rozelle suggested making it a package deal—one in January '72, the other in January '73—but that was rejected. Deliberations lasted more than three hours. The tone shifted when Davis stood and said, "Wait a minute. What happens to this game if the Cowboys are the home team?"

The Cowboys were just in the Super Bowl and were good enough to get back. That didn't matter to NFC owners, because if Dallas made it to the Super Bowl that meant their team didn't. But each AFC owner had to think about their club playing the Cowboys in Texas Stadium.

Then an NFC owner shot back, noting that Miami was only two games off the Super Bowl last year. On the 14th vote, they finally had a winner. "Everyone suddenly agreed there was one team which surely wouldn't be in the game," said New England Patriots owner Billy Sullivan. It was settled: Super Bowl VI would be held in New Orleans.

# Black Dallas, White Dallas

EIGHT YEARS AFTER THE assassination of President John F. Kennedy and seven years before television introduced J. R. Ewing, the city of Dallas was still struggling for an identity in 1971.

Kennedy's death, and the subsequent killing of his accused assassin, led Dallas to be known as the "City of Hate." The nickname was bolstered by how slowly barriers were coming down between the black and white communities.

If you were black, not even being a star on the Dallas Cowboys helped you find a decent place to live.

"The Negroes on the Cowboys can only find roach-infested houses," running back Don Perkins said in 1968. "The problem hasn't improved a bit in the seven years I've been there. There's been quite a lot of building for Negroes, but I would have to describe most of it as low-income housing. It is certainly not even up to middle-income standards."

Once Perkins brought the issue to the forefront, other black players spoke out, too.

"Every year, I mean *every year* I been on this team, it takes me two months after we get back to Dallas for me to find a place to live," defensive back Cornell Green said.

"And where is it? Umpteen trillion miles from the practice field, and from where everybody else is," receiver Bob Hayes said. "The tough part is after the game when the white players head north and the colored players head south. We play together and love one another—why not live together?"

Later in '68, emboldened by passage of the federal Fair Housing Act and tired of the same old, same old, defensive back Mel Renfro and his wife tried to move near team headquarters. They found a place they liked and were told to come back a few days later to sign the lease. When Mrs. Renfro returned to fill out the paperwork, she was told that policy changes would prevent them from moving in. The apartment manager also told Mrs. Renfro how much she enjoyed watching Mel play.

Renfro filed a lawsuit against the builder, the realtor, and the salesman. State Senator Oscar Mauzy called Renfro and volunteered to be his lawyer. Tex Schramm and the Cowboys were slow to support Renfro because they didn't want to irk anyone. They only got behind Renfro once they realized he was going through with it no matter what. The Renfros were vindicated in court. They brought attention to a delicate, shameful subject. Housing options improved, but only a little.

Dallas leaders also were in no rush to comply with federal rules requiring integrated schools.

In 1970, a black man named Sam Tasby was furious that his daughter couldn't attend a school near their home because it was meant for whites. He filed a lawsuit, and a federal judge demanded public schools in Dallas become more racially diverse. Starting in September 1971, black kids were sent on buses to white schools, with police on hand to make sure it went over smoothly. Progress remained slow. The courts did not declare Dallas schools fully desegregated until 2003.

The housing and school issues were merely new cracks in a racial divide that went back more than a century. In 1860, a fire destroyed downtown Dallas and three black men were hung because of it. It turns out that the fire may have been an accident, but it was a convenient opportunity for slave owners to show who was in control and how vigilant they could be to protect their authority. In 1916, Dallas became the first city in Texas with a law allowing segregated housing, making it legal for whites and blacks to each have their own neighborhoods. The state Supreme Court threw out the law a year later, but in 1921 the city council passed a new law that essentially restored it. The same year, the Ku Klux Klan announced its presence in Dallas when the letters KKK were burned on the forehead of a black hotel worker who allegedly had sex with a white woman. Dallas would soon have the nation's largest Klan chapter; the police commissioner and other city leaders were members. The KKK's power dwindled by the late 1920s, but its sentiments were still going strong in 1971. Blacks who moved into all-white neighborhoods had their homes burned or bombed.

Schramm thought sports helped race relations more on accident than other institutions did on purpose. He pointed to all the changes the Cowboys already had forced.

"Who integrated the Dallas hotels? We did, when we brought in NFL teams. Who started integrated seating in Dallas? We did, in the Cotton Bowl, and nobody even noticed," said Schramm, who'd been with the Los Angeles Rams when they signed black players into an all-white league, then drafted the first black players.

Yet for all the progress Schramm was touting, the Cowboys had blacks room with blacks, and whites with whites, until 1968. The change came after Perkins spoke out.

Race wasn't as much of a wedge in the locker room as it was elsewhere in Dallas, but that doesn't mean everyone was holding hands and singing kumbaya. Black players wondered whether guys from the Deep South were racist, and some white guys were curious about blacks simply because they hadn't been around many before.

That was the case with Bob Lilly. Growing up in West Texas, then Oregon, then playing at Texas Christian, he mostly had white teammates. He had no idea of the struggles blacks faced. Calvin Hill, Renfro, and Pettis Norman told Lilly stories that gave him a better understanding. He ended up putting a sign above his locker that read, "Walk a mile in another man's moccasins before you judge him."

Hill explored his own feelings toward his white teammates one afternoon early in the 1971 season when offensive lineman Forrest Gregg joined the team.

Gregg, who is white, had been teammates in Green Bay with Herb Adderley, a black cornerback who'd joined the Cowboys the previous season. When Gregg arrived, Adderley hugged him.

"Wow," Hill thought. "Who would I hug if I went to another team and one of my teammates from the Cowboys joined that team?"

5

# Roster Maintenance

SUCCESS CAN BE EXPENSIVE. The more a team wins, the more players want to be paid. And the Cowboys came away from their first Super Bowl with all sorts of contract issues.

Running back Calvin Hill was expecting a raise for the third and final year of his initial contract. Fellow running back Duane Thomas wasn't happy with the second year of his deal. Receiver Bob Hayes, defensive back Mel Renfro, and defensive tackle Jethro Pugh didn't have contracts.

There was no free agency. NFL teams were still protected by the reserve system, the pro sports equivalent of indentured servitude: Whatever team brought a guy into the league could pretty much keep him as long as it wanted. The only way a player could choose to leave was by "playing out his option." Doing so meant playing a season without a contract and getting paid 10 percent less than the previous year in hopes that another team would want him the next season. Even if a team did want to sign someone else's player, it had to work out both a contract with the player and compensation for the jilted team. If the teams couldn't strike a deal, NFL Commissioner Pete Rozelle could set the terms. So it was a risky proposition all the way around.

The Cowboys' top priority in the offseason between the 1970 and '71 campaigns was Hayes.

"Bullet Bob" had gone from a star at the 1964 Tokyo Summer Olympics to a dominant NFL rookie in 1965. He was such an unparalleled deep threat that zone defenses were created solely because of him. But they still couldn't stop him. In 1970, Hayes scored a touchdown every 3.4 catches and averaged a league-best 26.1 yards per catch, his best ever and the fifth-best in league history—all while playing out his option.

"I took the ten-percent cut in salary and risked getting an injury that could have hurt my future," Hayes said in March 1971. "I feel I've gone this far now and there's no way I'm going to turn around."

The Cowboys also knew there was no way he was going anywhere.

Should another team strike a deal with Hayes, the Cowboys would refuse all trade proposals or bring things to a stalemate with ridiculous demands. The bidding team would then have to ask Rozelle to intervene—and no team was foolish enough to ask for his help in an argument with the Cowboys.

The relationship between Schramm and Rozelle went back to 1952, when Schramm was named general manager of the Rams and hired Rozelle to replace him as publicity director. When Schramm left for CBS, Rozelle replaced him again as GM. Since becoming commissioner, Rozelle had Schramm secretly negotiate the merger with the AFL and put him in charge of the powerful NFL Competition Committee.

In March 1971, Hayes' attorney, Steve Falk of Miami, claimed the Cowboys were spreading rumors that his client was a troublemaker. Schramm countered that Falk was the troublemaker for trying to sour Hayes on playing for the organization.

"Bob wants to stay in Dallas with his teammates, and that's where we want him to stay—if they pay him what he's worth," Falk said. "He's been underpaid from the moment he signed with the Cowboys. But he won't be underpaid in 1971."

A few weeks later, Hayes said, "I like Dallas and I like the team. But I like money better." The day that quote appeared in the newspaper, the Cowboys traded for Gloster Richardson, a speedy receiver whose specialty was the deep ball.

Hayes officially became a free agent on May 1. Schramm had previously said that date had "no practical significance" to the Cowboys, then emphasized it by being on vacation. Gil Brandt was put in charge while Schramm was gone, and he too was out of town that day.

There was talk of Hayes, a Florida native, being interested in the Dolphins. The rival Redskins were another supposed target. The New York

Jets were a logical destination because Joe Namath needed another deep threat. As June approached and Hayes was still available, several Canadian teams considered bidding for him.

Things dragged on for so long that Tom Landry gently took Hayes' side.

"Some of these players with agents get way out on a limb. That's not the case where Bob is concerned," Landry said. He also wrote in his annual offseason prospectus, "Our receiving corps is still built basically around Bob Hayes, primarily because of what Bob has done in the past. He has been an excellent touchdown producer. He puts a lot of strain upon the defense, forces them to double or adjust their defense to him, so he is the key."

On June 24, a deal was done. It was for five years, with a base salary of $55,000 per season and incentives that could bring it up to $85,000. Hayes also received a $25,000 signing bonus to make up for his 1970 salary cut and to soothe any lingering wounds. There were provisions for a big raise if he was ever traded and compensation if he suffered a career-ending injury.

"Tex Schramm said we were mishandling Hayes. Well, we have mishandled him into being the highest paid receiver in pro football," Falk crowed. He was able to pat himself on the back all he wanted because Cowboys' top brass skipped the press conference announcing the signing. Schramm stayed in his office just down the hall, and Landry was on vacation.

Two days later, however, Schramm and Landry showed up for another press conference, one to announce the arrival of another Hall of Fame–bound receiver.

—★—

For the last four seasons, Hayes' on-field sidekick was Lance Rentzel. He was the receiver who punished defenses that loaded up trying to stop Hayes.

Rentzel was the kind of guy who seemed to have it all. He was rich, smart, talented, and suave enough to marry Joey Heatherton, an actress/singer/dancer whose best talent was looking pretty. But his life was far from perfect. Rentzel also was an exhibitionist—a "sex pervert," he later called himself.

In 1966, while playing for the Minnesota Vikings, Rentzel was caught exposing himself to two young girls in St. Paul, Minnesota. He pleaded guilty to a morals charge. A municipal court judge could've put him behind bars but only told him to get psychiatric care. The story hardly got out, and the Vikings traded him to Dallas. The Cowboys knew about his past and simply hoped for the best. Everything was fine until November 1970. A week before Thanksgiving, Rentzel exposed himself to a 10-year-old girl. A witness got his license plate number, and the car was traced to Rentzel. About 10 days later, he was arrested for indecent exposure to a minor. Rentzel voluntarily placed himself on the team's inactive list. He didn't play again that season, missing out on the Super Bowl.

In April 1971, the 27-year-old Rentzel pleaded guilty and received a five-year, probated sentence and was ordered to continue receiving medical and psychiatric help. His legal status settled, everyone wondered whether the Cowboys would bring him back.

"I can't end my athletic career this way," Rentzel said.

The Cowboys dumped him in May as part of two separate trades the club viewed as a package deal: Rentzel to the Los Angeles Rams for tight end Billy Truax and receiver Wendell Tucker; and tight end Pettis Norman, offensive tackle Tony Liscio, and defensive tackle Ron East to the San Diego Chargers for receiver Lance Alworth.

Boiled down, it was Rentzel for Alworth—a young Lance for an aging Lance. Still, considering the circumstances, it was quite the shrewd move.

"I can't think of a better combination for touchdowns than to have Alworth on one side and Hayes on the other," Landry said.

Alworth had been the AFL's biggest star, the top receiver in a league known for passing. His great hands, great moves, and great speed earned him the nickname "Bambi." The trade brought out such gushing tributes from the Chargers that it seemed as if they'd sent him straight for enshrinement in Canton, Ohio.

"I think he is the greatest player at his position that ever was. I love this boy like I do my own son," San Diego coach-GM Sid Gillman said. "He's good at everything he does. Give him a golf club and in a month he'll be able to play with the pros. . . . He has taken batting practice with the Padres a couple times, and they tell me in five easy lessons he could do all right in baseball, too."

So why'd they trade him?

Alworth was turning 31 in August, and his personal life was a mess. In the last 18 months, he filed a $5.6 million lawsuit against his own team, filed for personal bankruptcy, got a divorce, and remarried. He went through a faux retirement early in training camp, came back out of shape, and ended up getting hurt. He also claimed team officials turned him into a pariah because of the lawsuit, which is why he contributed so little—the fewest catches and yards since his rookie year. However, he still averaged 17.4 yards per catch, so he hadn't completely lost it. Landry studied his limited action and declared, "When he was healthy, he was as brilliant as ever."

Alworth showed what he thought of the deal by having an answering service block all incoming calls, even Landry's. The Cowboys knew he'd get over it because he couldn't pass up his $55,000 salary.

Indeed, once Alworth came to peace with the trade and factored in his financial situation, he showed up in Dallas sounding like a new man.

"I just couldn't resist having a shot at the Super Bowl," he said. Alworth added that he'd dropped weight and added speed and strength through a new fitness regimen. "In essence, I think this is the greatest thing that ever happened to me." Alworth spoke at a news conference held in the private club at the team's office building. Schramm was there and Landry, too; the coach even chauffeured Alworth and his new bride from the airport. Days after the low-key announcement about Hayes' deal, this red-carpet treatment was stunning.

"There was no slight intended," Schramm said. "I was working on something while Hayes was there. Oh, I could have come out and patted him on the back, but the press conference was held mainly to give everyone an opportunity to talk to Hayes."

This wasn't about race. It was more a reminder to anyone else considering taking on the front office.

—★—

Back in January, during Super Bowl week in Florida, Duane Thomas liked to relax on the beach behind the team's hotel. He hopped a concrete wall separating the hotel from the beach, walked to the edge of the water, and plopped into the sand. With his playbook on his lap, Thomas would sit and stare across the Atlantic Ocean as if he was in a trance.

A few sportswriters walking the beach saw him one day and stopped to chat. They asked Thomas what he was thinking.

"I think about what's out there. Over the water. New Zealand's over there. This morning I was thinking about New Zealand," Thomas said.

The writers were expecting him to say something about the Baltimore Colts, or the upcoming game in general. So they asked if he was excited about playing in the ultimate game, the Super Bowl.

"Why should I be?" Thomas said. "How can it be the ultimate game if they play it next year, too?"

Point made. But what about New Zealand?

"Steve Kiner says it's a good place to retire to," Thomas said.

Kiner was Thomas' roommate and a rookie just like him. Why would guys at the start of their careers be thinking about the end of their careers?

"That's the best time to think about retiring," Thomas said.

What seemed like a quirky conversation wasn't. In early May, Thomas returned from a trip to Bermuda and called Steve Perkins of the *Dallas Times-Herald* to say he was quitting. Over money, of course.

The problems went deeper than Thomas wanting a raise as a reward for his stellar rookie season. And rather than rationally explaining his financial jam, Thomas went on the attack.

"Nobody in the front office cares about what happens to the players. It's all business, the dotted line," Thomas said. "Then, when you get in the season, you're supposed to be one big family, pulling together. How do they figure?"

Thomas was furious that the team tried getting out of paying him a bonus for being rookie of the year. The club argued that Thomas didn't win the most recognized version of the award, the one given by The Associated Press. His selections came from *Football News* and *Pro Football Guide*. Schramm eventually gave in, but the damage was done.

"I was glad I could share my talents with other people, thrill them with the excitement of my running," Thomas said. "But you always hear about the fairness of the game, and I think a player has to be treated fair, too. . . . They look at you not as a person but as a specimen."

Thomas' main gripe was the terms of the two years remaining on the contract he'd signed the previous year.

"What did I know? I had an agent, okay, but after I signed and he got his cut I haven't seen him since," Thomas said. "I had an obligation to put out my best, every minute, for the ball club—and I did. Well, I feel like the club should have been obligated to me, obligated to be honest with me. They've been in the business longer than I have. It seems like all they're interested in is keeping me down. Well, they can't keep me down if I'm not going to be there, and I won't be there. . . . I'll get a job, and at least I'll stay sane."

Thomas had just changed agents, from the New York shyster who swindled him to a California agent who also represented Mel Renfro and Jethro Pugh. The new agent was headed to Dallas soon to try working things out.

"I'd hate to see him retire at twenty-two years of age," Gil Brandt said. "It would be a great loss. But I've learned long ago not to speculate on what a player will do."

—★—

The first move to reload the roster for 1971 came a few weeks after the Super Bowl. The draft.

This was being called "The Year of the Quarterback" because of how many good ones were available. The top three picks ended up being QBs: Jim Plunkett, Archie Manning, and Dan Pastorini. Solid starters were found in later rounds, too—Lynn Dickey and Ken Anderson in the third and Joe Theismann in the fourth.

Considering how the Super Bowl went, observers wondered whether the Cowboys would try getting a young quarterback. They did, but it was only Steve Goepel of Colgate, taken 311th overall.

Picking twenty-fifth in each round—second-to-last—Dallas had the first clunker of a draft in franchise history. The Cowboys took 19 players, and only four made the roster. None lasted very long.

The Cowboys also spent the offseason renewing their never-ending search for a reliable kicker.

Their most memorable hunt was in 1967, when they visited 28 cities over six weeks on a cross-country tour dubbed the "Kicking Karavan." The best leg they found belonged to a guy from practically their own backyard, the Dallas suburb of Garland. Mac Percival was a 27-year-old high school basketball coach whose wife had signed him up for a tryout. The Cowboys ended up trading him to the Bears, and the next year he led the NFL in field goals. Dallas didn't keep any candidates for itself.

This offseason, the hunt went overseas in search of a soccer-style kicker like Kansas City's Jan Stenerud, Chicago's Horst Muhlmann, and Miami's Garo Yepremian. They were among the league leaders thanks to backgrounds in *futbol*, yet none had been a high-level soccer star. So, Schramm wondered, how would an elite European soccer player do?

With that thought percolating, Schramm and Brandt were visited by Bob Kap, the former coach of the Dallas Tornado of the North American Soccer League. He'd come to sell them paintings. He left as the ringleader of Kicking Karavan II, European edition.

Kap and part-time scout Bob Ford, a veteran of the original Karavan, started by visiting the Spanish island Majorca in January, during soccer's equivalent of baseball's spring training. The leg they were most impressed by belonged to Toni Fritsch of the Vienna Rapid club.

Fritsch was beloved in his homeland as "Wembley Toni" because he scored two goals in Austria's 3–2 victory over England at Wembley Stadium in 1966, the year England won the World Cup. By 1971, he was only 26 but knew his soccer career was winding down and was intrigued by the idea of playing American football. He also discovered he was pretty good at it.

"I have only three, maybe four good years left in soccer," Fritsch said. "This other business, I can kick 'til I am old man."

In April, Brandt and assistant coach Ermal Allen went to Vienna to check him out themselves. Fritsch made 17 of 18 field goals from 40 yards, then kept making kicks from beyond 50 yards. On kickoffs, he kept putting the ball over a fence about 4 feet high and roughly 75 yards away.

"I shook his hand, took him right back to my hotel, and signed him on the spot," Brandt said. "Then I called Tom and Tex and told them we had a kicker."

—★—

The division rival Washington Redskins had a busy offseason, too.

George Allen was hired as head coach and given free rein to hire, fire, and acquire players. By the start of training camp, he brought in 18 veterans, many of whom had played for him on the Los Angeles Rams. He pretty much recreated his L.A. defense in D.C., with all the starting linebackers following him from coast to coast. To make these radical changes, Allen traded 20 draft picks, declaring, "The future is now."

Landry called Washington "the team to beat in our division."

"The Redskins already have that splendid offense. Now George is getting busy on toughening the defense," Landry said. "That's always been their problem, but that figures to change. If Allen gets everything together the way he's trying to, the Redskins will be a lot of trouble."

# Duane, Calvin & Walt

IN 1969, THE COWBOYS astounded everyone by taking a running back from Yale in the first round of the draft. Calvin Hill turned out to be the NFL's top rookie that season. He put himself in even more exclusive company, too, rushing for exactly the number of yards Jim Brown gained his rookie season (942). He finished second only to Gale Sayers in the NFL that season, and if he hadn't hurt a toe, Hill would've been the first rookie to crack 1,000 yards.

So it seemed strange for the Cowboys to even discuss taking another running back with their top pick in the 1970 draft.

"Is he better than Calvin Hill?" Tom Landry asked at a meeting to evaluate draft candidates.

"If Duane Thomas comes here, he will be your halfback," scout Red Hickey said.

Landry had to think about this. Hill was good enough to help Dallas win a championship. And now there was a chance of having him and someone better? There had to be a catch, and there was. Hickey discussed the volatile personality that came with this phenomenal athlete.

"Tom, I'm telling you, if Thomas is still there when our pick comes, take him—if you think you can handle him," Hickey said.

"You say he's better than Calvin," Landry said.

"Yes, he'll be your halfback," Hickey said.

"Then, Red, I think I'll try to handle him," Landry said.

Hill remained the starting halfback in 1970, picking up where he'd left off his rookie year—playing great when healthy but also sidelined by injuries. That gave Thomas a chance, and he lived up to Hickey's high praise; he also showed some of the peculiar personality Landry had been warned about.

Then there was the third member of the backfield—fullback Walt Garrison, the Cowboys' cowboy.

His favorite rodeo event was bulldoggin', also known as steer wrestling, and it showed in the way he played football. His style and skills were best summed up by his buddy Don Meredith: "If it was third down and you needed four yards, if you'd get the ball to Walt Garrison, he'd get you five. And if it was third down and you needed twenty yards, if you'd get the ball to Walt Garrison, by God, he'd get you five."

What a trio: Hill the intellectual, Thomas the deep thinker of another variety, and the good ol' boy, Garrison.

—★—

Thomas was born in Dallas, the middle child of five children for Lauretta and John Franklin Thomas. John was a big, strong man who was whispered to have fled his hometown of Marshall because he'd killed a man. He owned a funeral home eight blocks from the Cotton Bowl but later lost the business and resorted to doing construction work and odds jobs. Lauretta was active in the kids' schools and encouraged them to get their education, pray, and learn music. She loved history, especially studying the persecution of others, from Jersey Indians to Jews. She dreamed of being a teacher but had to clean houses to help support her family.

Finances became so tight that when Duane was in fourth grade, he was sent to live with Lauretta's sister in Los Angeles. He returned for a bit in sixth grade, then came back for good in high school after quarreling with his aunt over his curfew.

In Los Angeles, Duane interacted with white kids for the first time, learning it was okay to speak to white adults without asking for permission. He also became a sprinter. He'd begun making a name for himself in local track meets when he returned to Texas.

He wanted to keep running track when he started at Lincoln High School. His brother, Sonny, who was two years older, was playing football.

They wanted to spend more time together, so they made a deal—Sonny joined the track team and Duane went out for football.

As a ninth-grader, Thomas caught the eye of a tenth grader on the track team, a girl named Elizabeth Malone. She described him as being "tall and, well, exotic looking. He had the mystique of coming here from another state." Before they finished high school, they were married and had a child.

On the football team, Thomas came under the tutelage of coach Robert "Rabbit" Thomas. He demanded that every player know everyone's assignment on every play. Thomas absorbed it all and, by his senior year, he'd become a 215-pound freight train, helping Lincoln win the city championship.

Thomas went on to play college ball at West Texas State in Canyon, a town 18 miles south of Amarillo up in the Panhandle. He was lured there by coach Joe Kerbel, an incredibly stout man with an equally large personality.

Kerbel was tough and domineering. He turned himself into the king of Canyon, feeling so entitled that he would speed past cops and wave, or load up on groceries and tell the clerks, "Put it on my bill."

"He had those people hopping around like grasshoppers," Thomas said.

Kerbel hit it off with Thomas' dad, which went a long way toward getting Thomas there. Kerbel, who was white, also was more willing to take on black players and junior-college transfers than most big-time football factories.

The year before landing Thomas, Kerbel brought in Eugene "Mercury" Morris. He left school as the leading rusher in NCAA history, which meant Thomas didn't become the featured running back until he was a senior. He gained over 1,000 yards, and Dallas wasn't the only team scouting him.

While football came easy to Thomas, life was hard. His sophomore year, his dad died of pancreatic cancer. Ten months later, his mom dropped dead of a heart attack, right in front of the family's home. His youngest sister had a nervous breakdown, an older brother had a serious kidney problem, and a younger brother lost three fingers on his right hand in a car accident. Everyone looked to Duane as their savior, including his wife and their children; they now had two.

Despite Thomas' tremendous physical ability, some NFL teams were scared off by everything else about him. For instance, he worked hard in practice, but squabbled with Kerbel and trainers. He also owed more than $1,200 to a credit card company. "This kid should be one hell of a pro back, but I'm not sure he will be," an unnamed scout told *Sport* magazine.

The Cowboys figured he was worth the risk. If he didn't pan out, they still had Hill. So they drafted Thomas with the twenty-third pick in 1970, wiped out his debts, and hoped for the best.

About a month into his rookie season, Thomas replaced an injured Garrison and gained 79 yards on 13 carries against Minnesota's tough defense. The next week, he had 134 yards on 20 carries against another of the league's top defenses, the Kansas City Chiefs. He gained 1,118 yards over his final 12 games, counting the playoffs.

Thomas made it look easy. He ran with a graceful, gliding style that's rare for someone so big. He even was graceful describing his success.

"When you run out there, you see shadows. Then there's a flash of daylight, and you move through it, like in a dream," he said. "I look at running as being like an art design. You can create anything you want. It can be a beautiful thing. Like life, appreciate the beauty of it."

Thomas' finances were a mess because he made the mistake of trusting the wrong guy, a New York–based agent named Norm Young.

Young paid black middlemen to persuade players to sign with him. It was only later that his clients would discover what a sleazeball Young was. A Pittsburgh player once pulled a gun on him, and others had sued him. Living in Canyon, Texas, Thomas had no way of knowing any of that. Gil Brandt knew, though. The first time he talked to Thomas about Young, Brandt said, "Whatever you do, don't give this guy power of attorney."

"It's too late," Thomas said. "I already have."

Thomas also agreed to pay Young 10 percent of his entire contact, including the playoff bonuses that are usually strictly for the player. Young then cut a deal with the Cowboys that included a $25,000 bonus on top of salaries of $20,000 each of the first two years, and $22,000 in the final year. There were incentives such as $10,000 for being named rookie of the year, $5,000 for making All-Pro, and $5,000 for gaining at least 600 yards.

Young took $11,200 from the first check. That covered his 10 percent of the signing bonus and all three years' worth of salaries and $2,500 more as reimbursement for an advance he'd given Thomas.

This was Thomas' first slap of the real world. When he made $20 working for his dad, he got $20. There were no taxes or anything else taken out. So even though he knew Young would get a cut, it was jarring to see how much. And then when taxes and other charges lowered each paycheck, it pissed him off even more.

Things were set up so that the Cowboys sent every paycheck to Young's agency. Part of the money they removed was to pay Thomas' bills. They didn't. Creditors started coming around.

After the Super Bowl, an IRS agent told Thomas he owed the government $10,000.

"At this point I'm ready to kill Norman," Thomas said. "He'd been sending me statements that he'd paid them. I tried reaching him. He stayed unavailable. I could never get through. Finally I talked to him one last time. He said he'd paid. I said, 'Norman, these people want 10k.' He said he'd take care of it. He never did. I had to borrow the money."

Brandt advised Thomas to buy his way out of the deal, so he did. It cost him another $7,500, pushing him further in debt. But it was the quickest way to get rid of Young.

Thomas hired Chuck DeKeado as his new agent. DeKeado asked the Cowboys for salaries of $70,000 and $75,000 for the two years left on the contract. Dallas' counteroffer was much lower and included a third year. Schramm also mentioned how the club had dealt with Hill when he outperformed his rookie contract.

"Don't compare me with Calvin," Thomas told Schramm.

Before Calvin Hill was born, his father, Henry, was a sharecropper in South Carolina—until the day he took a drink of water that wasn't approved of by the farm owner's son. A fight ensued and Hill had to flee. He sent his wife, Elizabeth, to Baltimore and caught up once he could afford to join her. He only had enough money to reach Washington, then hitchhiked the rest of the way. They made their home in Turner's Section, an area just outside of town, in the shadow of a Bethlehem Steel plant.

Henry Hill had only a second-grade education. He learned how to read and write from Elizabeth, a homemaker and seamstress who had taught several of her siblings, even though she hadn't finished high school. As parents, they were determined for their only child to use education as a vehicle toward a bigger, better life.

Young Calvin read anything he could, even the set of encyclopedia books his father bought to help nourish his son's mind. He ended up earning a scholarship to the Riverdale School in the Bronx, where he excelled in academics and athletics; the football team had three undefeated seasons thanks mostly to Hill. He chose to continue studying and playing at Yale, and he helped the football team go 8–1 and 8–0–1 in his final two years. He was such a gifted athlete that while dabbling in track during the spring semesters, he set school records in the long jump and triple jump.

Hill planned to attend divinity school after college. He'd need a summer job first, though, and thought about trying to sign with his hometown team, the Colts. That's how sure he was that he would not be drafted.

On draft day, Hill called teammate Bruce Weinstein and pretended to be from the New York Giants. He said the club had just taken Weinstein in the second round. The prank worked until Hill started laughing. So when a guy claiming to be Gil Brandt called to say that Hill was a first-round pick by Dallas, Hill figured it was payback.

"Until Tom Landry got on the phone," he said. "After talking to Landry, I was almost in shock."

The Cowboys' scouting computer proclaimed Hill the fifth-best prospect in the 1969 draft. Scouts and coaches ranked him eighth. Taking him at No. 24 was an easy choice for Dallas, even if no Ivy League running back had been taken that early in 20 years.

At first, Landry didn't know what to do with Hill. He tried him at tight end, then linebacker. When a couple of running backs got hurt, Landry put Hill in the backfield.

Going into his first exhibition game, Hill feared being exposed as just another Ivy Leaguer, like the critics said. He quickly proved he belonged, both in the NFL and at running back. Postgame handshakes from veteran teammates eased his fears.

"That's when I first began to quit worrying about whether the Dallas Cowboys had made a mistake by drafting me in the first round," he said.

In his first regular-season start, Hill was named the NFL player of the week. In his second, he broke the club's single-game rushing record. In his third, he accounted for 206 yards of total offense before halftime. Then he dislocated the big toe on his right foot, starting a frustrating cycle of a player who could be great when healthy, but who kept getting hurt.

Hill played through the toe injury with a steel bar inside an oversized shoe for support. He wasn't as effective, and the toe ended up becoming infected, landing him in a hospital for more than a month. There was plenty to console him—a spot on the All-Pro team, the AP's Offensive Rookie of the Year Award, voted the favorite player by fans, and chosen as bachelor of the year. Dr Pepper hired him to tour the country holding rap sessions with black youths, giving advice and encouragement to help deal with whatever problems they were facing. He also was given use of a Chevrolet from a local dealer.

After the 1970 season, the dealer wanted the car back.

Thomas was the new sensation; Hill was old news.

Hill hurt his back one week, then gained just 10 yards on 10 carries the next game. He seemed to be running toward pileups instead of holes. Teammates wondered whether he'd ever be the same again. Then he hurt his shoulder, and Landry gave up on him. He moved Thomas to halfback and Hill to the bench. The Cowboys didn't lose again until the Super Bowl.

Against the Colts, Hill returned the opening kickoff 14 yards and hardly got back onto the field.

His only play from scrimmage was being used as a decoy on the game's pivotal play, when Thomas fumbled on his way into the end zone and Baltimore players convinced the officials they'd recovered it. Being a spectator in the most important game of his life, against the team he grew up rooting for, made Hill's heart ache.

"I think if there ever was a game that I was mentally and physically ready to play in, it was that one," Hill said. "I was really set. I was psyched up."

He channeled his disappointment into a desire to win back his job in 1971. Landry said Hill would have to prove his durability, so he bulked up, adding 10 pounds, much of it muscle from lifting weights. He was a solid 230 pounds and hardly lost any speed. He even grew an inch. Yes, at age 24.

"I knew I was getting taller," he said. "My pants were getting shorter."

Hill was growing as a person, too.

In 1969 and '70, he'd taken classes at the Perkins School of Theology at Southern Methodist, getting the divinity training he'd planned on getting after graduating Yale. His aim was to help those who weren't as fortunate as him. In the summer of 1971, Hill decided the downtrodden needed lawyers more than preachers, so he started to think about switching career paths. He spent time in courtrooms to get a feel for the environment. What struck him most was that public defenders either didn't care about their clients or didn't have enough time to learn to care about them. He knew that wasn't a problem for folks who could afford to pay for their own representation. Seeing this injustice within the justice system, he realized this was more of his calling. "I'd like to see law work the same for everybody," he said. "If some of the poor and underprivileged realize the law can also work for them, too, then I think society will be held together much better."

Hill had another reason to think about law school—his new bride, Janet, was considering it, too. She was teaching math at W. T. White High School in Dallas, but was thinking about going to Columbia.

At the start of training camp, Hill revealed his simple goal for the season: to play all 14 games. Everything else—including the contract he was due after the season—would take care of itself, as long as he remained healthy.

"My attitude right now is just as it was when I was a rookie. I'm challenging for a position," he said. "Last year was a disappointment. But it's not the tragedies a person experiences, only how he reacts to them."

At 6-foot, 205 pounds, Garrison wasn't particularly big. He certainly wasn't fast. But there may not have been a tougher son of a gun in the NFL.

"I've seen him have great games when others as physically banged up would not have even bothered to suit up," Landry said.

Like Super Bowl V. Garrison went in with a chipped collarbone, a badly sprained ankle, a bruised hip, and so many other bumps and bruises that it took 36 yards of tape to get him ready. He became the game's leading rusher.

There was plenty of country bumpkin in him, too. How many guys carry spittoons in their car? How many manage to spill it on a woman they're taking out for the first time? How many end up marrying her?

Garrison grew up in Lewisville, which is now a sprawling Dallas suburb with more than 100,000 residents. But in Garrison's youth, he recalls it being "so small they had both city limits signs on the same post. There was one main street, and the biggest deal that ever happened was when they paved that street."

He started riding bulls and bucking horses in eighth grade, competing in dusty rings every spring after playing football in the fall. Even while playing football, he broke colts after school to pick up some extra money.

He wasn't much of a football prospect coming out of Lewisville High. Years later, he asked University of Texas coach Darrell Royal why the Longhorns didn't recruit him. "Well, Walt, we took a look at you and you weren't any good," Royal said.

Garrison got only one college scholarship offer, and it was not because of his football prowess. It was because he worked the graveyard shift at the American Nut Company. The story is pretty convoluted, but it involves the owner of the nut company being the brother of the governor of New Mexico, and the lawmaker using his connections to get Garrison a scholarship from Oklahoma State University.

"Daddy said, 'If they don't want you or you're not good enough, come on back home. But if you just quit 'cause you're not tough enough—just keep going north.' And he meant it," Garrison said. "We grew up never having a whole lot of money. I used to borrow to go to rodeos. He figured I had a chance to go to school and maybe have a pro career, and he meant for me to make the most of it."

Garrison did, earning all-conference honors twice. The Cowboys drafted him in the fifth round in 1966, and he felt bold enough to make big demands for his signing bonus: first-class airline tickets for his parents to see him play in the East-West Shrine game and a two-horse, in-line trailer.

"What the hell is that?" Brandt said.

"It's a trailer where the horses are one behind the other," Garrison said.

For $2,200, the Cowboys bought him the best two-horse, in-line trailer Garrison could find. They also threw in a new Pontiac Grand Prix. Garrison got the car in green and white to match the trailer, and had the dealer put on a shiny chrome trailer hitch. When he brought the car to team head-quarters, Tex Schramm went behind it, got on his hands and knees, and said, "I want to see the trailer hitch that cost me one hundred and fifty dollars!" Garrison ended up trading in the Grand Prix for a pickup truck.

Horses and rodeos meant so much to Garrison that he developed a sneaky routine his rookie season.

The night before home games were spent at the Holiday Inn on Central Expressway. There was a team dinner at 6:00 p.m. and curfew wasn't until 11:00 p.m., so Garrison would slip out and take off for Mansfield's Cowbell Arena to enter the bulldoggin' event. He got away with this several times. Then someone called the team to say how nice it was of the Cowboys to let Garrison compete the night before a game. Garrison soon found himself in Landry's office, getting told, "We don't do that."

The night before a game in Pittsburgh that season, Garrison was resting in his hotel room when Meredith and other veterans took him out on the town. It was a rite of passage—getting a rookie drunk the night before a game. Garrison was hung over the next day and happy to be stuck on the bench. Except, with about two minutes left, Landry sent him in, and Meredith sent him into the teeth of the Steelers' defense. Meredith kept calling the same play—"31 trap"—and letting Garrison get smacked around. When he trudged back to the huddle after one of his poundings, Garrison looked as bad as he felt.

"Let me tell you something," Meredith growled. "You ain't nothing but a little pussy. You're hurtin'? Shit! You're nothin' but a little pussy. But I can't call you that in public so from now on I'm gonna call you 'Little Puddin.' But that means 'Little Pussy.' So every time I call you that you'll know what I'm talkin' about."

Meredith retired following the 1968 season, as did Don Perkins. That turned Garrison into the starting fullback. In '69 and '70, he blocked for the best rookie running backs in the NFL and did darn well handling the ball himself. He also was becoming better known for his personality and the fact he was the Cowboys' cowboy.

In 1971, NFL Films sent a crew to watch him go bulldoggin'. Wearing a heavy camera attached to a Cowboys helmet, Garrison lost his balance and caught a steer's horn in his mouth. It took about a dozen stitches to the stop the bleeding.

"Some people play golf. Me, I enjoy bulldoggin'," he told NFL Films. "Rodeoing helps me stay in shape in the offseason. Dangerous? Not really. There aren't many ways you can get hurt. The events don't last long enough. Calf roping takes the longest, and that's only to twelve seconds. Bulldoggin' lasts three to ten seconds. Heck, you can hold your breath or stand on your head in that little time."

Throughout the interview, Garrison dipped snuff and had a dashboard full of Skoal cans. Execs at U.S. Tobacco decided he'd be a great spokesman for their company. Garrison took their offer to Schramm, and he didn't like it one bit. He thought it would be bad for Garrison's image—meaning, really, the team's image. So Garrison turned them down. A year later, U.S. Tobacco again extended the invitation. This time, after learning there was no NFL rule against it, he signed up, starting a relationship that would make him more money than football ever did.

As training camp approached, Garrison had a chance for a more prominent role in the offense. With Thomas "retired" and with Hill's trouble staying healthy, Landry might have to rely on Garrison's creaky legs more than ever. With leverage like that, Garrison could've become another running back looking for a raise. Nah, not his style.

"If the Cowboys paid me what I was worth," he said that summer, "I'd lose money."

# Mr. Cowboy & Killer

DEFENSE WAS THE BACKBONE of the Cowboys' success. Bob Lilly and Lee Roy Jordan were the backbone of that defense, the Doomsday Defense.

Every offense getting ready to play Dallas worried first about keeping Lilly out of the backfield. Strong and quick, he was the perfect defensive tackle for any system, especially Tom Landry's.

Widely considered the team's best player, Lilly was also its hardest worker. The way Lilly saw it, he got paid to practice; that was work. Games were the reward, the fun part.

Consider his impact on the franchise this way: He arrived after Dallas went 0–11–1 in 1960. The Cowboys won the first two games he played and, because he never missed a regular-season game in his 14-year career, they'd literally never won a game without him when he retired. Hence the nickname, "Mr. Cowboy."

"A man like this comes along once in a lifetime," Landry said. "He is something even a little bit more than great. Nobody is better than Lilly."

Jordan was the vocal leader. His personality and position required it.

He was the middle linebacker, the quarterback of the defense. Landry created the job when he developed the 4–3 defense, and only gave it to guys he trusted. The lineage started with Sam Huff on the New York Giants, then Jerry Tubbs in Dallas. Jordan arrived in 1963, and he was deemed worthy to take over in 1966.

Jordan was relatively small at 6-foot-1, 220 pounds. He made up for it with a high football IQ and a ferocious style. He worked hard to keep his mind sharp, taking home a projector and several canisters of game film to watch every single night. As for the personality, well, that came naturally.

"We'd play intrasquad games, and the running backs would fasten their chin straps tight because Lee Roy tried to kill everybody," running back Walt Garrison said. "When he'd hit you, your mouthpiece would fly out of your mouth. It didn't matter if it was his own teammates. He'd hit his grandmother if she had a helmet on. That's why we called him 'Killer.' Lee Roy just loved to kill you. Six days a week, I hated Lee Roy. But on Sundays, when he was on my side, I loved him like a brother."

When the Cowboys were 5–4 in 1970, Landry was so disgusted that he told the team to go play touch football. Jordan and Lilly made it happen, as much for a stress-buster as an in-your-face to the coaches and everyone else who didn't believe in them. The club needed less interference and more encouragement anyway. Jordan and Lilly knew it could only come from within the locker room, that the only people who mattered were their teammates. They were going to treat practices as if they were games. If that didn't get them ready to handle the competition, nothing would.

It worked, all right. The Doomsday Defense allowed only 46 points over the seven-game winning streak that carried Dallas to the Super Bowl. In the NFC Championship Game, the Cowboys allowed only 10 points to a 49ers team that led the NFL in scoring.

"What we did last year pulled us together," Lilly said prior to the '71 season. "We built something, and no one is going to be able to take it away. I was never as proud of being a member of this team as I was last year. We finally found the secret to getting along. We finally showed ourselves that football can be fun."

Winning a championship would be much more fun.

"I used to worry about it all the time and we never got there, so I gave up," Lilly said. "But I tell you, that's one game that makes it worth playing. If you ever go, you damn sure want to go back."

Jordan came by his demeanor the old-fashioned way. As the fourth boy among seven kids, he needed a fighting spirit to hold his own growing up in the tiny town of Excel, Alabama. The Jordans grew cotton, vegetables, and sugar cane. They turned the cane into syrup and traded it for groceries. They also raised hogs, turkeys, cattle, and chicken.

Football was always his thing. He started on the high school varsity while in eighth grade, and was recruited to the big state school, Alabama, to play for Paul "Bear" Bryant. As a junior, Jordan was a big reason the Crimson Tide went undefeated and won their first national championship under Bryant. As a senior, Jordan was a unanimous All-American pick. He closed his college career with 31 tackles in a shutout of Oklahoma in the Orange Bowl. He would retire with the most tackles in Cowboys history.

"Lee Roy takes it mighty personal when anybody comes at him with a football," Bryant once said.

When Jordan arrived in Dallas, the Cowboys were still struggling for a team identity. The club also was lacking leadership in the locker room.

"That surprised the hell out of me," he said. "I mean, I kept waiting for somebody to come up, to stand up and take over, and nobody did. . . . I was used to somebody taking charge from when I played at Alabama, and coach Bear Bryant wanted somebody to do that. It was me. I'd be the leader, the holler guy. I'd be the one to yell at players. It wasn't there with the Cowboys, and I missed it. So after a couple of years, when I saw the need for it and just did it, things started to work better. The whole atmosphere changed, and I was a lot more comfortable."

Jordan led by any means necessary. When a Philadelphia player broke Don Meredith's often-broken nose, he got revenge with a clothesline takedown of Eagles running back Timmy Brown. The collision broke Brown's jaw and relieved him of some teeth.

The turnaround in 1970 was his greatest feat as a leader. His signature moment came in the NFC Championship Game against San Francisco. Early in the third quarter, the game was tied at three and the 49ers were about to snap the ball near their end zone. Jordan looked around the huddle and hollered, "Somebody's gonna make the big play! Somebody's gonna stop them!"

"And then who does it?" Lilly said. "Lee Roy himself."

Jordan intercepted a pass on the San Francisco 17 and returned it to the 14. Duane Thomas ran for a touchdown on the next snap, putting

the Cowboys ahead for good and on their way to the Super Bowl for the
first time.

—★—

Lilly was a country boy, too, raised in the West Texas town
of Throckmorton.

His dad, John Ernest "Buster" Lilly, was a mechanic with a passion
for football. He also was the victim of a drunk truck driver as a
teenager. His thigh bone was crushed so severely that doctors used
a steel plate to put it back together. The leg ended up 1 1/2 inches
shorter than the other, requiring him to wear a specially made shoe
for balance. It hurt him every day for decades. Once Bob was playing
for the Cowboys, he asked team doctors to take a look. They removed
the plate and chiseled out an infected part of the bone, finally giving him
some relief.

When Bob was a boy, Buster did some scouting for the Throckmorton
High varsity. Coaches thanked him by passing along a beat-up football so
he could play catch with his son. They started going to games when Bob
was eight, and they occasionally made the several-hour trek to Fort Worth
to watch college games at TCU, the alma mater of Buster's favorite player,
Slingin' Sammy Baugh.

Bob describes himself as being thin, underweight, and uncoordinated
when he started high school. Not very good at football, either. But he loved
the game and forced himself to get better. His body filling out helped. So
did strength built by hauling hay and other chores, which he did more of
once his dad got into the land-clearing business.

He figured that after high school he'd go into the military. Then, after
his junior season of high school, Lilly received a letter from Baugh. He was
coaching at Hardin-Simmons in Abilene and wanted Lilly to play for him.
Suddenly, he realized college might be an option.

Hardin-Simmons wasn't the only school that saw this prodigy. TCU
coaches were keeping tabs on him, too. Assistant coach Allie White
actually discovered him at a volleyball game. White was there scouting
someone else, but came away raving about Lilly.

But before his senior year, the Lillys took off for Oregon.

A drought turned the land around Throckmorton into dust, shriveling
Buster's business. Relatives in Oregon found him work in the town of

Pendleton, so he sold practically everything he owned, built a trailer to haul the rest, and headed to the Pacific Northwest.

White kept after Lilly. He sent him a postcard offering a scholarship, and Lilly accepted. He and a friend jumped into an old Studebaker and drove 1,800 miles to campus.

Lilly became such a force he was dubbed the "Purple Cloud" and named an All-American. His strength became so legendary that people talked about the time he picked up a Volkswagen Beetle in a parking lot and carried it to the steps of a nearby building.

The ever-humble Lilly insists it didn't happen. Well, it did, but not exactly like that. "I came into the parking lot, and there was a Volkswagen in my spot," Lilly said. "I didn't pick it up. I just moved one end at a time until I had moved it off my spot."

The Cowboys lucked into him.

They were supposed to have the second pick in the 1961 draft but had traded it. They wouldn't pick again until No. 16. Lilly was still available at 13 when Cleveland was stuck figuring out what to do. The guy they wanted was headed to the AFL. So Tex Schramm offered Dallas' first-round pick in 1962 for this selection right now. It was the first of many draft-day coups for Schramm and the Cowboys.

As a rookie, Landry put Lilly on the end of the defensive line. Playing out of position on a lousy team, Lilly broke five ribs, a wrist, and a thumb, sprained both ankles, and hurt a knee. And he still made the all-rookie team. Landry kept him at left end through the first half of 1963. Finally, Landry moved Lilly to right tackle. By the next season, Landry was calling Lilly among the finest tackles in the NFL and certainly the quickest. It was as if he could go from snap to full speed before the guy trying to block him had even made his first move.

A big evolution for Lilly and the Cowboys came in 1965, when Landry added a wrinkle to his 4–3 defense. He called it the "Flex."

Because Vince Lombardi had everyone running to daylight, Landry decided to fabricate some shutters. He put his four defensive linemen in a zigzag formation—the right end and left tackle in the traditional spots, but with the right tackle and left end a few feet back. The distance meant a few extra steps to get to the line, but they had a better idea of where the play was headed once they got there. The defense was less likely to throw a running back for a loss, but they also were less likely to give up big gains.

That was the flexible part: bending a play back against the way the offense wanted it to go.

As for rushing the passer, the Cowboys had schemes named for dance steps. The "Cha-cha" was when Jethro Pugh—who lined up at the other tackle spot, immediately left of Lilly—jumped out first, into the gap between the center and guard. As soon as the center moved toward the guard, Lilly bolted through his vacated spot. When the Cowboys used the "Limbo," Lilly was the guy gobbling up blockers, this time a guard and tackle. That gave George Andrie—who lined up immediately right of Lilly—a clear path into the backfield.

Landry's schemes were tough to learn. Once mastered, they were far tougher for offenses to exploit.

In '65, Lilly's second full season at tackle and first in the Flex, Dallas avoided a losing record for the first time, going 7–7. The Cowboys won 10 games and the division the following year. They kept winning, too, launching what would become the greatest feat of Landry's career: 20 straight winning seasons.

Midway through the 1967 season, Lilly and his wife Kitsie celebrated the birth of a daughter. The week the playoffs opened, Kitsie found the baby dead in the crib, having stopped breathing in her sleep. She was buried the next day, and Lilly rejoined his teammates for a victory over Cleveland. A week later, he played the Ice Bowl with a heavy heart.

The story was hardly mentioned in the newspapers. It was typical of the era, and Lilly appreciated it. He also was grateful not to have much publicity about his marriage falling apart in 1970. The football aspect of that story was that Lilly's job became his refuge.

"I'd just go out to the field and work my ass off and get my mind on football," Lilly said. "And I think maybe I had the best year I've ever had. That's funny, isn't it? I guess you compensate."

Entering his eleventh season, Lilly remained in terrific shape, plus had a wealth of experience to draw upon. The combination made him as dominating as ever.

"I'm taking my shots now. Not dirty, understand. But I'm not letting anyone stand around and sightsee," he said. "Holding is something I put up with for too many years. Holding can be eliminated by different methods of rushing the passer. I use my own hands a lot more. When that fails, you start belting them around the headgear and it tends to eliminate holding."

Lilly always was looking to refine his performance, seeking little advantages he could gain here or there. So when he noticed that he blinked whenever the ball was snapped or whenever he hit an opponent, he decided that had to stop.

"Blinking causes the loss of approximately a millisecond—which may not seem like a lot, but in football it could mean the difference between getting the advantage over your opponent or allowing him to get the advantage over you," Lilly said. "So when attending practices or meetings, I would gently touch my eyeballs over and over until I got the point where I would no longer blink. The players used to make fun of me, but before long they were doing it, too."

Lilly had once targeted 1971 as his final season. He'd even thought about retiring if the Cowboys had won Super Bowl V. But the game was still fun, still as profitable as anything else he could think of doing. And he had a burning desire to be a champion.

Lilly had an idea of what it would be like—the hugs, the smiles, the thrill of victory. And a championship cigar. He rarely smoked, but he'd seen Mickey Mantle fire up a stogie after winning a title and thought it seemed like the thing to do. Lilly's business partner and pal Bud Cooper was a cigar smoker, so he gave Lilly a nice Cuban cigar to enjoy after Super Bowl V. Following the loss, Lilly didn't dare light it. Although he went straight from the Super Bowl in Miami to the Pro Bowl in Los Angeles, Lilly took the cigar with him. He brought it back to Dallas and kept it on ice for safekeeping. Every time he opened his freezer in 1971, the cigar was there, a fuse waiting to be lit.

# Craig vs. Roger

O N FEBRUARY 5, 1971, the quarterback of the Dallas Cowboys celebrated a birthday.

Both of them.

Craig Morton turned 28, Roger Staubach 29. Yet from a football perspective, Morton was the veteran; he was coming off his sixth season in the NFL, Staubach only his second.

Morton had it made. At 6-foot-4, 220 pounds, a bachelor with curly hair and a dream job, he was the envy of most men in Dallas and the desire of most women. His bed was only empty if he wanted a good night's sleep.

"Craig was a party animal. In fact, he was the whole zoo," Walt Garrison said. "That boy could rock 'n' roll, let me tell you. He spent money like it was fertilizer, and he had a couple thousand head of cattle. And, boy, he had some good-looking girlfriends. He didn't have a wife or family and he was the quarterback of the Dallas Cowboys, which was glamorous as hell. And he had a big contract. So why not enjoy it?"

Bob Lilly considered Morton an all-pro partier.

"His pursuit of fun, drink, and women was at the top of his priority list," Lilly said. "Craig proved he was a great athlete—he could stay out all night and still make practice in the morning, not to mention being able to casually throw seventy yards as though it were twenty."

Morton's rise to the role of starting quarterback pretty much followed Tom Landry's perfect scenario.

A first-round draft pick from Cal-Berkeley, Morton spent four years learning the team's intricate system while watching Don Meredith run the team. Morton started more games during his apprenticeship than Landry preferred, but it made him ready as could be when Meredith retired in the summer of 1969.

Sure enough, the Cowboys had a seamless transition, going from 12–2 in Meredith's final season to 11–2–1 in Morton's first season in charge. The next season was 1970, which culminated in the team's first trip to the Super Bowl. A few weeks after losing to the Colts, Morton seemed to have plenty to celebrate as he blew out the candles on his cake.

If only it was that simple.

The popular sentiment was that the Cowboys made the Super Bowl *despite* their quarterback. The game was remembered as the "Blunder Bowl," and Morton's blunders were the worst of all. Three of his final six passes were caught by members of the Baltimore Colts, helping them turn a 13–6 deficit midway through the fourth quarter into a 16–13 victory.

There was little appreciation for the fact Morton had gotten Dallas within minutes of a championship while playing through the agony of a pinched nerve and floating bone chips in his throwing elbow. Few people seemed to care that he would be having surgery to put his wounded wing back together, or that he could return better than ever. Even some of his teammates were grumbling that Staubach deserved a chance. Landry said he was considering it, too.

So on February 21, Morton let everyone know how he felt. He wrote a guest column for the *Dallas Times-Herald* that ran under the headline, "The Best Is Yet to Come." He retraced the steps in his career, the years "devoted to learning and waiting out some very, very frustrating moments," and got a lot more off his chest.

> In my fourth year an unusual but persistent creature arose from the stands of the Cotton Bowl. His name was "Boo-bird." He started in small numbers but as time passed he multiplied into the thousands. . . . The Meredith Boo-birds have switched their allegiance to Morton, and many of the Morton supporters now have chosen another. I have come to realize the deep hurt and frustration that Don once felt and which may have put an early end to a great career.

At first I felt all the personal things that booing represents. I accepted them and made this rejection a personal challenge. Despite my personal commitment, injuries greatly affected my throwing. First came the dislocated shoulder with which I played 11 games in 1969 and became the fifth-ranked quarterback in the NFL. Then, in 1970, I played some eight games with a bruised and infected elbow and again wound up as the No. 5 quarterback in football. I could never really accept being called the worst quarterback in football and receiving much of the criticism and blame for losses which in my mind weren't all my fault.

I do not write to complain, but to relay to the fans the absurdity that surrounds the personal life of a celebrity. Many people consider me aloof and carefree. Some say I need a wife to settle me down, still more consider me a playboy, others have voiced added opinions. Perhaps in other eyes I do touch some part of these typecastings.

But when I look at myself I see a sensitive, quiet, dedicated person who enjoys people and has always given as he has received. I probably have become more withdrawn the last two years because of many unpleasant moments in public. I know all this goes with being an athlete, and I accept it as such. I have accepted criticism and blame without comment, and I have been the first to praise others where praise is due. I have always done these things and will continue to do so as it is part of my real self.

This past year was without question one of great frustration. First, being benched was a blow. But it was one from which I had seen Don come back. I was booed soundly, but accepted it for I had seen Don fight against it. I heard and received unbelievable words and letters, but learned to accept them because another— Don—had come before me. You see, those who criticized forgot that they weren't original. I had studied under the best and was prepared for their unknowledgeable forecasts, bits of "inside information" and the "real scoop of victory and defeat."

I did achieve something with the help of a great football team that only a handful of quarterbacks have accomplished: a trip to the Super Bowl. I am extremely proud to have been a part of this, and it will be the highlight of my career until the day of victory in this game. I love Dallas and its people, but I will not change my beliefs or goals for those who scorn and criticize me. You see, I enjoy my own company. Although I do have many faults, as all of us do, I try to understand them and correct them just as the birds that hover above and about the Cotton Bowl.

In conclusion, I have one prediction that will shock some, be laughed at by others, and perhaps agreed upon by a few. But it will not elude me. Craig Morton will be the best quarterback in football.

—★—

For Staubach, being 29 was a huge number for a guy still trying to prove he belonged in the NFL.

At 21, Staubach was the best player in college football, the winner of the Heisman Trophy. But he still had another year at the U.S. Naval Academy, then a commitment to serve four years in the navy. He spent one of them in Vietnam and was discharged on July 5, 1969, the very day that Meredith retired.

The Cowboys had taken a flier on Staubach in the 1964 draft, grabbing his rights in the tenth round. Tex Schramm would never be so bold as to say he knew Staubach would be worth the wait. But it seemed like a risk worth taking.

The club had to outmaneuver the AFL's Kansas City Chiefs to secure his rights during his years in the service. They won him over with a $10,000 signing bonus and a salary of $500 a month while he was in the navy, with guarantees for another bonus and a solid salary whenever he came out—as long as he was still good enough to make the team.

While in Vietnam, Staubach got tractors to level a field into a semblance of a playing surface so he could throw around the football Gil Brandt sent him. The field was dubbed Staubach Stadium, complete with a wooden sign bearing that name. The ground was still so rough that the ball got torn up, forcing Staubach to write Brandt asking for a replacement.

In 1967, on his way home from Vietnam, Staubach visited Cowboys training camp in Thousand Oaks, California, for a few days. Landry checked out his form and gave him some things to work on. Over the next year, Staubach saved up his leave time so he could experience a full training camp.

Staubach didn't tell anyone then, but those 15 days in the summer of '68 were a huge test for him.

He and his wife, Marianne, were happy with their navy life. However, football was his first love, and he wanted to see whether he was still good enough to compete with the pros. If so, he'd stick with the plan of joining the Cowboys. If not, he would continue serving his country.

A game featuring mostly rookies from the Cowboys and Los Angeles Rams made the verdict clear. Staubach completed 10 of 14 passes, including touchdowns that covered 48 and 51 yards. He also scrambled four times for 28 yards.

"This guy can play in our league," Rams coach George Allen said. "He throws well long and is an exceptional runner. He reminds me of Fran Tarkenton, except he has a stronger arm."

Watching Staubach sweat through two practices a day during his time away from the military, players were divided into two schools of thought. They either respected his dedication or questioned his sanity.

"I'm glad it's you instead of me against this guy," Meredith told Morton. "Anybody who takes a vacation and comes to two-a-days has got to be a little weird. He's gonna get your job."

Staubach headed back to his base in Pensacola, Florida, with a present from Landry—a playbook. This was a big deal because Landry rarely let go of such a thing. But he realized Staubach was a keeper and that he had some catching up to do.

Staubach put it to good use as quarterback and backfield coach for the Pensacola Goshawks, a team from his naval base who played small, four-year colleges. He used Dallas' formations and numbering system—even-numbered plays going left, odds to the right—so it would become second nature.

In the spring of 1969, knowing Staubach was headed their way, the Cowboys traded third-string quarterback Jerry Rhome. When Meredith retired a few weeks later, Staubach was up to No. 2.

He ended up starting the 1969 opener because Morton broke a finger.

Dallas beat St. Louis, but the job still belonged to Morton. He returned the next week, and over the rest of the season Staubach only was used to finish lopsided games.

He nearly had a chance for a bigger role when Morton slightly separated his throwing shoulder. But Morton didn't dare take any time off to recover. Perhaps Meredith's crack about Staubach taking his job echoed as Morton forced himself to play through the pain. A week after the injury, Morton persevered so well that he threw five touchdown passes, prompting owner Clint Murchison Jr. to recommend he have a sore shoulder every week.

Morton's first season in charge ended the same way Meredith's last season did: with a first-round playoff loss. So Landry decided to shake things up.

He sent out a questionnaire asking players what should be done differently. Changes followed, although not necessarily the ones recommended by responses to the questionnaire. The biggies were the hiring of a strength and conditioning coach and setting "performance levels" for each player; failure to meet them landed a player on the bench, regardless of the player.

Morton was coming back from shoulder surgery, so he lacked his usual arm strength early in 1970. That prevented him from meeting his performance level. Sticking to his vow, Landry benched him. Staubach again started the opener.

He led the Cowboys to a win, then won again, earning a third straight start. Dallas trailed St. Louis only 3–0 when Staubach threw his second interception of the game. Landry likely had been looking for an excuse to go back to Morton, and this was it. It also became the first time in Staubach's career that he'd been pulled from a game.

Staubach knew what long odds he faced to keep the starting job that season. Landry had lectured him about the fact that in the modern era of the NFL, no starting quarterback had won a championship in his first three years. The most inexperienced starter was Joe Namath, who'd won the previous Super Bowl in his fourth year. So when the team was slumping along at 5–4 and Landry debated which quarterback to pick, Staubach wasn't surprised Morton got the nod.

But now, as the '71 season approached, things were different.

There was the chat with Landry on the airplane home from the Super Bowl. And turning 29 served as another reminder to Staubach that he couldn't wait much longer.

—★—

Coming off the lousy performance in the Super Bowl, Morton needed all the good publicity he could get. Throughout the 1971 offseason, he kept going the other way.

It started innocently enough in early March with some comments to a reporter in Abilene. Perhaps it was a slow news day because a big fuss was made over what he said—that he couldn't handle another year of Landry calling plays for him, even though the coach had done so throughout the run to the Super Bowl; he also seemed to dismiss the possibility of losing his job to Staubach.

"He's going to have to do a lot more than he has," Morton said. "It's nothing I really think that much about—you know, he has to beat me out, I don't have to beat him out."

A few days later, Morton had surgery on his right elbow, and all went well. While some questioned why he didn't do it sooner, the important thing was that it was done. He was supposed to be healed for the start of minicamp, certainly by training camp.

He was released from Baylor Hospital on a Saturday morning with his elbow in a cast. He had a date that night, and the woman drove. She stopped for gas at an all-night service station off Central Expressway. What happened next depends on who is telling the story.

According to officers D. E. Mayner and R. C. Hawthorne, Morton stood beside the parked car and peed in the parking lot, despite a men's restroom being only about 10 yards away. According to Morton, no such thing happened. But everyone agrees a foul-mouthed shouting match followed. Morton was placed under arrest on a misdemeanor charge of "indecent conduct and abusive language." He was taken to jail and released after paying a $50 bond.

"It's so ridiculous, it's absurd," Morton said. "We pulled up to get some gas, and I got out of the car. My date was driving, and I told her to pull closer to the gas pump. Then the two policemen came up and told me I was under arrest. I thought they were kidding. I said I hadn't done anything. They told me to get in the car. I still thought they were kidding. Then one of them grabbed my right arm and bent it behind my back. I told him to take it easy, I just had that arm operated on. They made me get in the patrol car, and we drove off. I admit that's when I started using abusive language.

I was pretty darned upset. This whole thing is a farce. I did not urinate in the street. That's a complete falsity, and it's not even in the charge given to my attorney. I have no idea what made those policemen come at me in the first place."

After the backlash from the Abilene stories, Morton knew how bad this would look in the newspapers.

"I wish everyone didn't have to read about it," he said. "This is a bunch of trash. But the damage is done. People probably won't read the retractions."

Morton was vindicated a few months later. The indecent conduct charge was dropped. He paid only a $15 fine after pleading no contest to the charge for cussing out the cops. Whatever satisfaction this might've bought him turned out to be short-lived because of what hit during the next news cycle.

"Dallas Cowboy quarterback Craig Morton is broke," read the first sentence of a United Press International article out of Oakland, California.

Morton had filed for personal bankruptcy protection and corporate bankruptcy for two bookstores and two sporting goods stores. He listed assets of $93,000 and debts of $546,000. He owed $50,000 to the Cowboys and was in trouble with the IRS.

"I had a guy keeping my income tax and [was] supposed to have paid it," Morton said. "Now I hear from the revenue service I owe them for three years. He never sent the money."

Around this time, his professional reputation took a blindsided hit.

*The New York Times* asked NFL coaches to pick any quarterback other than their own that they could have for the upcoming season. The poll drew 22 anonymous responses. Namath was the winner. Morton was the loser; a 28-year-old starting quarterback in the most recent Super Bowl got a grand total of zero votes.

Staubach, meanwhile, was enhancing his image as someone too good to be true—the college star who married his childhood sweetheart and served his country before starting his pro career.

Right after Morton's arrest, Staubach was in the headlines, too—for the uplifting speech he gave at a Salvation Army luncheon. A few weeks later, he was pictured in a newspaper ad for Camp Rio Vista, listed as the athletic advisor. Staubach wasn't trying to start a positive-PR campaign, but it probably seemed like it to Morton and his supporters. Consider some of these selections from Staubach's clip file:

- May 9, *Irving Daily News*: "Cowboy Staubach says 'God center of his life'"

  "There is a simple solution to all of our problems and that is belief in Jesus Christ," Staubach said in a speech at Public Schools Stadium. "I just wanted the people of Irving to know that here is an athlete, parent, and businessman who makes God the center of his life."

- May 27, *Dallas Times-Herald*. Staubach asks locals to fly flags in support of an organization seeking the release of prisoners of war in Southeast Asia.

  "These men need faith in God, faith in their families, and faith that people in the nation care about them to get them through," Staubach said.

- May 30, *Dallas Times-Herald*. Featured in a photo promoting Dallas' "Bag Your Trash" campaign.

  Staubach, in short sleeves and a tie, is shown handing a bag of trash to Raymond Wilson, the sanitation department foreman.

- June 19, *Dallas Morning News*. A story runs about Garrison and Staubach hosting a football camp for kids.

  "I really like this, but Roger is better with the kids than I am. He's been here before," Garrison said. The story notes that in 1970, Staubach ran the camp by himself.

- June 21, *Longview Daily News*: "Landry Isn't Staubach's Only Coach," reads a headline spanning the entire page atop a story about Staubach being the guest speaker for Religious Heritage Day, part of Titus County's 125th anniversary celebration.

  "It takes a fine defense to put the offense in a good field position," Staubach said. "In the game of life, God is like that strong defense who has put you in a good field position. He's given us the Bible, tradition, and a great coach named Christ. But it's up to us to get that ball across the goal line; and I'm talking about salvation. . . . I make every decision like I think He would make them. I guess that includes the decisions I make on AstroTurf as well. Speaking about next year, I'm looking forward to a great season.

My only hope is that I pray a little harder this year to go one game better."

Yet there was one story Staubach hid from the public.

About two months after the Super Bowl, Roger and Marianne Staubach were expecting their fourth child, a fourth daughter. They'd decided to name her Amy. A week past her due date, Marianne Staubach checked into Presbyterian Hospital. She hadn't felt any kicks for a few days.

"There's been a serious problem here," the doctor said. "We can't find the heartbeat of the baby. It's like a thousand-to-one shot the baby is still alive when we can't hear the heartbeat. Of course, we've had situations where the heart is in a position where we couldn't hear it. But these situations are rare. Very rare. I just wanted you to be prepared for what we might find."

The baby came out looking perfect. But she was stillborn. The umbilical cord was shorter than usual and doctors surmised it had strangled her. She was buried in a small box, the words "Baby Girl Staubach" etched on the grave marker.

About 10 months earlier, Staubach's dad died of diabetes. Now he'd lost a baby, too.

"We never even knew her," he said.

Throughout the summer, Marianne woke up in tears. Daughters Michelle, Stephanie, and Jennifer were saddened, too. All Roger and Marianne could tell the girls was that their sister was in heaven. Some nights, during their bedtime prayers, the girls would ask God to bless Amy, too.

—★—

Morton believed what he'd told the Abilene paper, about the competition for his job rankling him.

Once his arm healed from the surgery, he knew he would end this supposed controversy.

The job was *his*, damn it.

"I'm throwing well enough now that nobody can take the job away," he said. "After this year there won't be any more of that stuff. I'll settle it once and for all. I'm tired of it. I earned that spot through a lot of years."

But Morton underestimated the drive of a guy trying to make up for lost time.

Staubach's straight-arrow persona belied the heart of a tireless warrior. The story about him wearing out footballs in Staubach Stadium wasn't just a charming anecdote; it showed his work ethic. The story about the Pensacola Goshawks shows a guy who doesn't just play for fun, he plays to win and tries getting better every chance he gets.

"I once told Craig Morton that I didn't know how he could sleep at night because he should know that Roger was up studying so he can take his job," Calvin Hill said. "If he were a running back, I'd be afraid even if he were third or fourth string and I knew he was after my job. He has that kind of spirit."

A challenge only made Staubach fight harder. Garrison put it this way: "If somebody did one hundred sit-ups, Roger was going to do one hundred and one. If somebody ran a mile in six minutes, Roger would do it in five fifty-nine. If somebody threw the ball sixty yards, he was going to throw it sixty-one." Bob Lilly said Staubach would race Bob Hayes in 100-yard dashes, then keep asking for another chance . . . and another, and another . . . until Hayes would just let him win so he could get off the field.

In the summer of 1971, Staubach faced two challenges. He had to convince Landry a third-year guy deserved the chance to lead a team, and he had to beat out Morton. Accomplishing one without the other wouldn't be enough.

Staubach's first chance to impress came at an April minicamp. Morton wasn't cleared to throw yet, so Staubach was competing against himself.

In 1970, he'd been told his delivery was slow. He showed up to this session having learned to hold the ball higher, closer to his ear. That gave him one of the fastest releases around. And he always put plenty of zip on the ball.

"He can throw a football through a car wash without getting it wet," passing coach Ray Renfro said.

Once doctors gave Morton the green light, he was amazed at how good his arm felt. He was back to his original throwing motion. His old velocity returned, too.

"I didn't get any tingle or sharp pain," he said. "I could wing the sideline pattern and also throw the bomb. I feel by the time training camp begins I should have a really strong arm . . . . Remember last year? I couldn't work out during the week, and it got to the point where our patterns had no timing. I shouldn't have that trouble any more."

Landry vowed to keep an open mind. His only pre-camp declaration was that both quarterbacks would start exhibition games.

"As far as Craig is concerned, we must assume that with his offseason operation he will come into camp with his arm ready to throw. And, if this is so, then we will feel that he will be what we anticipated in the past, and he will be efficient and operating effectively. We must go on this assumption," Landry said. "But we do feel that Roger will make a very substantial challenge to the position. It will be only through the preseason games that we will be able to determine whether or not his challenge will be sufficient to take over the number one spot."

The pressure to get this right was starting to mount. Some of the heat came from that old Cowboys gunslinger Dandy Don. Meredith had dealt with Landry's infuriating wrangling with his career for too many years. While Morton wrote that the Boo-birds drove away Meredith, the coach in the fedora was plenty accountable, too. In fact, a few more encouraging words from Landry might've quieted those jeering fans. Landry and Meredith were bound to butt heads because they had opposite views about life, on and off the field. Landry never accepted that someone as carefree as Meredith might also truly care. He under-valued both Meredith's incredible toughness and his rapport in the locker room. Landry won all their arguments, of course, because he had all the power. So maybe Meredith was just jabbing back now that the dynamics of their relationship had spun around. Coming off his popular debut season on *Monday Night Football*, he had all the power. Everyone liked hearing what he had to say about everything, especially a topic like this.

Then again, maybe Meredith was just speaking his mind when he spouted a few theories about Landry's handling of quarterbacks to the *Los Angeles Times* in a story headlined, "Meredith Raps Cowboy Coach for QB Policy." "Landry would never come out and designate his number one quarterback. And I think that's wrong because it's the one position in which he should say, 'This is my man,'" Meredith said. "It can't help but have a negative effect on the rest of the team if he doesn't do it. . . . I knew I was number one, but I don't know if anyone else ever did."

Meredith kept the heat on in a follow-up article by Steve Perkins of the *Dallas Times-Herald*.

"In that organization, the quarterback is always going to get the brunt of the criticism," Meredith said.

CRAIG VS. ROGER   85

But isn't that typical in football?

"No," Meredith said. "Some places, they fire coaches."

—★—

On July 11, Marianne Staubach and the girls drove Roger to Love Field to send him off to California for the start of what promised to be a career-defining season, one way or another.

Morton was supposed to be on the same flight. But he wasn't there.

He was already in California, already checked into training camp.

★

# Flawed Perfection

# And So They Gathered

ONCE THE STING OF losing Super Bowl V faded, thoughts turned to getting ready for the 1971 season. Right away, folks realized something. Maybe next year really was *the* year for the Dallas Cowboys.

Team owner Clint Murchison Jr. felt so good about the outlook that during a spring chat to the Irving Chamber of Commerce, he said: "The 1971 Cowboy team will not only be the best in the league. It will furthermore be the best in the history of the NFL. This team, I predict, will score points like the 1951 Rams and play defense like the 1963 Chicago Bears." Those Rams averaged 32 points per game; the Bears allowed a record-low 144 points.

Dallas certainly had a schedule that set it up to be successful. The road map for the upcoming season looked like something Commissioner Pete Rozelle mapped out as a favor to his old pal Tex Schramm.

Eight of the 14 games would be against division foes. That left six games to be filled in. The group Dallas landed won only 32 percent of its games in 1970. By comparison, Philadelphia's nondivision foes won 66 percent of their games in 1970. So the Cowboys were not only expected to be among the best teams, they also would have the easiest nondivision schedule.

Even the order of those games set up nicely for Dallas. There were so many softies the first two months that a 7–0 start seemed very possible.

The preparation for it all began in earnest with training camp on the campus of Cal Lutheran in Thousand Oaks, California. Rookies started working out on Saturday, July 10. Veterans had to be there the following Friday.

As late as July 1, starters Mel Renfro, Jethro Pugh, Craig Morton, Chuck Howley, Walt Garrison, John Niland, and Blaine Nye didn't have contracts. Neither did top pick Tody Smith or second-round pick Isaac Thomas. And Duane Thomas was still "retired."

"All over the NFL, the salary pinch is on," said Los Angeles attorney Ron Barak, Smith's agent. "But Dallas is leading the league. This is one department where the Cowboys are Super Bowl champs."

Schramm harrumphed, "We never have any trouble signing a good player."

Schramm also downplayed the club's decision to give safety Cliff Harris a new contract with one year remaining on his original deal. Harris had gone from an undrafted rookie out of NAIA Ouachita Baptist to starting the opener as a rookie, then starting the Super Bowl in his second year. He had outperformed his measly original contract and deserved being properly compensated. Thomas hadn't come from obscurity or surprised anyone by starting the Super Bowl; he'd been a first-round draft pick and was being paid to perform at a high level. Still, Thomas declared, "I'm not going to camp unless they give me a raise."

—★—

If he had everyone signed and healthy, Tom Landry knew he had the makings of an outstanding club, his best yet. If anything, he had too much talent at the skill positions—three proven running backs, two future Hall of Fame receivers, a future Hall of Fame tight end, and a capable backup . . . and one ball for all of them to share.

"It could be a problem only if the individuals become jealous. If that happens, we don't have any teamwork," Landry said. "I hope our only problem is so much offense that everyone wants to help the other guy."

Even if everyone got along swell, it would take time to get in synch. Lance Alworth and Billy Truax were newcomers. Lance Rentzel and Pettis Norman would be missed. And there was that minor detail of picking a starting quarterback.

Landry's thoughts about the quarterbacks were a moving target.

He referred to Roger Staubach as being ready to "actually go in there and carry the team," adding that "all Roger has ever needed is experience." Then Landry said Staubach had to outperform Craig Morton, and not just statistically.

Landry wanted Morton to throw every day to make sure his arm could handle the wear and tear, to "work himself out of the mental shock of the Super Bowl. . . . That takes time," Landry said.

Once Morton had a healthy arm and a clear head, then Landry could evaluate him. But it was clear that the coach held his incumbent starter in high esteem.

"All I can say about Morton is that he was hurt for two years and did a fine job considering," Landry said.

Dealing with the status of being conference champions was another challenge for Landry.

In the limited history of teams that reached the Super Bowl, only the Green Bay Packers made it twice in a row, and that was back in Super Bowls I and II.

Landry brought this up during his opening speech of training camp. He told players not to rely on their past success or their potential to carry them through the fall. The 1970 season provided fresh examples of what can go wrong, and what can go right. Which path the 1971 team would follow was up to them.

"People striving, being knocked down and coming back . . . this is what builds character in a man," Landry told the club. "The Bible discusses this at length in Paul. Paul says that adversity brings endurance, endurance brings on character, and character brings on hope."

—★—

California Lutheran University is about 45 miles north of Los Angeles and just a few miles inland from the Pacific Ocean. It opened in 1961, shortly after the master-planned community of Thousand Oaks grew from the brushy scrubland of the Conejo Valley.

The matchmaker who lured the Cowboys was a dormitory housemother.

She'd been a dorm mom at St. Olaf College, the Lutheran school in Minnesota where the Cowboys trained in 1961. When she transferred to Cal Lutheran, she told the people in charge about the great deal they could have. An NFL team would pay $50,000 to spend about six weeks on campus when nothing is going on there anyway.

The Cowboys were up for it because the climate was perfect. Afternoon temperatures got into the 80s, warm enough for players to break a good sweat, and evenings were in the 60s. It never rained in July or August, and there was almost always a breeze. Humidity wasn't an issue.

Los Angeles was far enough not to be a distraction, but close enough to help. The Cowboys sent their morning practice films to Universal Studios for processing and had them back in time to watch that night. As for nightlife in and around Thousand Oaks, there wasn't much—another plus as far as the team was concerned. The local hotspots were Los Robles, a restaurant-night club that overlooked a golf course, and Orlando's, a pizza joint-discotheque. Players and coaches had a deal: Los Robles was home turf for the bosses, Orlando's for the players, although the pizza place became happy hunting for coaches and other front-office types after the players' curfew.

Because Orlando's was *the* place for the players, it became *the* place for women in the area—young and old, small and big, single and married. Orlando's became known as "Peyton Place West" because of all the soap opera-esque characters that hung out there and the story lines that sprung from the place.

"The brasher members of our rookie contingent discovered early on that the words 'Dallas Cowboy' were magic: 'Hello darlin', I play for the Dallas Cowboys. Wanna fuck?' proved to be an effective come-on with many of the local barflies and snuff queens," defensive end Pat Toomay said.

Like all NFL teams at this time, the Cowboys brought in plenty of fresh blood—50 rookies, enough to field a team. That's exactly what they did, taking on the San Francisco 49ers' collection of newcomers. Dallas won 34–7, and Landry chalked it up to Dallas having had a few more days of practice and several more players.

By Friday, the deadline for veterans to arrive, Morton, Renfro, Nye, Pugh and second-year linebacker Steve Kiner all showed up, despite not having contracts.

The only no-shows were Thomas and Chuck Howley.

Howley didn't have a contract. He was 35 and had been talking about retiring for several years. He also was the reigning Super Bowl MVP, and Landry believed he was playing better in his mid-30s than he did in his mid-20s. He clearly had some good years left.

"I don't think the contract he's been offered is the basic problem," Landry said. "I could be wrong, but I think he has a fair offer and that he thinks it's fair. Chuck is a very level-headed guy."

Landry and linebackers coach Jerry Tubbs called with recruiting pitches. Center Dave Manders phoned to say, "Get your tail out here."

Howley did, only four days late.

"I've asked myself if I could maintain the same level this season," Howley said. "Could I do it over again? I think I can or I wouldn't be out here."

He blamed his delay on making sure he had the right people running his uniform rental and cleaning business so that he could devote his full attention to football.

"I had decided to retire four or five weeks ago because of business difficulties," he said. "I had to make a decision to play football another year or prepare for the rest of my life."

Howley's return meant only one veteran was still holding out. With only one year under his belt, Thomas was hardly a veteran.

Now that Thomas was backing up his threats, the Cowboys had to at least consider that he wouldn't return.

"This would be the first time I ever saw a player retire after his first year, but it's possible," Landry said. "Every man on the street knows his value to us. But say Calvin Hill comes on and gives us a performance like he did in '69. How much damage has there been then?"

Running backs coach Dan Reeves offered to settle things himself.

"Just give me a blank check," Reeves told Schramm.

"All right," Schramm said. "And we'll just take the difference out of your salary."

At this point, Thomas' absence was still a laughing matter.

—★—

On the first Sunday after veterans reported, fans in Dallas awoke to a copyright story in the *Times-Herald*: "Morton Played Under Hypnosis."

Cowboy quarterback Craig Morton worked with a Dallas hypnotist for the last 12 games of the 1970 season on an experiment in post-hypnotic suggestions.

Edward J. Pullman, 58-year-old director of his Southwest Hypnosis Research Center, met with Morton once a week during this period and used hypnosis on game days when he talked with Morton on the phone. He said the practice was without the knowledge of coach Tom Landry or Cowboy officials.

"The object was to relieve Craig of game pressures, boost his confidence, free him from further injury by conditioning him to relax on the instant of body contact, to keep his elbow from being a conscious hindrance and just generally to open up the full potential of his abilities," Pullman said.

What a revelation for a guy fighting for his job and for the support of the fans.

"This is likely to be a controversial subject with most people," Morton said. "I look on it with an open mind. Any educated man would acknowledge that experiments with the subconscious [are] fascinating. . . . Every day you read about advancements of hypnosis in medicine—but you really have to believe in it for it to work."

Morton said he had no idea whether it helped him. He also was done trying it.

"I have no thoughts about the subject right now," Landry said. "Football is a mental game, and if it helped him, that's fine with me."

The whole thing started when Morton bought a painting by local artist Nancy Sims. She wound up coming to his house the day after a game, when he was still in bed recovering from the pounding he'd taken. His sister and mother entertained Sims, and they began talking about the many problems in Morton's life.

"I know someone who could help Craig," Sims told them.

It just so happened that she'd been watching a Cowboys game on television with Pullman. Seeing Morton struggle with accuracy and injuries, Pullman had mentioned, "If only I could work with that guy. I know I could help him."

Pullman had been working with hypnotism for about 25 years and said he had about 100 regulars. Although he hadn't worked with other professional athletes, there were several stories of baseball players who'd had great success with it. Then again, the St. Louis Browns were once hypnotized to think of themselves as pennant winners; they finished last.

Morton was interested but skeptical. So he sent his sister for a session with Pullman to see if he could snap her out of the blues she'd been feeling. Soon, friends noticed she had more spunk. So a few nights before a game at Kansas City, Morton drove to Pullman's house to give it a try.

"He was in such pain," Sims said. "He almost had to be helped out of the car. His legs were straight and taut. He could barely walk or bend his knees."

Morton called Pullman the morning of the game to trigger the post-hypnotic suggestion. The words that unlocked it: "Black salt." According to a recording Pullman made, here is what followed:

> You're in a deep sleep, but you can hold the phone. You feel fine. You must remember everything I told you, all the suggestions I gave you. You must be perfectly relaxed and calm and have all the ability you need to work the game today. Everything that I gave you must come through today and you're going to be amazed at the results. You will experience no pain. You're going to fall and not get hurt.

Just before kickoff, Morton took three deep breaths to remind him of everything he'd learned that week from his coaches and from Pullman.

Voila. Morton completed 50 percent of his passes for 160 yards, his best of the season in both categories. He threw an 89-yard touchdown pass to Bob Hayes and didn't throw an interception. The Cowboys won 27–16. He moved around so well that Sims recalled an announcer accusing Morton of faking all his injuries.

"I'm really excited," Morton told Pullman in a phone call after the game. "None of the fluid has come back on my elbow, which is kind of amazing because it usually balloons right up. I had my knee twisted a bit, but it went right away."

Pullman believed his work was the key that unlocked this performance.

"You can't take an average person and through hypnosis enable him to throw a football accurately or powerfully. But you can clear away the distractions that may be preventing an athlete from performing to his full potential," Pullman said. "It is like a file drawer in which all the papers have been filed out of order. This can put all the papers back in order."

The Wednesday before Super Bowl V, Morton was in his Fort Lauderdale hotel room when he called Pullman in Dallas. Again, the hypnotist taped the conversation.

> Pullman: How's your arm?
> Morton: Not so good. It's pretty sore.
> Pullman: Well, we've got to get that taken care of.

Pullman then took Morton through "a ten-fold program that will enable you to beat Baltimore and win the championship." It included health and wisdom, football skills, and strategies. The end of the program went like this:

> Nine. You will break all your past records in this game against Baltimore and be the first Cowboy quarterback to win the Super Bowl championship. Ten, and last. You're going to do all the things we worked on and all your coaches told you to do, because you have the ability, the intensive desire to win this great victory for yourself and the team.

If only Pullman's hypnotism had worked as well as it had earlier in the season.

Morton also allowed a woman who called herself a "natural psychic medium" to delve into his past lives.

Her powers revealed that in the nineteenth century, he owned and trained thoroughbred horses in Ireland. In the fifteenth century, he'd been a German general. And back at the start of recorded time, he was a leader in the Anglo-Saxon wars. She envisioned him taking troops into battle from atop a high knoll. She saw him pierced by a spear; it didn't kill him, but affected this incarnation of him whenever he sat down. She asked whether he ever felt such a pain. Morton said he did.

Leadership and injuries; yep, that sounds about right for a quarterback. Morton got a laugh out of the reincarnation aspect of his "treatment."

Wacky as it all was, this story had a short shelf life. It started on a Sunday and was forgotten after what happened Wednesday morning in Dallas.

# Duane Goes Off the Deep End

DUANE THOMAS INVITED REPORTERS to the Press Club in downtown Dallas. Wearing a decorative African shirt called a dashiki, bell-bottom jeans, and sandals, he was relaxed, comfortable.

And he had a lot to say.

He started by describing his contract demands.

> I want a new contract for $80,000 base pay and I don't want any incentive clauses in it. I think, everything considered, $80,000 is pretty cheap. But we are about $50,000 apart. I proved myself last year, and I think I'm entitled to a new contract. I'm the best. The entire Cowboys organization is totally eliminating the fact that I am an artist. After all, they never would have made it to the Super Bowl without me, and they never will make it again unless I play for them.

Then came his disdain for his bosses.

> Tex Schramm is sick, demented, and completely dishonest. Tom Landry is a plastic man, actually no man at all. Gil Brandt is a liar. They were completely dishonest with me in our contract

negotiations prior to last season, and therefore I feel no moral obligation to withhold my end of that contract.

He insisted things would be the opposite had he performed poorly as a rookie.

Had I not had a good season last year, then I certainly wouldn't have expected the Cowboys to hold up their end of the original three-year contract. I'd have quit. I wouldn't have asked them to pay me more than I deserve.

He brought it all back to race, blaming his white agent for cheating him on his original contract.

I was misinformed, just like all black players are misinformed. I don't doubt for a minute that the Cowboy organization paid off my agent—or, rather, my ex-agent. . . . The problem in general is that I'm black. If I was white, it would have been totally different. They would have done me justice. They have done this to all black players and have exploited black players all along. They're always comparing me to Calvin (Hill) and Jimmy Brown. MY NAME IS DUANE THOMAS!

Then came the big finish.

I've stated my position and they know what I want. Now it's up to them. I wouldn't mind being traded. I'm tired of being treated like a stupid animal, and I think these people have been trying to crook me. They don't want to pay me what I deserve, and they aren't actually paying me at all. Hey, the public is paying me. It's the public that pays the bill. Maybe I'll ask to be traded eventually, but I won't play for less money for someone else. . . . If I do not play football, then I'll do some social work, helping my people. But I don't have any deadlines or anything. I'll just wait and see what happens.

This performance lasted almost 45 minutes. Schramm had an assistant fetch a recording of the whole news conference from radio station KLIF, then played it over the phone to a gathering of team officials and reporters in the media room at Cal Lutheran.

When Landry heard himself referred to as a plastic man, he melted into a smile.

When Thomas pointed out that Schramm had never played in the NFL—"Why, you can look at him and see that," Thomas said—Schramm laughed. As for the attack that Schramm was "sick and demented . . . totally dishonest," Schramm said, "Well, he got two out of three."

Schramm also put out the following formal statement: "I'm sorry to hear the sentiments expressed by Duane. But he certainly has the right to express his views. It will remain for the press and fans to assess the validity of the charges and accusations made by Duane."

The Cowboys were in a difficult situation. They were never planning to give Thomas much of a raise and certainly couldn't now, or else others would resort to such extreme tactics. Even if Thomas reversed field and decided to play for his existing deal, he wouldn't be welcomed in the locker room. Players were angry that he considered himself the reason Dallas made the Super Bowl and that he'd be the reason they returned. Even fellow black players who may have agreed with the exploitation argument were disgusted by his selfishness.

The only option left was to trade him. And that wasn't a very viable option.

"I don't think we'll have a lot of clubs knocking down our door to want Thomas when he wants $80,000 a year and meanwhile castigates all the top people in the Dallas organization," Schramm said.

Thomas' eruption had been building. A few nights earlier, he had a practically incoherent interview with Channel 4's Dick Risenhoover. Chuck Howley saw it before flying to training camp.

"I was embarrassed for Duane," Howley said.

Everyone had a theory of what was behind all this erratic behavior. Most said drugs. Many thought he was being influenced by the wrong people, perhaps radical black Muslim groups. It could've been a combination. Or maybe he'd just gone nuts.

Disgraced agent Norm Young tried clearing his name, denying that he or the Cowboys exploited Thomas. He said, "nobody twisted his arm to sign," either with his agency or with the Cowboys. Young also suggested success had gone to Thomas' head. In about 18 months, he'd gone from "a very mild-mannered chap; I could hardly get two words out of him" to someone who "must feel like he's king of the hill now."

"I don't know what he's trying to prove," Young said. "I think he's created a monster. He's said words he won't be able to retract."

The day after the news conference, Thomas' family pastor visited him to see if he could help. The pastor took Thomas to the Cowboys' business offices.

A secretary called training camp to let club officials know about their surprise guests. Landry ended up on the line. It was a one-sided conversation, with Thomas doing the talking.

"After all that had been said already, I had to listen more than do any talking," Landry said. "I understand him . . . up to a point. He was somewhat apologetic, if he hurt anyone. Whether he was apologetic for the whole thing, I can't say that, no. He did express the possibility he'd come back."

If the Cowboys still wanted him, that is.

"There are but three alternatives: Do nothing, and let him sit; trade him; or take him back if he expresses a desire to come back," Landry said. "I'm not leaning in any one direction at this time. . . . I always got along with Duane. I know he grew up the tough way. It was a hard and tough struggle for him. Now I don't know if he can accept anyone looking out for his best interests."

The Cowboys let it be known how many little things they'd done for him. Like paying traffic tickets and catching up on alimony when officers came around with arrest warrants. A story in the *Fort Worth Press* included a reference to the Cowboys having "cancelled checks made out to various municipal, state and federal agencies to prove they've bailed Thomas out of several jams."

Chuck DeKeado, Thomas' agent, was still negotiating with the Cowboys. He said the team budged on some incentive clauses, but they were relatively minor. The real news was that the Cowboys were talking about the contract at all.

A few days later, NFL Commissioner Pete Rozelle visited camp. Thomas' status obviously was a big topic of discussion, but the commissioner steered clear of that subject.

"I'm afraid that's a club problem," he said.

Thomas was among 16 holdouts across the league. The commissioner said these things have happened before and would happen again.

"But," he said, "they've never been *this* heated."

—★—

Two days later, the Cowboys traded Thomas' best friend and roommate.

Steve Kiner wanted out. He was a linebacker who hardly played as a rookie in 1970 because he was stuck behind Howley. During Howley's absence, Kiner got a taste of playing with the starters and decided that was where he belonged. So the day Howley arrived from Dallas, Kiner went straight to Landry's room and asked to be traded.

"It wasn't hard to find a team that wanted Steve. A lot of people know his potential," Landry said. "I didn't want to see him go, but in fairness to the boy, I just about had to. He almost went nuts sitting on the bench last season."

Kiner was sent to the New England Patriots for a fourth-round draft pick. Considering Dallas took him in the third round, it wasn't a very good return on the club's investment.

Then again, Kiner hurt his own stock by getting into a brawl with officers at a rock concert in Tennessee during the spring. It was a lot like Morton's case, with the initial headlines and accusations falling apart. Kiner wound up being fined $50 for resisting arrest; charges of disorderly conduct and being under the influence of alcohol and drugs were dismissed. He'd already been branded a free spirit because, as a rookie, he didn't pick up his signing bonus until after the season.

Still, it seemed strange for Dallas to give up on a talented second-year player when all three starting linebackers were in their 30s and the guy directly ahead of him was the oldest of the bunch. That is, unless the club considered Kiner to be among the bad influences on Thomas.

"No, that didn't enter into it," Landry said. "Steve was just anxious to play somewhere. If Howley had stayed retired and he had lost out in the competition for the job, he would have demanded to be traded then. That's how strong he was on the subject."

Landry also mentioned that Kiner "is the type of guy who would be an asset to us only if he were a starter." Interpretation: If Kiner was a backup again, he'd be nothing but trouble. And the Cowboys had enough of that.

—★—

A week later, a wild rumor swept through Cal Lutheran: Duane Thomas' Black Muslim friends were going to kidnap Schramm. A posse of security guards surrounded him that day, just to be safe.

About 5:00 p.m. on a Thursday afternoon, a black Cadillac pulled up to training camp and out stepped Thomas and another man, his driver. Schramm came to greet them and sent word for Landry to come over once the afternoon workout finished.

Thomas was wearing jeans and the same dashiki from his Dallas news conference. He shook hands with Schramm, but his friend refused. The man's name was Mansfield Collins, but he was introduced as Ali ha ka Kabir.

Reporters asked Thomas if he had anything to say. He stared for a few seconds, then said he had no comment.

Thomas and his friend met with Schramm for about an hour. Landry joined them for the final 45 minutes.

Thomas said he would return only if his friend could get a tryout and stay with Thomas in his dorm room. Told that wasn't going to happen, Thomas asked to be traded. No, demanded was more like it.

"Duane was aggressive and at times intense in the conversation between us," Schramm said. "That was one of the most unusual things I've ever experienced. Nobody had any idea where Duane was and, suddenly, he's there with this guy in a long robe. The two just stared at me. I wasn't sure whether to bow or run. We refused the tryout, and they left again."

In a formal statement about the meeting, Schramm said: "We told him our position remains the same—our first responsibility is to our football team and the goals we have set. We told him that if we can benefit the Cowboys and at the same time accommodate him, we will be happy to do so. We certainly have no personal animosity toward Duane. As far as his relationship with the Cowboys, he gave no indication of any change in the sentiments he expressed in Dallas."

That night, Thomas came up with another plan. He called DeKeado and said he was going to report to camp just to put pressure on the Cowboys.

"I'm going to force their play," Thomas told his agent. "They want to get rid of me. If the guys feel the way they do, they'll have to get rid of me."

Around 4:00 a.m., Thomas called Steve Perkins of the *Dallas Times-Herald*—the same reporter Thomas had called to announce his retirement—and said he would be reporting to camp at noon.

"The only reason I would come back is for my people—the black people," Thomas said. "Whatever happens to me from now on will be up to the Cowboys."

At 10:00 a.m., Thomas called Perkins again.

"I have decided not to report today because I feel spiritual about this," Thomas said. "I'd rather sacrifice my career so other black players will have a fair shake—not only at Dallas, but at other places in the league. . . . I came out yesterday to talk to them because I was the victim and Tex Schramm had made me out to be the culprit. I was telling him to take his foot off my neck. I have to say the same about this because where I display strength on the field, I have to show strength off the field."

Thomas' plan worked. The next day, he was traded—to New England, reuniting him with his pal Kiner. The deal was not conditional on the Patriots signing him to a new contract.

"He is their property," Schramm said. "Period."

Along with Thomas, Dallas sent offensive lineman Halvor Hagen and rookie receiver Honor Jackson. In return, the Cowboys got a future first-round pick and running back Carl Garrett, who in 1969 had beaten O. J. Simpson for AFL rookie of the year.

The Patriots knew what they were getting into because of their new director of player personnel—Bucko Kilroy, who'd been a scout for the Cowboys the last six years. He'd been at the pre-draft meeting when Red Hickey said Thomas was a supreme talent with attitude issues. Hickey also had told Landry to draft him only if he thought he could handle Thomas' personality. Kilroy and the Patriots apparently felt their coach, John Mazur, was up for the challenge. A former quarterback at Notre Dame and a former Marine, Mazur knew all about discipline.

Garrett was thrilled with the trade. Born in Denton, raised in Fort Worth, he grew up a Cowboys fan. His parents still lived in the area, so they could see him play regularly. The only thing better than the homecoming was the promotion in the standings—from the team with the NFL's worst record last season to one that came within a few minutes of winning the Super Bowl.

Garrett called it "maybe the best thing that could have happened to me." He also had a message for Thomas: "Anybody can run through a hole. Thomas is going to find a big difference with the Patriots. He's going to miss those blockers there. He won't be reeling off those 150 yards a game."

—★—

Thomas was working out on a beach near Los Angeles when he got word of the trade. He asked for an extra plane ticket for a friend and the Patriots refused. Instead, Kilroy and general manager Upton Bell would escort him across the country.

They arrived Sunday night at Patriots training camp on the campus of the University of Massachusetts, in Amherst. An introductory news conference was held. Asked for an opening statement, Thomas said, "I'm here."

"I can't say how long it will take me to adjust to the Patriots. You know there are adjustments that must be made. I'll just try to do the best I can," he said. "I admit I have a different attitude toward professional football after a year of experience. But I don't think I have to prove myself to anyone."

Thomas told Bell he wanted to practice Monday, so they brought in team doctor Burton Nault for a physical on Sunday night. Once Thomas got to his room, something told him not to unpack.

"I figured I should check things out first," he said. "I didn't want it to be another Dallas. . . . I especially wanted to meet the brothers and check them out."

In the dining hall, Thomas heard someone yell, "Hey, Duane, come over here for a minute." He said he would, right after he got some fruit.

"I'm John Mazur," the man said, standing to greet him.

"All right," Thomas replied.

"I'm John Mazur, the head coach," the man said.

"Right, man," Thomas said. "Nice meeting you, you know."

The conversation never got on track. Thomas felt Mazur was trying to impress him. For instance, Mazur said he wasn't prejudiced, then added, "I'm a Polack."

Before practice Monday afternoon, Mazur gave the club a pep talk. He told the group, which now included Thomas, "I don't want any free spirits around here. And I won't tolerate any. All I want around here are football players who want to win."

Mazur had the club run a few wind sprints, then lined up the offense. He eventually called an I-formation play with 235-pound fullback Jim Nance lined up behind the quarterback and Thomas behind Nance.

Thomas dropped into a stance with his hands on his knees. Before the snap, Mazur approached Thomas.

"Here, we want a running back to get down in a three-point stance, with his hand on the ground," Mazur said.

"In Dallas, they taught us to get down in a stance with both our hands on the knees, so we could see the line," Thomas said.

"Well, here we do it my way, in a three-point stance," Mazur said.

"Maybe so," Thomas said. "But I'm doing it my way."

"No, you're not!" Mazur said "You're going to get out of here right now. Get the hell in the locker room!"

Mazur told Bell to get rid of Thomas. But how?

The Patriots ended up releasing a statement saying Dr. Nault "developed certain questions concerning Duane Thomas' general condition. These concerns tended to be confirmed in the brief practice that followed. Mr. Thomas has since withdrawn from training camp after declining to complete his physical examination."

Nault added, "The portion of the examination Thomas refused to undergo included a urinalysis and a blood test."

Schramm had made it clear the trade wasn't contingent on a contract. But New England wasn't giving up on Thomas because of contract problems. Nor was this about the physical, despite the Patriots' claims. If they had legitimate concerns with Thomas' condition, he wouldn't have even been allowed on the practice field. Plain and simple, this was a personality conflict. In that case, the Patriots should have been stuck with him.

The Cowboys didn't push it, though. Likely at Rozelle's prodding, they voided the swap of running backs, taking back the rights to Thomas and sending Garrett back to New England for an awkward reunion with his offensive linemen. The Patriots got to keep Hagen and Jackson, and Dallas got New England's second- and third-round picks in 1972. The first-rounder that had been swapped went back to the Patriots.

"While there were no conditional aspects associated with the Duane Thomas trade, under the unique circumstances that developed I felt compelled, both from a moral and ethical standpoint, to affect a solution that would not work an undue hardship on either club," Schramm said in a statement.

Now the Cowboys faced the same sticky situation as a few weeks ago. Maybe worse, because trading Thomas was no longer an option; they'd tried that, and it didn't work.

Thomas had lost any leverage for a new contract. Even if he was to return, the Cowboys would have to give him a thorough physical to make sure the Patriots didn't turn up some sort of complication.

Refusing to take a blood or urine test was a clear admission of drug use. The *Los Angeles Herald-Examiner* even wrote a story under the headline, "Was Thomas under the influence of drugs?"

However, Thomas said he was never asked to pee in a bottle or give any blood. He told the *Herald-Examiner*, "I don't take anything, and I don't drink. I wondered why other players were taking [pep pills], but that's their thing not mine. I'm a strange guy. I'm walking around wondering what the hell people are doing. People shouldn't worry so much about understanding me. They're mixed up. I know who I am."

Stuck in another stalemate with the Cowboys, Thomas switched agents again. He hired Al Ross, the agent who had represented basketball Spencer Haywood in a drama that resulted in the U.S. Supreme Court establishing the "hardship rule" that allowed players in need of money to play in the NBA without waiting for four years of college.

Ross tried portraying Thomas as misunderstood.

"He does not eat meat—does that make him weird? He eats only one meal a day—does that make him weird?" Ross said. "He has been misinterpreted because he does not want to be exactly like everyone else. He wants to be an individual. If that makes him weird, then a lot of people are weird."

As the regular season approached, Thomas and the Cowboys remained a world apart. Then President Nixon enacted a wage freeze that affected everyone in the country. Whatever your salary was on August 15, it had to stay that way for 90 days.

Ross, however, planned to seek an exception for his client because, "there are so many problems connected with Duane's case, he shouldn't be penalized." He talked about getting President Nixon to intervene. That's how silly these negotiations had become.

Some of it would've been funny if it wasn't so maddening.

- The Cowboys offered a bonus for gaining 1,000 yards. Ross' response: "Why not make it ten million yards? Who needs all these incentives? Pay a guy what he's worth. That is incentive enough!"
- Ross hired a respected Los Angeles physician to give Thomas a physical. The doctor declared him perfectly healthy. The Cowboys suggested a psychiatric evaluation. Ross' response: "Thomas will take a psychiatric examination if everybody else in the league takes one, including the coaches."
- Ross eventually got face time with someone important. Not Nixon or even NFL Commissioner Rozelle, but Rozelle's right-hand man, Jim Kensil, the executive director of pro football. They should've met on a schoolyard considering the way things played out. Kensil called Ross an "agent, or I don't know what you are." Ross replied, "You're nothing but a flunky."

In early September, Thomas and Ross went their separate ways. Thomas still didn't have the deal he wanted. Ross was tired of all the advice Thomas' other friends were giving him.

Whoever and whatever was influencing Thomas, the grip was strong.

"I could say money was what I wanted at first, but now it is not only money," he said. "I realize that there are black people all over the world starving, and I want to do something. I can't stand to see people suffering because I don't like to suffer myself. I realize the betterment of one man is the betterment of another. You have to do it while you are on top. That's why I asked for more money. I might not be here tomorrow. They want my services now? Well, let them pay me now."

# Heroes & Zeroes

EVERY AFTERNOON OF TRAINING camp, reporters and coaches got together in a dorm room to unwind and shoot the breeze over some beers and snacks. It was known as the 5:30 Club, and it was a tradition Tom Landry brought along from his days with the New York Giants.

Landry liked having a private, social setting for his assistant coaches to sit and chat with the beat writers about what was really going on with the club. Theories were tested and stories were swapped. All off the record.

There are some good stories to be told about the guys on this team. While the season wasn't always riding on the success or failure of some of the more colorful characters, each had an important role. For every one of them, there was a game or a play when they were the most important guy on the field.

—★—

The Cowboys traded for Mike Ditka in 1969 not so much for his skills as a blocker or a receiver. They wanted his toughness. His rage.

Ditka's temper could flare at any time. Like the night he and some teammates went to a restaurant and saw a table with chairs stacked on top. Rather than taking them down one at a time, Ditka swiped across the table with his forearm, sending the chairs sprawling. Then he called everyone over to grab one and sit down.

At the team's annual golf tournament, Ditka always won the club-throwing competition. Dan Reeves could vouch for that skill, as the two played rounds of golf that tended to feature clubs getting hit as hard as balls. The same happened when they played racquetball; games turned into cuss-fests, with racquets slammed, thrown, and broken.

Ditka was primed for a big year in 1971. The tight ends were expected to catch more passes this season, so he came to camp weighing 231 pounds, the slimmest he'd been since his junior year at Pitt. He was in great shape, too. No longer would his jarring hits end up punishing him the most. No longer would he fear pulling a muscle every time he went out for a pass.

"I just figured this was my eleventh year in the league—it was time for me to put up or get out," he said. "I think I have a lot of football ability left and I'd like to repay the Cowboys. They've been great to me."

Ditka was among the first tight ends who could block like a lineman and catch like a receiver. He was the NFL's Rookie of the Year in 1961 and helped the Bears win a championship in '63. A perennial Pro Bowler, he was traded to the Eagles in '67 and endured two miserable seasons until being rescued by the Cowboys.

"After what happened in Philadelphia, I really didn't know whether I could play as I used to. When they take away your desire, there's not much left," he said. "When I first came to Dallas, I felt I wanted to prove I could be the best again. But I no longer want to prove that. I want to prove I can get into our offense and do a good job. When this thing's all over and they look at the films, they can tell what kind of job I'll do, blocking and catching. I want to go to [the Super Bowl] and win that game and be an integral part in playing the game. I couldn't care less about being all-pro. I've been there before and it got me nothing. The measuring stick, the only measuring stick, is what your teammates feel you're contributing to the team and what the coaching staff feels you're contributing. The Super Bowl is the reward, not all-pro."

His stance on the Duane Thomas melodrama was no surprise.

"This team is not going to worry about one guy," Ditka said. "One guy didn't take us to the Super Bowl and it's foolish for anyone to believe that. If you want to pick one person, then you have to go all the way down the defensive lineup by name. I also saw too many tough catches by Bob Hayes and Lance Rentzel and too much great blocking from the offensive line to believe one man did it. If one person did, it just might be the man coaching us."

Ditka was considering going into coaching. But not yet. He still had two seasons left, and he was going to make damn sure they were productive. Just ask San Diego defensive end Jeff Staggs.

Staggs and Ditka tussled during a training-camp scrimmage. Thinking he'd gotten the better of the old man, Staggs snarled and said, "You're living on your laurels!" Seeing the blood dripping from Staggs' nose, Ditka knew otherwise.

—★—

Herb Adderley was the team's second-best vocal leader, a notch behind Lee Roy Jordan. Everyone respected the two championship rings Adderley earned playing for Vince Lombardi and the Green Bay Packers, and everyone appreciated a man who answered the telephone with the greeting, "Peace, love, and happiness."

Adderley arrived in 1970, and the Cowboys went to the Super Bowl for the first time that season. His three interceptions helped, but so did the champion's attitude he brought to the locker room.

When Dallas slogged along the first half of the '70 season, and players were dreading Landry's Monday film sessions, Adderley took charge like a guy who'd been there forever.

"It doesn't have to be this way," he said. "Get off your butts and stop crying in your soup. Let's get out and kick some butt."

Mel Renfro said that when Adderley spoke, "guys started standing at attention."

"Their antennae went up, almost immediately," Renfro said. "Herb was so fiery, and he had such confidence. He had come up under those Lombardi days where winning wasn't everything, it was the only thing. And that's what he instilled in us; 'Guys, you can win, and you're gonna win. *We're* gonna win.' And that was all there was to it. He was always a team guy. It wasn't that he bridged a gap between black and white. It was a team thing. There was no color there."

Adderley had been a star running back growing up in Philadelphia, then starred as a runner and receiver at Michigan State. The Green Bay Packers took him with the twelfth pick in the 1961 draft—one slot before Dallas took Bob Lilly—and converted him to a defensive back late in his rookie year.

Adderley had the speed and moves to stick with any receiver, which fit perfectly with Lombardi's one-on-one coverages. Landry, however, believed in a controlled, zone defense. But he knew what he was getting when he traded for Adderley and allowed the future Hall of Famer to do things his way.

"No doubt about it, I've been a gambling type for years," Adderley said. "I've always considered life itself a gamble. It's like a football game in many respects . . . you never know what's going to happen next."

— ★ —

Run. Catch. Block. Throw. Return punts. Hold on kicks. Coach while still playing.

Dan Reeves did it all.

On a day off in 1971, he even helped out in the ticket office.

Reeves did all he could because he lacked a specialty. He wasn't good enough to start anywhere, but he was versatile enough to be a backup at several spots. That's how he lasted eight seasons on knees that were each operated on twice.

"I haven't lost much speed because I didn't have much speed to lose," he said.

Reeves became a player-coach in 1970. In '71, he oversaw the running backs while also serving as the fourth-string running back, third-string quarterback, and holder on placekicks. When injuries thinned the ranks· at receiver during training camp, he filled in there, too.

"He simply has the knack for doing the right thing at the right time," Landry said. "It's a gift."

Reeves' work ethic stemmed from working on the family's farm in Americus, Georgia. A summer spent riding a mule to plow peanut and cotton fields taught him all he needed to know about that kind of life.

He started college at 16 and a year later was the starting quarterback for South Carolina. He rolled out a lot and ran plenty, but he also set school passing records. The NFL didn't need any of those types, though, and he wasn't drafted.

The Cowboys invited him to training camp in 1965. He played defensive back, then flanker before getting a shot at running back. He reminded Landry of Frank Gifford, his old teammate on the New York Giants.

"He just keeps doing something special for you," Landry said. "Reeves has a heart for the game and a nose for the goal line."

Reeves' perspective on things changed once he became a part-time coach. He discovered how little he knew about football and how much work goes into coaching. He also discovered he loved it, and he was pretty good at it.

"He tells me when I do something wrong, and he doesn't say anything when I do something right," said Garrison, who'd been Reeves' roommate from 1966 to 1969. "He's a regular coach."

—★—

The morning after Super Bowl V, Renfro, Bob Lilly, and John Niland flew from Miami to Los Angeles for the Pro Bowl. Sitting next to Niland on the cross-country voyage was Norm Schachter, the lead official in a game the Cowboys might've won had the crew gotten right a call on a fumble into the end zone early in the third quarter.

"Norm, you guys blew it yesterday," Niland said. There was no response. In fact, no more words were spoken between them the entire four-hour flight.

A few days later, Niland spoke at a high school in Los Angeles. The principal was supposed to pick him up, but someone else did. It was only once he was at the school and about to meet the kids when he discovered who the principal was—Norm Schachter.

A few months later, Niland had a surprising encounter with someone else while in Europe on a Bob Hope trip that counted as his annual obligation to the U.S. National Guard.

Along with Ralph Neely, Niland visited several army bases and showed the highlight film of the Super Bowl. Before leaving Dallas, Niland mentioned to a socialite friend that he would soon be in Italy. She said she was going to be there at the same time and suggested he visit her villa outside Venice. Niland took along the phone number and indeed had some free time while in Venice.

The woman sent over a driver, and Niland headed out, expecting the villa to be a cottage. It was more like a mansion. And when the door opened, he was greeted not by his friend, but by one of her friends—Jane Murchison, the wife of the Cowboys' owner. Make that, the recently separated Jane Murchison.

After 25 years, she had tired of her husband's serial adultery, as she called it. In demanding a divorce, she told him: "I can understand a few women here and there, Clint, but thousands of women? No." So, now it was her turn.

Although Niland was married—to a model, even—he eagerly spent a few days in the villa with the companionship of his two female friends, living up to his nickname, "Johnny Nightlife."

Niland's life always was one adventure after another.

He grew up in Amityville, New York, on Long Island, in an area described as an "industrial ghetto." His house was boxed in by a coal company, a milk company, the oil company, and the telephone company. He worked at a gas station when he was 11, then delivered newspapers. Throughout high school he worked at Al's Delicatessen, earning 50 cents an hour and all the food he could eat. That's how he grew into being an offensive lineman.

"I went for sandwiches mostly. I used to make real interesting combinations like roast beef, bologna, liverwurst all thrown into one, with Swiss cheese and top it off with a little potato salad on the side. It was a whale of a sandwich," he said.

When he was 16, Niland discovered he was adopted. He only found out when he needed papers to get his driver's license.

He recalls only one book in his home while growing up, a Time-Life book about World War II. He read it often, but never understood the significance until many years later, when he was watching a TV show about the real-life family that inspired the Oscar-winning movie *Saving Private Ryan*. That family's real name was Niland.

Niland went from Long Island to Iowa City, Iowa, on a football scholarship. The Cowboys took him fifth overall in 1966, and as of '71, it was still the highest Dallas had ever drafted. He practiced every day lined up against Lilly. That forced him to get better quickly.

Away from football, Niland had a South American ocelot as a pet and took vacations to exotic locales. He also repeatedly found himself in situations most folks never face, such as chasing down a guy who robbed a jewelry store and capturing a horse that escaped a trailer and was running free on a highway.

He always had offseason jobs. A favorite was working for a start-up UHF station. He went around handing out loop antennas just so people could tune in the station. He also swept the studio's floors and sold ads. One of his tricks was going around to car dealers and offering to star in their own commercials. In need of programming, the UHF station filmed high school football games on Friday nights. Niland did some of the commentary and had to deal with irate mothers protesting to the station about the things he'd say. He later landed a lucrative job with Pepsi that mostly involved giving speeches.

Much of the money he got for promotional appearances went to a special fund—a scholarship program for kids at his high school in Amityville.

"It's just my small way of paying back," he said.

—★—

Dave Edwards was always the "other" guy.

He was the third linebacker after Lee Roy Jordan and Chuck Howley, the giver of colorful nicknames besides Walt Garrison, and Ditka's business partner in the Sportspage Club, a bar-discotheque that opened in the summer of '71. As one of the players living in the Four Seasons apartment complex when Pete Gent lived there, traces of his antics are among those fictionalized in the book and movie *North Dallas Forty*.

"It comes up every year about my being less noticed than the other guys," he said. "It really doesn't bother me that much. I can't be worrying about that all the time. It's just the way it goes on a lot of teams."

Edwards was a damn good football player. His career got a boost in 1969, when linebackers coach Jerry Tubbs came up with the plan of always lining him up over a tight end so he could use his strength to maul the guy. Being a run-stopper didn't make for many highlights, but teammates and coaches understood his role and appreciated how he well he played it.

"They could never get a clear block, no matter who it was," Bob Lilly said. "He could stand 'em right up on the line of scrimmage—Jackie Smith, Ditka, even John Mackey at Baltimore. They couldn't push him around."

Coming out of Auburn, Edwards was drafted by the AFL, but not by an NFL team. He signed with the Cowboys as a free agent in 1963 and stair-stepped his way into action: from the taxi squad (the precursor to the practice squad in today's NFL) as a rookie, to part-time player in '64, to starter in '65. He'd missed only one game since becoming a regular.

—★—

Toni Fritsch was the least likely member of the Dallas Cowboys. Short and balding, he was breaking in a potbelly. Fresh from Vienna, he hardly spoke English.

Don Talbert took it upon himself to teach his new teammate a few phrases.

Lesson 1: The guy in the striped shirt is known as "Asshole." So when Fritsch went out for the kickoff of the first exhibition game, the referee handed him the ball and he politely said, "Thank you veddy much, Meester Asshole."

Lesson 2: "God damn" means "good morning." That one was easy for Fritsch to break in.

"God damn, Coach Landry," Fritsch said.

"What?" Landry said.

"God damn, Coach Landry!" Fritsch repeated, trying his best to get it right.

"Where's Talbert?" Landry said.

Reeves was Fritsch's roommate in 1971, which certainly didn't help.

"The poor guy has to learn two more languages—my Americus, Georgia, talk, and then he's got to translate that into English before he can translate into German," Reeves said in his syrupy drawl.

One of Reeves' duties was taking orders for pre-game meals. Going door-to-door, he had plenty of the usual requests for steak and eggs. Fritsch's preference?

"Wienerschnitzel!"

Fritsch's ignorance about American football was evident in the way he wore his uniform. His helmet was described as looking like as astronaut's lid. Fritsch called it "a perfect fit."

"A little hard to get on, but after it's on, it's all right," he said.

He worked out in the helmet, a T-shirt, silver football pants without pads, high-top soccer shoes, and dark blue wool socks.

"I kick well in these socks," Fritsch said. "Tomorrow I try the white ones. Also the shoulder pads. I will take things a little at a time."

Fritsch was an easy target for jokes and fun. Like the night he was sent out for pizza. Just before curfew.

Realizing he was going to be late, and in trouble with Landry, Fritsch hit the gas. He was going 85 miles per hour when he zoomed past a policeman. Fritsch had no wallet or driver's license. When he pleaded to be released so he could get back for curfew, the officer didn't believe this 5-foot-7 Austrian played for the Cowboys. The team T-shirt he was wearing hardly qualified as a veritable means of identification.

"Me Dallas Cowboy," Fritsch pleaded. "Keeker."

"Sure you are, buddy," the cop said. "And I'm the Lone Ranger. You're going to jail."

Gil Brandt ended up getting Fritsch back to camp. He had to pay the speeding ticket and the team's penalty for breaking curfew.

"Goddom," Fritsch told Walt Garrison. "One cold pizza for you bastards cost me six hundred forty-five marks!"

Fritsch seemed to make up for it with free beer.

He could be found enjoying a brew in his room as early as 7:00 a.m. He'd just sit around, watch TV, and relax while teammates were getting ready for their grueling day. For exercise, he preferred skipping rope. When told to lift weights, Fritsch said, "I kick with my foot, not with my arms." He loved this new athletic endeavor that required so much less running than soccer.

Most of the beers he sucked down came from the nearby room of Cliff Harris and Pat Toomay. They kept a refrigerator stocked with a couple of cases and began noticing how often they had to restock it. So one night they put a cup above the fridge with a sign that read, "If you take a beer, put some damn money in the cup." Fritsch couldn't read the sign but realized it had something to do with the money. So, he helped himself to a few bucks. And another beer.

"Players make joke with me, I make joke. We have good time," Fritsch said. "I think Dallas Cowboys is great team."

On a 40-man team, they can't all be heroes. There are bound to be a few zeroes, as Toomay discovered one night during training camp in 1971.

Walking down the hall of a practically abandoned dormitory, looking for something to do and someone to do it with, he detected what sounded like a television. He followed the sound into a room where he found Larry Cole asleep on one bed, Blaine Nye on his back but still awake on another bed.

Nye was an offensive guard who had a bachelor's degree in physics from Stanford, a master's degree in physics from Washington, and that summer had begun working toward a master's in business administration from Stanford. The only time fans asked for his autograph was when they mistook him for Bob Lilly. Earlier this camp, he'd been disgruntled over his contract, but only after he signed it. He wanted to get paid as much as Niland, even though Niland was more experienced and far more accomplished. Nye claimed he no longer cared about playing and was considering going back to school full time. It doesn't take an MBA, however, to realize he could get paid to play in the fall and take classes in the spring and summer. So he came back after spending five days at his parents' home on the other side of Los Angeles. To soothe his ego, the Cowboys arranged for him to get a free rental car from some Pontiac dealers who happened to be visiting camp that week.

"Things said when I was mad are not carved in marble," Nye said. "Nothing was unreasonable, but I was just pretty stubborn about it."

Cole was a big, blonde defensive lineman who reminded Garrison of Joe Palooka, the heavyweight boxer from the funny pages. His curriculum vitae differed a bit from Nye's. Upon matriculating from Granite Falls High School in Minnesota, where the football team was nicknamed the Kilowatts in honor of a local power plant, he went to the U.S. Air Force Academy. He was dismissed for failing to turn in friends he knew were cheating, so he went to the University of Houston, then to the University of Hawaii. The Cowboys drafted him in the sixteenth round in 1968, and he became the starting left end as a rookie. He also had a tendency to grunt like a caveman, earning the moniker, "Lurch."

When Toomay stumbled into their room, Nye declared, "Welcome to the Zero Club."

Toomay plopped onto a third bed in the room, and Nye continued with the formal introductions.

"This is the Zero Club, and we're organized," he said. "I am el presidente, Cole is vice president, and you are hereby appointed social secretary."

Toomay began carrying out his duties by suggesting they go to a movie.

"Ah, ah, ah. Hasty, hasty," Nye said. "Let's think about it. The shock of going to town may be too much for Cole. Round up the transportation and wake us up when you're ready."

Toomay tried borrowing a car from one of the scouts. The best he could find was a rookie running back who was going to town with his girlfriend in her car. Soon enough, the happy couple was hauling three linemen crammed into the back seat of a Toyota Corolla.

The Zero Club watched *How to Frame a Figg* starring Don Knotts. Since they had no car, they walked back to the dorm. Cole pondered out loud what some of their teammates were doing.

"All those studs are out on the town tonight, and they probably think they're having a good time—nice restaurants, good wine, live entertainment—but they're not. We are," Cole said. "We're having the good time, aren't we, Blaine? Aren't we having a GODDAMN GREAT TIME?!"

The ensuing wrestling match made for quite a nightcap.

The Zero Club eventually got some publicity, which in turn drew requests for membership. That violated their charter. Showing interest automatically eliminated candidates.

"We just tried to make a virtue of our liability," Toomay said. "We figured out it was like Joseph Heller wrote in *Catch-22*: There was a useful purpose in cultivating boredom. It can extend your career, because the more bored you are, the more time slows down and the longer you can last."

Toomay liked to challenge things. He wondered aloud why televangelists give their own address when asking followers to send money to Jesus. His insistence on trying to find a shortcut to anything prompted the nickname, "Ropes," because he knew all the ropes. He also was a hard-core liberal, leading to some strong discussions with Nye, a Republican.

A military brat, Toomay was a quarterback all the way through high school. When he got to Vanderbilt, coaches decided his size, speed, and arm were best suited at defensive end.

"I only had two problems as a quarterback," he said. "The first was I couldn't throw short. The second was I couldn't throw long."

He was eager to join the Cowboys because he figured he would thrive under Landry, who reminded him of his dad.

He became disillusioned pretty quickly.

The way Toomay saw it, Landry shut himself off from the team, treating players as little more than pawns in his own chess game. While Landry upheld the Christian principles he espoused, the coach turned a blind eye toward all the shenanigans going on in the organization. That contradiction irked the deep-thinking Toomay. He kept a journal during the early years of his career and turned it into a book, *The Crunch*. He later wrote a novel called *Any Given Sunday* and had a role in the movie of the same name.

—★—

Everyone had a quirk or three.

George Andrie didn't play football his senior year at Marquette; the school dropped the program after his third year.

Punter Ron Widby played for the New Orleans Buccaneers in the American Basketball Association in 1967 and 1968.

Kicker Mike Clark was so tired of losing with the Steelers that he retired. He was selling pharmaceuticals in Longview, Texas, when the Cowboys called to say they'd given up a third-round pick to get him. In his second season with Dallas, he whiffed on an onside kick. In a playoff game. Thus his nickname, "Onside." He showed up to training camp in 1971 fresh off earning his wings from the Confederate Air Force, a Texas group that flies World War II–era planes. He was eager to show off what he could do with a B-24, but couldn't persuade any of his teammates to go up for a ride.

Cornell Green was a star basketball player at Utah State, good enough to have his jersey retired. But he didn't play any football. That's why when he joined the Cowboys in 1962 he didn't know how to wear a uniform. An injury during his first preseason was traced to him wearing his hip pads upside down. In the first quarter of one of his first preseason games, facing the reigning champion Packers, he forced Boyd Dowler to fumble and recovered the ball. He came off the field with a big grin, thinking, "Hey, this isn't going to be so tough." He indeed became a solid cornerback, then in 1970 moved to strong safety to open a spot for Adderley.

"I enjoy it," Green said as he prepared for his second year at safety. "I have somebody to talk to now, the other safety. Used to be when I played cornerback, I only had the wide receiver to talk to. And sometimes he wouldn't talk to me."

Tex Schramm liked Green enough to put him on the payroll during the offseason, breaking him into the front office. "That guy has something inside—fortitude, guts, and he's just plain stubborn," Schramm said.

Then there was center Dave Manders.

He blocked for Adderley at Michigan State but wasn't drafted. He accepted an invitation to Cowboys training camp in 1962, when it was held in Marquette, Michigan, and lasted just a few weeks. He'd been fed up with football because of a tough senior year in college. A broken nose during camp was the last straw. He quit.

Landry, Schramm, and offensive line coach Jim Myers tried talking him into staying. His pregnant wife and mother-in-law showed up to visit just as he was going out the back door. He hitchhiked 80 miles to his parents' house in Iron Mountain, Michigan.

Manders got a job with General Mills, and eventually he began playing football again. He got as little as $37.50 and as much as $100 per game over two seasons with the Toledo Tornadoes and Grand Rapids Blazers of the United Football League. His passion for football was stoked enough that he considered giving the NFL another try. Around Thanksgiving 1963, he filled a pay phone with quarters and called Gil Brandt.

"I didn't have enough guts to call collect," Manders said.

He introduced himself sheepishly, saying, "You may not remember me, but this is Dave Manders."

"The center from Iron Mountain, Michigan," Brandt said.

The Cowboys sent him a plane ticket to training camp in 1964. Manders cared so much about making the club that he broke out in hives.

He earned a job all right and became a starter the next year. The year after that, he made the Pro Bowl. By 1971, he was a team captain.

# Coaching Brilliance or Sheer Confusion?

WHILE THE DUANE THOMAS saga played out, the Dallas Cowboys hardly missed him. Calvin Hill was getting Thomas' carries and making the most of them.

Hours after Thomas was traded, the Cowboys played a scrimmage against the San Diego Chargers. Hill let everyone know the running game was in good hands by gaining 42 yards on just seven carries. In the first exhibition game, he had 55 yards on 12 carries and caught a pass for 28 yards against the Los Angeles Rams.

"Hill? Hell, it was a mountain," muttered Los Angeles' defensive lineman Deacon Jones.

A few weeks later, against Cleveland, Hill pretty much was the Dallas offense. He carried 21 times for 167 yards and caught two passes for another 36 yards. On the second play of the game, he had an 89-yard touchdown run, the longest in his life.

The increased workload was Hill's favorite part.

"I feel like Hubert Humphrey did when Lyndon Johnson decided not to run," Hill said. "It feels so strange Duane isn't here after I've been thinking about going against him all the offseason. I never thought he'd carry it this far."

Newcomer Lance Alworth had only seen Thomas from afar. Having watched Hill up close, Alworth said, "I can't see how anybody is better than Calvin Hill. He really pulls away when he gets in that secondary, like nobody you've ever seen. I think he's even quicker than Thomas."

Hill came to training camp taller, heavier, and healthier than ever. Wiser, too.

The Yale graduate understood the game better after two seasons in the NFL, and he knew all too well the agony of losing his job because of an injury. So he was determined to regain his starting job, regardless of whether Thomas was there.

"You have to fight for what you can get in this world, and Calvin is a fighter," said Henry Hill, Calvin's father.

In that sense, Hill would've preferred beating out Thomas. He certainly had motivation: Thomas' declaration that the Cowboys needed him to become champions insinuated they couldn't win with Hill.

"We may not make it to the Super Bowl this year," Hill said, "but it won't be because Duane isn't here."

Tom Landry was hoping Hill would break his habit of leaving his feet, trying to catapult over defenders in short-yardage situations, like near the goal line. Landry hated seeing Hill go airborne because it made him more vulnerable to getting hurt. Landry liked to say Hill was big enough to gain four or five yards just by falling forward. So Hill tried teaching himself to flip off the mental switch that made him jump. He lay in bed at night visualizing times he could jump and repeated to himself, "I'm not going to do it."

"Then, in a game, I don't worry about it, because I think I have my mind conditioned," he said.

All in all, Hill should've been thrilled. Everything was snapping together for him. But he refused to see it that way. He knew Thomas could return any time. He knew he was one play from getting hurt again. After all the ups and downs of his first two seasons, he knew better than to get comfortable.

—★—

Tody Smith, the first-round pick who'd become the longest rookie holdout in franchise history, watched the Cowboys play the exhibition opener against the Rams. He kept his eyes on the guys playing his position, defensive end.

Pat Toomay, entering his second season, did well. So did Bill Gregory, a fellow rookie taken in the third round. That's when Smith realized he needed the Cowboys more than they needed him. He signed three days later.

His arrival created a pleasant dilemma—too much talent.

AFC teams sent scouts to watch the Cowboys practice and play even though the deadline for trades between the conferences had passed. They were there strictly because they figured Dallas' leftovers might still be good enough to make their squads.

"It's occurred to me that this ball club is like a mighty river," Hill said. "You can scoop a pail or two out of it and it still keeps rolling along."

"That's the kind of philosophy Calvin learned at Yale," Lee Roy Jordan said. "But, you know, I think he's hit the thing right on the head."

Talent wasn't the only thing overflowing. Good vibes were, too.

"They're just in a great frame of mind, enthusiastic about the season," Landry said. "And you have to be encouraged when you look at the defense, the way they're moving and hustling."

All the rookies were signed and, eventually, the veterans, too. (Thomas had a contract, he just didn't like it.) Mel Renfro dropped his threat of playing out his option and signed a new deal. He even said, "I think they did real well by me." Craig Morton got a new contract just before the federal wage freeze hit. Jethro Pugh was the lone unsigned player at the time, and now he couldn't do anything about it anyway.

"I feel like we're picking up where we left off in the Super Bowl," center Dave Manders said. "We're getting the job done here."

—★—

Every throw Morton or Roger Staubach made was scrutinized in person and on film, the result jotted down. Detailed records were kept from the start of camp in hopes a wealth of data would make the decision obvious for Landry. Or at least help justify whoever he picked.

The first big test was an intrasquad scrimmage in late July. Morton and Staubach took turns running the first-team offense against the second-team defense and vice-versa, with all drives starting at the 20-yard line. Each got two stints with the first team and two more with the second team. A fifth round would be the reward for whichever quarterback looked best.

"That was clearly Staubach," Landry said. "He was sharp, but he mostly stays sharp."

Staubach finished his three series completing 14 of 22 passes for 225 yards and two touchdowns. Morton went 3 of 11 for 69 yards and one touchdown in his two chances.

Round II was a scrimmage with San Francisco.

Staubach went 23 of 43 with an interception, but also had 10 passes dropped. Morton was 25 of 45 with two interceptions and five passes dropped.

"Roger appears to do better in individual work and Morton does better in team work," Landry said.

There was one last scrimmage before the exhibition season. Against San Diego, Morton was 8 of 12 for 69 yards, Staubach 9 of 12 for 107 yards. Landry called it "a peer draw," which was pretty much the overall score for the three rounds so far. Staubach was slightly ahead, but not by the overwhelming margin he needed.

"I rated both of them pretty equal in passing—one best one day and the other best the next—in camp," Landry said. "But Morton, of course, is still ahead in experience."

Landry also mentioned that while he preferred to pick a main man by the start of the regular season, he wasn't going to rush into a decision.

"We don't necessarily have to be established at the quarterback position by our first game," Landry said. "We have two very impressive quarterbacks, and I may decide to just sit and wait before choosing either of them to be number one."

Passing the first checkpoint of their race in a dead heat, Staubach knew he was behind.

As the incumbent, Morton got to go first at everything—practices, scrimmages, and the exhibition opener. Staubach understood. He just wanted to play more to show Landry how much he'd learned.

Staubach had become a more fundamentally sound passer, just like coaches wanted. He stuck with the quicker release he'd showed off at minicamp. He was more conscious about stepping forward in the pocket before he threw. And he was scrambling less.

"He's looking like a quarterback," Landry said.

Staubach knew how much Landry hated seeing his quarterback turn into "Roger the Dodger," and he realized he was risking getting hurt—which, in this case, would mean handing the job to Morton. So even though it might help put points on the board, Staubach tried to stay put. He also discovered he didn't have to run as often. That experience Landry valued so much really did make a difference. The game was slowing down for him.

"People who used to fly past me . . . well, I know who they are now," Staubach said. "Before, I knew I could run and throw and thought I wouldn't have any trouble. There's a lot more to it than that. You're beating your head against a wall if you don't know what you're doing."

—★—

On a Friday night in Los Angeles, Morton took the first big step in rehabilitating his career.

In his first game since the Blunder Bowl, his first game since elbow surgery, his first game since getting arrested for public urination, filing for bankruptcy, and revealing he called his hypnotist before games last season, Morton was back under center to open the exhibition season against the Rams in front of 87,187 fans at the Los Angeles Coliseum.

And on his first series, all he did was hand the ball to his running backs.

His first pass came on the second play of the second series, a dart to Bob Hayes. Morton led Dallas to a touchdown on that drive, then showed perfect touch on a lofted pass to Mike Ditka for another touchdown. Morton left after six drives, having put up three touchdowns and a field goal.

"My arm gave me no trouble, that's the big thing," he said.

Morton completed 10 of 14 passes for 121 yards. Among his misses were a drop and a deflection. While Staubach played well (9 of 18, with a touchdown to Hayes), it didn't matter. If Morton kept playing like this, the competition was over.

He knew it, too. Playing cards with Reeves, Garrison, and Ditka on the plane back to Dallas following a 45–21 victory, Morton said, "It's going to be a very good year, you watch and see."

For the next game, at home against the New Orleans Saints, the quarterbacks' roles were reversed. Staubach started and Morton came in with the backups.

Staubach opened the game conservatively—three runs, then two sideline passes. On the next snap, he dropped back close to his 20-yard line and heaved the ball nearly to the other 20-yard line, where Hayes was waiting for it. He easily took it into the end zone for a 69-yard touchdown. Staubach topped that with an 81-yard touchdown strike to Margene Adkins and connected with Adkins again for a 10-yard touchdown. It was 27–0 at halftime.

Landry credited Staubach for hitting the deep passes, but noted "he missed the short ones." Indeed, he completed 7 of 17 passes for 186 yards, but four were dropped and another drew a pass interference penalty. Staubach certainly liked the ratio of three touchdowns among seven completions.

"I'd like to have those three in New Orleans. Next January," he said.

Morton played the entire second half. Surrounded by lesser players, his outing was ugly at times. Like when he turned for a handoff and no one was there to take it. He ended up running into the left guard. Certainly that was someone else's mistake; maybe two or three people were to blame. He went 4 of 10 for 66 yards and an interception, and the big lead Staubach left behind turned into a 36–21 victory.

"We had so many players mixed in, everything went wrong," Landry said.

Landry wanted to give Morton a better chance to succeed in the next game, at home against Cleveland. With a national television audience watching, Morton struggled again, this time while surrounded by the starters. Landry stuck with him anyway. Staubach thought he was going to play in the second quarter; he warmed up in the third, but never left the sideline. While Dallas won winning 16–15, this game raised more questions about the quarterback competition than it answered.

How can both guys have a shot if one guy didn't take a snap? And why didn't Staubach get a snap? Did this make it clear Landry was slanting the competition in Morton's favor?

"It's hard to pull a quarterback when it's their game," Landry said. "There just wasn't a situation where it was fair to substitute. Morton was competing to win the ball game, and I just had to let him have the chance."

Morton had completed 5 of 15 passes midway through the fourth quarter. Those Cotton Bowl "Boo-birds" were singing. But he justified Landry's faith with his performance over the final minutes. He had a 68-yard drive that set up a potential go-ahead field goal that was missed, then marched Dallas 39 yards to set up another field goal that won it with 26 seconds left.

"Not playing much last week showed," Morton said. "It was not a great performance, but we did come back and win."

There was another important message here. Experience counts.

"The last five minutes, Craig did a fine job of play calling," offensive lineman Ralph Neely said. "They didn't know pass or run, the way he was mixing them up. He'd pass left, run right, pass right, run left. They didn't know what was coming."

A few days later, Landry said he would've stuck with Staubach under the same circumstances. He also said Staubach would start the next game, in Houston.

On the opening possession, Staubach marched the Cowboys 75 yards for a touchdown. Then everything went against him. First, Houston's defense swallowed the Dallas offense. Then, early in the second quarter, a pass clanged off Adkins and was intercepted. It was Staubach's first turnover of the exhibition season and it earned him a spot on the bench. In came Morton to finish the first half.

What? Morton got the chance to clean up his mess. Why didn't Staubach get the same opportunity, like Landry had promised?

"It wasn't the same," Landry said. "It's a matter of 'feel' with me. I had a different 'feel' for the situation tonight. I had meant to change right at the quarter, but Staubach had the drive going. I had already told him before the previous series that Craig would be coming in."

Landry's logic was convoluted. He said, "If Roger hadn't had their first good drive under his belt, I would probably have left him in there." That means Staubach was benched because he'd put up a touchdown; had he done nothing but struggle, he would've stayed in.

Was this coaching brilliance? Or sheer confusion?

Staubach returned for the second half. He finished 7 of 14 for 108 yards with an interception and lots of regret.

"This surely can't put me ahead of Craig," Staubach said.

As a squad, the Cowboys were flat this game. They didn't throw, run, block, tackle, cover, or kick very well. Landry suggested it could've been a hangover from beating Cleveland. Or maybe players were looking ahead to a Super Bowl rematch with Baltimore. Still, they beat Houston 28–20 to improve to 4–0.

"We play this bad and win," an assistant coach said, "we might never lose again."

# Ready or Not

**M**IDWAY THROUGH THE EXHIBITION season, the training room became awfully crowded.

Lance Alworth's ribs were a mess; a hit against Cleveland left him with torn cartilage in front and three broken ribs in back. Margene Adkins would have taken his place, but he broke a bone in his foot. Reggie Rucker had a torn muscle in his thigh. Depth at the receiver position was so thin that Landry turned to Dan Reeves just to have enough bodies in practice.

Tight ends couldn't fill in because both of them were banged up. Mike Ditka broke the bone that connects the ring finger to the wrist. Billy Truax injured the nerve next to his Achilles' tendon.

Mel Renfro twisted a knee. Backup Mark Washington was out with a badly sprained knee. Herb Adderley and Cornell Green weren't about to move to the right side of the field, so rookie Ike Thomas was given a battlefield promotion from third-stringer to starter.

Add in offensive lineman Bob Asher being out for the year with a knee problem, and all that optimism was draining away.

"Worries have a way of cropping up," Tom Landry said.

The 4–0 record in exhibition play was deceiving, too. The last two games were stinkers.

"Most of our mistakes come from lack of concentration," Bob Lilly said. "I don't think we have concentrated real good since the Los Angeles game. It seems to happen to us every year. Our concentration suffers when we leave the West Coast and come home. I guess it's because you leave an atmosphere that is strictly football and come back home and get all caught up in other activities and other problems."

—★—

To replace Asher, Landry turned to a future Hall of Famer.

Forrest Gregg had been a star at SMU before his standout career creating daylight for Packers to run through on Vince Lombardi's best teams. The last two seasons, he split his time playing tackle and coaching the offensive line. He'd been considering retiring when the Packers pushed him that direction by putting him on waivers. Nobody claimed him.

What a stroke of luck. Landry needed an offensive lineman and here was a guy who'd been All-NFL for eight straight seasons at both guard and tackle. He was living in a Dallas suburb and remained in shape, running three miles, three times a week, around the track at Lake Highlands High School. Landry offered Gregg quite a deal: Play two games, then decide for himself whether he wanted to stick with it.

The call surprised Gregg. The offer thrilled him.

"I've always had so much respect for the Cowboys, and I've really admired the things they do on offense," Gregg said. "I couldn't resist trying to be a part of it. They're a great team, another reason I had to try. If I can't make a contribution to the team, I'll know it, and I won't go on."

—★—

Fans howled over how obvious it was their guy should be the starting quarterback. Landry could only wish it was that easy.

The man many thought was wired like a computer couldn't solve this problem.

"I have no criticism of either one. They are both doing well," he said a few days after the Houston game. "I think it is important to have one quarterback if neither is doing too well, but it isn't that important to have a top guy if both are doing well.

"But, it'd sure help me in these press conferences if I had one quarterback."

By sticking with Morton when he struggled against Cleveland, then pulling Staubach at the first sign of trouble against Houston, Landry made it clear that he trusted Morton more.

As much as the former naval officer had progressed, he was still in his third NFL season, and Landry couldn't get past the fact no third-year quarterback had won a championship.

Yet Landry also knew Staubach was no ordinary third-year quarterback. He was 29, with the physical skills and mental makeup to become the first third-year quarterback to win a championship, especially with this team around him. So Landry continued to fret and to float the idea of using both of them.

How?

"I don't know," he said. "I would just play it by ear. I'd use them how I saw fit. I wouldn't alternate them in a game, no."

He did that before, with Eddie LeBaron and Don Meredith. He'd also gone through other bouts of uncertainty at quarterback, always with bad results.

In 1965, the Cowboys were 2–5 as Landry struggled to pick a starting quarterback. He gave the job to Meredith and the Cowboys went 5–2 the rest of the way. Last year, Staubach started the first three games, and things didn't get straightened out until after they were 5–4.

Despite that reservoir of bad experiences, Landry was climbing the high dive, ready to plunge into that murky water again. His only way out was if the final two exhibition games produced an injury, a meltdown, or the greatest performance in NFL history. He could only hope that facing the last two Super Bowl champs in the final two exhibition games would provide some clarity.

—★—

A few days before the Super Bowl rematch in Baltimore, Landry announced Morton would play the first half, Staubach the second. This was a slight change in procedure. Before, each was supposed to be ready at all times. Now, they had advance warning.

Whether this was some sort of experiment or change for the sake of change, Landry wouldn't say.

While in Baltimore, Staubach took a side trip to Annapolis to visit the U.S. Naval Academy. He spoke to the team, then saw the squad in the stands at the game that night. They had plenty of room to spread out as only 22,291 fans bothered to show up on the Friday night going into Labor Day weekend.

Again, Morton and Staubach played to a duel in Landry's eyes. Staubach was better, but not by enough.

- Morton was 11 of 19 for 146 yards and an interception. The Cowboys outscored the Colts 10–7 on his watch.
- Staubach was 12 of 17 for 193 yards and two touchdowns. The Cowboys outscored the Colts 17–7 on his watch.

Landry was impressed by a particular play, a third-and-goal from the 11. No one was open, but Staubach handled it like a polished veteran, not a ready-to-run, quarterback-in-training. Forced out of the pocket, he kept looking for a receiver. He ended up finding Hayes for a touchdown.

"He wouldn't have done that last year," Landry said. "He had broken field in front of him, a shot at running over the goal. Yet he stopped just at the line of scrimmage and passed the ball to Hayes. It's encouraging that he's still looking for receivers that late in the play and not at how far he can run before he gets tackled."

Staubach didn't have a single rushing attempt against the Colts.

—★—

The final exhibition game was filled with intrigue and subplots. Fans, too—74,035, one of the biggest crowds ever in Dallas for a game that didn't count.

The Cowboys and Chiefs were both undefeated. Unlike the twenty-first century approach of resting starters in the preseason finale, these teams were playing to win—or at least to keep momentum going into the regular season.

With both teams among the top contenders in their conference, there was talk of this being a possible Super Bowl preview. There also was an undercurrent of history, too.

Back in 1960, the Cowboys and Dallas Texans shared the Cotton Bowl. Now the franchises were meeting in what would be the final pro football game there if Texas Stadium could be ready for the home opener on

October 3. Even if delays might return the Cowboys to the Cotton Bowl, the Texans-turned-Chiefs weren't coming back.

The Morton-Staubach marathon also was headed for the finish line, or so they hoped.

Landry went with another flip-flop in his deployment, giving Staubach the first half and Morton the second.

Staubach had two long drives that ended with touchdown runs by Calvin Hill. He also had an interception caused by his arm getting hit while he was throwing. Dallas trailed 17–14 when he finished. Staubach also had to deal with swelling in his right thigh. He hurt it during training camp, but couldn't afford to mention it and risk losing any playing time. It had bothered him more in the last week or so. It was diagnosed as a ruptured blood vessel.

Morton completed only three of nine passes, but that included a 70-yard, game-winning touchdown to Gloster Richardson in the final minutes.

"I had some fine series and some other ones," Staubach said. "But Craig threw the winning touchdown pass, and that counts a lot."

Said Morton: "Who'll start next Sunday? I have no idea. You never can tell what's going to happen."

—★—

All along, Landry said he would follow his gut. He would consult the statistics, but, he told reporters, "I don't look at them the same way you fellows look at them."

Their numbers were extremely close, and the team's performance was similar under each quarterback:

|  | CMP | ATT | YDS | TD | INT | Y/A |
|---|---|---|---|---|---|---|
| Morton | 41 | 81 | 618 | 2 | 4 | 7.6 |
| Staubach | 44 | 83 | 714 | 6 | 2 | 8.6 |

|  | Team TD | Team FG | Team PTS |
|---|---|---|---|
| Morton | 7 | 7 | 70 |
| Staubach | 9 | 3 | 72 |

Staubach was more efficient and had more touchdowns while playing less. Morton had more total scoring drives. He also pulled out victories in the final minutes of two games, which loomed large to Landry. Staubach never had the chance to show what he could do in those situations.

Morton had settled any doubts about his health. His surgically repaired elbow held up great, and the shoulder operated on the previous year was back to full strength.

Staubach had also settled doubts. He fixed the biggest flaw in his motion, harnessed his instinct to take off running, and showed the poise and maturity befitting his age, regardless of his experience.

"I think either Staubach or Morton are capable of doing the job to get us back in the Super Bowl," Landry said.

Perhaps.

But only one could start the opener.

—★—

The morning after the exhibition finale, Morton caught an 11:00 a.m. flight to San Antonio.

He was headed to Santa Rosa Medical Center to see Bill Miller, an 11-year-old boy he'd never met.

Bill had leukemia. Doctors expected the disease to claim him two years ago, but the kid was a fighter. His spirit won over everyone he met. Now the disease was fighting back. Bill was readmitted to the hospital almost a month earlier and appeared to be giving up. He rarely smiled, hardly talked. So his father, Dick Miller, turned to Dan Cook—the main sports columnist in town and sports anchor of the local CBS affiliate—to see if he could help arrange a visit from Morton, Bill's favorite player.

Bill picked the right guy. Morton was a softie when it came to things like this. Although his heart broke every time he visited people in the hospital, from sick kids to Vietnam veterans, he went anyway because he understood it wasn't about him.

Dick Miller and Cook picked up Morton at the airport and took him straight to the hospital. Because Bill's resistance was low, Morton had to slip a surgical mask over his mouth and nose to make sure no germs were spread. This also made him unrecognizable.

"He's here, Bill. This is Craig Morton," Dick Miller said.

"Are you really Craig Morton?" Bill said.

"Yes, I am," the man behind the mask said. "And I came to San Antonio just to see you."

"Really? You are Mr. Morton?" Bill said.

"Take off your mask for a moment, Mr. Morton," Mrs. Miller said.

Bill's smile returned.

The boy kept smiling as he looked over the goodies Morton brought—a football autographed by all the Cowboys and some color pictures. Morton asked the boy about hospital life, and Bill asked Morton about throwing the winning touchdown pass the night before.

When someone brought up that it almost was time to head back to the airport, Morton announced, "I wonder if all of you here would mind leaving the room for a few minutes so Bill and I can have a few words together."

Here is how Cook described the rest of the visit:

> After five minutes alone with Bill, the Dallas quarterback strolled out and walked toward a group of nurses at the desk.
>
> "Which one of you is Margaret?" he asked.
>
> The pretty black one stepped forward, seemingly shy and perhaps a bit frightened. "I'm Margaret," she said.
>
> "Look, let's get something straight. Next time Bill gets mashed potatoes, we've got to have more gravy on them. Okay?" asked Morton.
>
> That busted up a bit of tension, and after Margaret agreed to more gravy everybody laughed. Morton then went back into the room, alone with Bill again.
>
> Half an hour later as we rushed toward the airport for Morton's 2 p.m. return flight to Dallas, my curiosity choked me.
>
> "Say, Craig, I know it's probably none of my business but would you mind telling me just what you and Bill talked about when you were alone back there?"
>
> For the first time that day Morton sort of stumbled for words.
>
> "Well, I guess you'd have to say it was kind of private. We just had a little personal chat. If Bill wants to tell you about it, that would be his business and okay with me. And by the way,

about those photographers you had at the hospital. They were certainly fine with me, but I think we should check with Bill again and see if he minds that sort of publicity. After all this is his day, not mine," Morton said.

As we told Craig goodbye at the airport, Mr. Miller said, "I can't thank you enough and you'll never know what this has meant to Bill."

And Morton answered, "It's meant a lot to me, too. It helped me as much as it helped Bill."

The next day, Bill told of his private session with the Dallas player.

"He told me that I was very brave and strong. He said he was proud of me and he was proud that I asked for him. Then he asked if we could say a prayer together and we did. After that, we just looked over the different autographs on the football he brought me and we discussed the different players. Man, he's great."

Craig Morton is still fighting for the first string job in Dallas today, but here in San Antonio he's got some votes for all-pro and the Miller family figures he is a shoo-in if they ever give an award to the quarterback with the most heart.

# A QB Decision—Sort Of

O N MONDAY, SEPTEMBER 13, the first Monday of the regular season, Tom Landry met individually with Craig Morton and Roger Staubach. He had some news to share.

Landry decided not to pick a starter. The job belonged to both of them, a two-quarterback system sort of like he had during the exhibition season, only with even less definition. Changes would come at his whim.

Landry would pick a starter by Wednesday of each week, but there would be no formula for who plays when. They would split the snaps during practice to keep both sharp.

For the opening game on Sunday in Buffalo, Staubach would start—if he was healthy. He missed practice Monday because of a bruise on his upper, inner right thigh, and doctors weren't expecting it to heal soon enough for him to play.

"Okay?" Landry said, giving the question everyone knew was a statement signaling the end of the conversation.

Naming Staubach the starter, yet probably having Morton start the opener, sounded like a way of making everyone happy. Quite the opposite. Staubach felt teased, Morton demoted.

Morton was furious. He'd rebuilt his arm and his confidence over the summer and still lost his job. Or at least sole possession of it. He was No. 1B, only starting the opener if No. 1A couldn't.

"I know Morton is burned up about this," Landry said. "You expect a guy to get mad if he feels he lost some ground. I hope he reacts the way I think he will. If he does, we'll be better off for it."

Staubach didn't like it either, but at least he was moving up. Landry acknowledged that Staubach had made up the gap with Morton, but he wondered how long it would last. Staubach knew how Landry felt about experience and his lack of it.

"It's like walking a tightrope. You have to be sure to stay up there," Staubach said. "I'm looking for the time when I take charge. This is the way I've planned it and the way I want to play. That time will come."

As the quarterbacks tried sorting through their quasi-starter status, Landry tried figuring out how to explain it to the media and fans.

Every Tuesday during the season, the Cowboys invited the media to the private club on the second floor of their office building along Central Expressway. They served a buffet lunch, with beer among the refreshments. When Landry finished eating, he answered question after question, giving as much insight and information as he chose about his club, the upcoming game, and anything else reporters wanted to know about. This first session of the regular season, there was no doubt what would be the main topic of conversation.

"There is a big misunderstanding of even my statement of going with two quarterbacks. Even the quarterbacks don't understand it," Landry said.

"Roger has a slight edge in probably some important categories of scoring, passing, so on. Wasn't much, really. To me it was not a putdown of Morton—it was an acknowledgement of Roger's competitiveness through the summer and the fact he was able to finish slightly ahead of Morton, which wasn't a very significant factor when you come right down to it. I have been on record with performance level. I have said that a backup man could not replace a starter without his superiority over him. A clear-cut superiority. Roger does not possess that over Morton at this time. Therefore, Morton did not lose his starting status with us. And this is the reason I have gone to the two-quarterback situation."

He was essentially continuing the preseason competition into the regular season. How much longer it would last depended on how long it took for someone to demonstrate a clear-cut superiority.

"I have to do what I think best for the team," Landry said. "Here's the unique situation—you could coach all your life and never face it, of two guys about the same age and the same ability. So I have to continue to go with them both at this time. It is not what I like because I know that I am going to be the one [who] is going to suffer from it. Because I am going to be second-guessed every decision that I make. I'm going to be second-guessed any time it brings losses, and there are always losses. Sometimes quarterbacks do not play well, just like Vida Blue doesn't always have his curve. But I'm willing to take that responsibility in order to establish one or the other as our starting quarterback for the future. . . . Things will be different next year. I'll go on record we won't do this again. The quarterback job will be resolved this year."

The day after the news conference, there was still some swelling and soreness in Staubach's leg. When he threw hard, the strain made it worse. Playing on it could've made things much worse, perhaps knocking him out up to six weeks. Landry called it "too big a chance to take," and gave Staubach the consolation prize of likely starting the second game, in Philadelphia, if he could throw hard without any problems by next Wednesday.

The season hadn't even started, and Landry already had his first quarterback flip-flop.

—★—

The Cowboys were two different teams depending on the quarterback. Both the Morton-led Cowboys and the Staubach-led Cowboys were very good teams, but they had different strengths and weaknesses. This made for an identity crisis from the start.

Each player had a quaterback he preferred for his own reasons. Maybe it was a receiver who liked the feel of a pass from Staubach, or a running back who liked how often Morton handed off. Whatever. The more important thing was that everyone believed in both quarterbacks. They just wanted Landry to pick one so they could adjust to that guy being in charge. It was the thought of jumping back and forth between the quarterbacks—between their leadership styles, their playing styles—that left everyone queasy.

What burned guys up was that this team was talented enough to win the NFC East with, say, Dan Reeves taking all the snaps. Heck, the Cowboys might have been better off being settled on Reeves than juggling Morton and Staubach.

Didn't Landry know that?

Everyone saw this team as a championship contender. After all the struggles and heartache of the last few years, why would he voluntarily make things more difficult? Wouldn't it be easier to do things the typical way: pick one guy and if things work out, great; if not, replace him with the other guy? The Vida Blue comparison didn't work. Baseball pitchers are routinely replaced, and it hardly affects everyone else. Maybe one pitcher gets more ground balls and another gives up fly balls, but fielders have to be ready for both on every pitch. In football, changing quarterbacks means a different voice in the huddle, a different cadence to the signals, and different plays that are run. Even on the same play, Staubach was more likely to move around the pocket, if not take off running, changing responsibilities for blockers and receivers.

Besides, if this was a good idea, more teams would try it.

"Your quarterback has to be your leader out there on the field," Falcons coach Norm Van Brocklin said. "If the players or coaches or the press or anybody else starts choosing sides on which of your quarterbacks is better, you can tear the guts right out of your ball club."

Van Brocklin understood the intricacies of a two-quarterback system as well as anyone.

From 1950 through 1952, he and Bob Waterfield split time for the Los Angeles Rams. They swapped every quarter, and the offense hummed along no matter who took the snaps. One of them won the passing title each of those seasons; in '51, Waterfield finished first, Van Brocklin second. The team thrived, too. The Rams reached the NFL championship game in 1950, won the title in 1951, and returned to the playoffs in 1952.

That '51 team was referenced by Cowboys owner Clint Murchison Jr. when he predicted the '71 Cowboys would win the Super Bowl with one of the best offenses ever. Tex Schramm thought highly of that '51 Rams club, too; he was their publicity director.

That success might've been the worst thing for future generations of quarterbacks because any coach bold enough or crazy enough to try a two-man system could always point to those Rams teams and say, "See, it can work." But that doesn't mean it was a good idea, even then.

"When Van Brocklin was in there, they hollered for Waterfield. When Waterfield was in there, they hollered for Van Brocklin," Van Brocklin said. "We were both hotter than a two-dollar pistol, so it worked great.

Besides, we had so much talent on that team we would have won with any system."

The tandem broke up because Waterfield tired of it. He quit football at 32 to go into show business, the same line of work as his wife, Hollywood pinup queen Jane Russell.

A few years later, the New York Giants tried a modified version of the two-quarterback routine.

In 1956, Don Heinrich started every game and at some point always gave way to Charlie Connerly. It worked well enough that the Giants won a championship. The assistant coach in charge of defense on that squad was Tom Landry.

—★—

Landry's history of struggling to pick a starting quarterback was as long as the history of the Cowboys.

The indecision started with the initial roster. Dallas signed Don Meredith before even landing the franchise, then took Heinrich in the expansion draft, figuring he could mentor the fresh-from-college rookie. Then Landry discovered he could get Eddie LeBaron, and he became the primary starter.

LeBaron and Meredith shared time for several seasons, but their relationship was different from what Morton and Staubach were going through. They were mentor and pupil; old-timer on his way out, youngster being eased in. LeBaron knew the drill; he had a similar relationship with Sammy Baugh as a rookie with the Redskins.

So as LeBaron saw what Morton and Staubach were going through, he could sympathize with both. But as a television analyst, and future general manager of the Falcons, he also saw things from Landry's perspective.

"There's never a serious problem with overabundance," he said. "Staubach is mature and intelligent enough to beat the five-year timetable. I believe he has arrived. Morton is throwing as well as I've ever seen him. The coach is faced with an odd situation. He has two fine, young quarterbacks both worthy of playing."

Meredith wasn't so kind.

Landry always had Meredith looking over his shoulder—either at a veteran like LeBaron or youngsters like Morton and Jerry Rhome.

Meredith always felt like he was merely renting the job of starting quarterback, never given the peace of mind that comes with owning the job. It burned him out, just like sharing snaps with Van Brocklin helped send Waterfield into retirement. Only worse: Dandy Don was 30 when he took his last snap, even younger than Waterfield had been when he called it quits, and Meredith didn't have a second career lined up. He spent a year as a stockbroker before stumbling into show business. Now he had the bully pulpit. He picked up where he left off in his last criticism of Landry.

"I'm somewhat disappointed, but I'm sure not nearly as disappointed as Craig Morton and Roger Staubach, not even to mention the thirty-eight other players who also are involved in that wishy-washy decision," Meredith said.

"It doesn't surprise me that he wouldn't want to go out on a limb and choose one, although his position as head coach would indicate to me that is his responsibility. . . . They're both talented individuals. They wouldn't be there if they weren't. But Landry's responsibility as a head coach is to pick a quarterback.

"Now, after he has spent this long with them he doesn't have any idea which one is best? Then get another goddamn coach."

"Morton vs. Staubach" was strictly business. There was one job, and both wanted it.

Otherwise, they got along great.

They became pals during the 1965 College All-Star Game. Morton was a friendly face for Staubach during his summertime visits to training camp while still in the navy. They enjoyed each other's company during the '69 and '70 seasons, even though they were so different on and off the field.

Most of all, and most importantly in 1971, they respected each other and understood the difficult situation they were in. There was no friction between them and no monkey business. Neither was politicking for the job—no lobbying of coaches, teammates, or reporters to put in a good word for them. That wasn't their nature.

Sure, they knew which teammates supported them and, by extension, who was rooting for the other guy.

From the beginning, Tex Schramm (center) and Tom Landry (left) built the Cowboys with the goal of being a perennial contender. Schramm's wise, wily personnel moves and Landry's coaching made that possible. Here they are at their first NFL draft, in December 1960, when they made Bob Lilly the franchise's first-ever pick. *AP Images*

Craig Morton was the first quarterback to start a Super Bowl for the Cowboys. They may have beaten Baltimore in Super Bowl V had he not thrown interceptions on three of his final six passes, turning a 13–6 lead into a 16–13 loss. *Focus on Sport/Getty Images*

On October 24, 1971, the Cowboys lambasted the Patriots 44–21 in the first game at their new home. Texas Stadium and its hole-in-the-roof design were so state-of-the-art in 1971 that the NFL almost voted it to host that season's Super Bowl. It would've happened had AFC owners not been worried about giving the Cowboys a home-field advantage should they reach the big game. *Charles Bennett/AP Images*

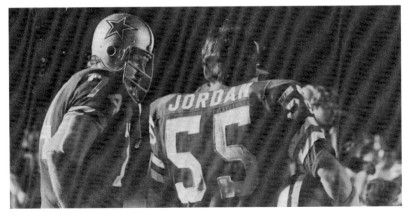

Bob Lilly (No. 74) and Lee Roy Jordan were the backbones of the "Doomsday Defense." Lilly was "Mr. Cowboy," and he led by example. Jordan was known as "Killer," and led with words and actions. *From the collections of the Texas/Dallas History and Archives Division, Dallas Public Library*

Jordan (No. 55, standing left), Lilly (No. 74), Chuck Howley (No. 54, middle right), and George Andrie (No. 66) were major reasons the Cowboys gave up the fewest yards-per-carry in the NFL in 1971. Landry often said that Lilly and Howley were better in their mid-30s than in their mid-20s. *Tony Tomsic/Getty Images*

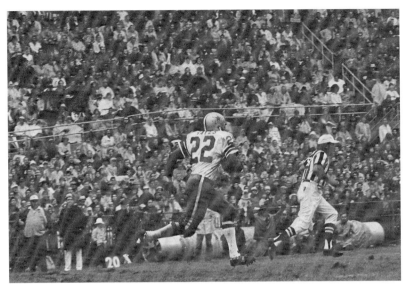

Seven years after winning a gold medal as the world's fastest man, "Bullet Bob" Hayes was still tough to catch. He opened the 1971 season catching a 76-yard touchdown against Buffalo. He led the NFL that season with an average of 24 yards per catch. *From the collections of the Texas/Dallas History and Archives Division, Dallas Public Library*

With Duane Thomas missing at the start of the season, a healthy Calvin Hill (No. 35) reminded everyone of his rookie of the year success in 1969. Here, guard John Niland (No. 76) leads the way for Hill during a rain-soaked game against the rival Redskins. *From the collections of the Texas/Dallas History and Archives Division, Dallas Public Library*

Lilly could dominate the most crafty veterans in the league, so Eagles rookie offensive lineman Henry Allison (No. 65, left) had no chance of stopping him during a September '71 game. "He'd just jump over my head and disappear," Allison said. *Focus on Sport/Getty Images*

Dan Reeves did it all for the Cowboys in '71—filling the roles of fullback, halfback, holder, running backs coach, emergency receiver, and third-string quarterback. *Tom Tomsic/Getty Images*

Morton (No. 14) and Roger Staubach (No. 12) led completely different lives and had different styles of playing quarterback. Landry had them alternate starts, then alternate snaps, before finally settling on Staubach. *From the collections of the Texas/Dallas History and Archives Division, Dallas Public Library*

Losing to the New Orleans Saints in mid-October showed how befuddled the reigning NFC champs—and their coach—were. *From the collections of the Texas/ Dallas History and Archives Division, Dallas Public Library*

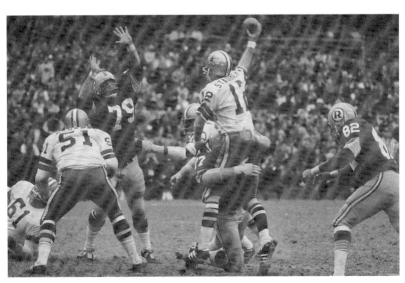

When Landry picked Staubach as his starting QB, Staubach said, "I won't let you down." He didn't. The Cowboys won their final 10 games, including the Super Bowl, and he was named the game's MVP. *Nate Fine/NFL/Getty Images*

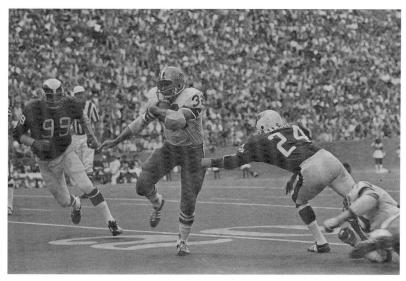

Walt Garrison (No. 32) was the Cowboys' cowboy, the toughest son of a gun in pads. In '71, he led the club with 40 catches and ran for 429 yards. *From the collections of the Texas/Dallas History and Archives Division, Dallas Public Library*

The "Doomsday Defense" allowed the third-fewest yards in the NFL in 1971. The Cowboys were the toughest team in the league to run against, and they knew how to get after the quarterback, too. *From the collections of the Texas/ Dallas History and Archives Division, Dallas Public Library*

In a first-round playoff game at Minnesota, the Cowboys were supposed to struggle against the Vikings and their "Purple People Eaters." With John Niland taking care of Alan Page, Duane Thomas (No. 33) and Staubach powered the Cowboys toward the Super Bowl. *From the collections of the Texas/Dallas History and Archives Division, Dallas Public Library*

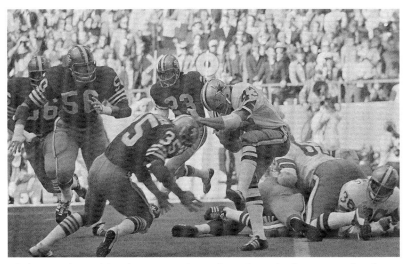

Cliff Harris (No.43) lost his starting free safety job to Charlie Waters when he went to military duty in 1970. In '71, Harris won the job back and became an entertaining punt returner. In his signature wild running style, "Captain Crash" exploded into the arms of the 49ers' Larry Schreiber (No. 35) on the opening play of the NFC Championship game. *AP Images*

Landry and Staubach made quite a tandem. Starting in 1971, the Cowboys went to the Super Bowl four times in eight years, winning twice and losing the others by four points each. Along the way, they turned "Next Year's Champions" into "America's Team." *AP Images*

"Leave me alone—I don't want to talk to anybody," Thomas told the first wave of reporters on Super Bowl Media Day. The only other words he spoke that afternoon: "What time is it?" *AP Images*

Cornell Green (No. 34) and the "Doomsday Defense" kept Bob Griese and the Dolphins out of the end zone in Super Bowl VI. That Miami club remains the only team not to score a touchdown in the Super Bowl. *AP Images*

Herb Adderley breaks up a pass intended for the Dolphin's Jim Kiick during the Super Bowl. A former Packers star, Adderley was among nine future Hall of Famers to play for the Cowboys in 1971. *Vernon Biever/NFL/Getty Images*

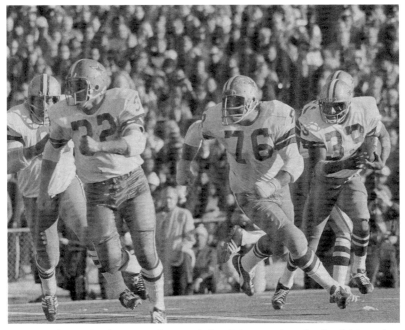

Garrison (No. 32), Blaine Nye (No. 61, behind Garrison), and Niland (No. 76) lead the way for Thomas as he heads downfield in the Super Bowl. Thomas was the most impressive player in the big game, running 19 times for 95 yards and adding 17 yards on 3 receptions. *AP Images/NFL Photos*

The thrill of victory, and of dismissing all the talk that he and the Cowboys couldn't win the big one, left Landry with a smile that many would never forget. Surrounding him as he's carried off the field are cornerback Mel Renfro (No. 20), receiver Bob Hayes (No. 22), and right tackle Rayfield Wright (No. 70). *AP Images*

Thomas should've been the MVP of the Super Bowl, but organizers didn't know whether he'd fulfill all the obligations. Turns out, he was so happy that—with Jim Brown's encouragement—he gave an interview to CBS' Tom Brookshier. The interviewer was so stunned he botched most of the questions. *From the collections of the Texas/Dallas History and Archives Division, Dallas Public Library*

When the phone rang in the winning team's locker room, Landry was expecting President Nixon on the other end. It turned out to be someone looking for CBS' Pat Summerall. Nixon eventually called, too. *From the collections of the Texas/ Dallas History and Archives Division, Dallas Public Library*

Lilly wasn't much of a smoker, but he brought a victory cigar to Super Bowl V. He took it home and put it away for the day he could really enjoy it. That moment finally came following Super Bowl VI, when all the ghosts that had haunted the Cowboys' past went up in smoke. *From the collections of the Texas/Dallas History and Archives Division, Dallas Public Library*

"But it didn't matter," Morton said. "As a quarterback, if you have any intelligence, you don't deal with that stuff."

Each tried to bring out the best in the other, realizing the team would benefit from their survival-of-the-fittest competition. As long as Landry didn't botch it.

★

# SECTION III

---

# False Start

# The Early Calm

AROUND 6:15 P.M. ON the Wednesday before the opener, a visitor entered Tex Schramm's office.

Duane Thomas was reporting to work.

As with everything else involving Thomas, it wasn't so simple. He would have to pass a physical, and the commissioner would have to reinstate him from the voluntarily retired list before he could rejoin the active roster. There were feelings to be mended in the locker room, and it would take a few weeks of practice for him to get in shape. But as long as Thomas was willing, those things could all be handled. The important thing was this first step—showing up for the first time since late July, when he and his pal Ali ha ka Kabir visited training camp.

"We have always said the door would be open when Duane fulfilled the necessary requirements of reporting and was prepared to join the team and contribute to winning the Super Bowl," Schramm said.

The way teammates felt about Thomas had changed in the two months since his inflammatory news conference. Time heals, but so does the reality of the regular season starting without a guy who could help them. They'd rather put up with him taking credit for wins than risk losing without him.

"If the man wants to come back and play football, why should we hassle him?" said receiver Bob Hayes, who had defended the organization against Thomas' accusations of racism. "We want him here. He's a teammate."

"I just hope any problems he had have been solved," offensive lineman Rayfield Wright said. "I would have hated to see that much talent wasted, and I'd like to see it benefit our club again."

— ★ —

Heading into the opener, things were falling into place.

There were some injuries and some shoddy performances in the exhibition games, but now it was showtime. With Mel Renfro recovered from a knee injury, all 11 defensive starters from the Super Bowl would be in the lineup against the Bills. Lee Roy Jordan, the heart and soul of the Doomsday Defense, proclaimed his unit ready.

"We won't be as sharp defensively as we were the last four or five games last season, but we'll be all right," he said. "We'll get there."

The only real position battle on defense this summer was at free safety, with Charlie Waters beating out his good buddy Cliff Harris.

Harris won the job in training camp in 1970, then was summoned to military duty late in the season. He was allowed to return for games, but Waters was there every day and became the starter. Their battle this training camp was the undercard to the headliner of Craig Morton versus Roger Staubach. Landry called the safeties "both one hundred percenters" because they gave their all on every play.

"There's not much difference between them," he said.

Harris picked up another job, becoming the primary returner of punts and kickoffs. While he didn't have the speed of incumbents Hayes, Renfro, and Thomas, he made up for it with a kamikaze spirit—running all over the place looking for something to hit, and hit hard, no matter whether he had the ball or someone on the other team did. "A rolling ball of butcher knives" is how Longhorns coach Darrell Royal described Harris; he eventually became known as "Captain Crash."

"Some of the coaches think I'm crazy," Harris said. "I feel the harder I run, the less chance I have of getting hurt."

Mike Clark remained the kicker, with Austrian import Toni Fritsch going on the taxi squad. The plan all along was to give Fritsch some time to adapt to a new country, a new culture, and a new sport. But he sure looked good in preseason—hitting a 46-yarder and a 50-yarder against New Orleans, while Clark missed a 47-yarder that game. Against Cleveland the following week, Clark missed a 19-yarder with 1:55 left that would've put Dallas ahead. He got another chance, though, and helped hold onto his job by making a 26-yarder with 26 seconds left.

"An old man taught me what to tell myself: 'To hell with the last one, make the *next* one,'" Clark said. "That's the only thought to keep."

The offense was still in flux, and not just at quarterback. Billy Truax was settling in at tight end, and Mike Ditka was playing through an injury. Receiver Lance Alworth was out because of damaged ribs, so another newcomer, Gloster Richardson, started opposite Hayes. Calvin Hill was ready at halfback, but there was less faith in his backups, Joe Williams and Claxton Welch. Depth on the offensive line was a question, too. Forrest Gregg stuck around, but it was clear why the Packers had let him go.

Still, the reigning NFC champs had every reason to expect great things. The 6–0 preseason set quite a tone. Only once before had the Cowboys been unbeaten in exhibition play—in 1966, when they went to the NFL Championship Game for the first time.

"We have," Landry said, "the best team we've ever had."

—★—

The Cowboys had never played the Bills, and many guys had never been to Buffalo. So the day before, a bunch of them did the tourist thing and visited Niagara Falls. It was a perfect way to prepare for the conditions on Sunday.

Rain turned the field to mud. Big chunks of turf came up. Maybe the bad traction was to blame for Dallas defenders running into each other all afternoon.

It started when Buffalo's Dennis Shaw lobbed a pass to Haven Moses down the middle of the field. Renfro closed in for the tackle when he was knocked out by Waters, giving Moses an easy 73-yard touchdown.

Then Shaw threw a short pass toward the sideline to Marlin Briscoe. Jordan collided with Herb Adderley, and Briscoe jogged 75 yards for a touchdown.

Still in the first half, Waters intercepted a pass and was leveled by Renfro.

At halftime, Landry replaced Waters with Harris. The Bills kept scoring, though, with Shaw hitting Briscoe for a 23-yarder that put them ahead 30–28 in the third quarter.

Then it was the Cowboys' turn.

On a third-and-goal from the 19, Morton was supposed to throw to Dan Reeves in the corner of the end zone but saw Reggie Rucker standing practically alone. So Morton threw to him for a touchdown that put Dallas back in the lead. Hill stretched it with two short touchdowns runs in the fourth quarter, and the Cowboys pulled away to win 49–37.

"The only reason I like it is that we won it," Landry said. "We made some unusual errors out there."

Dallas drew 13 penalties for 129 yards. The defense limited O. J. Simpson to 25 yards on 14 carries, but gave up four touchdown passes. Richardson and Buffalo cornerback Bob James were ejected for fighting, then Hayes left with muscle spasms, leaving Landry no choice but to use Reeves at receiver.

"I wouldn't say they were double- or triple-covering me," Reeves said. "Once I looked up and could swear they had the defensive end assigned to me."

Morton kept the Cowboys pretty efficient.

On the opening drive, Hill went right for 8 yards, Walt Garrison went left for a career-best 34 yards, then Hill went right 2 yards for a touchdown. Hill finished with 22 carries for 84 yards and four touchdowns, tying a club record.

Morton completed 10 of 14 passes for 221 yards and two touchdowns. He misfired only once in the second half. In the fourth quarter, he threw a reverse screen pass to Garrison, which symbolized how good he felt. He hadn't called that play since hurting his shoulder on it during a game in 1969.

"I'm happy," Morton said. "My arm felt good. I know Roger will probably start next week. We just have to go along with it until we find out how it's going to be."

The 86 combined points was the most in any game the Cowboys had ever played. But all that mattered was starting 1–0. Several other playoff contenders—San Francisco, Los Angeles, Oakland, and Kansas City—were all upset in their openers.

"I think the most important thing is that we stayed in there," Landry said. "I think we will get better. We're just not sharp yet. We've done just enough to get by. I'm still encouraged with the offense. It's been scoring all summer. When the defense tightens up a bit, like late last year, we'll be in pretty good shape."

—★—

The commissioner reinstated Thomas on Tuesday, giving the Cowboys 10 days to put him on the active roster or the taxi squad. He wasn't ready to practice because of an infection in his leg, so there would be an extended breaking-in period for him.

"You can't tell how his reflexes will be after this layoff. You've got to wait and see," Landry said. "Anybody who misses any work at all, even injured players like Mel Renfro, it takes them a while to get back in the groove after coming back."

Thomas' physical condition rarely was an issue. The question was his attitude, especially after the last few months.

"His attitude is fine with me," Landry said. "He's no different now than what he used to be when I talked to him."

What about him calling you "a plastic man, actually no man at all?"

"I haven't asked for an apology, and he hasn't offered one," Landry said.

The other big news on Tuesday was rain, with more in the forecast. This mattered because the parking lots at Texas Stadium weren't fully paved. Now, there was no way the lots would be ready for the game against Washington a week from Sunday. So the new target for opening the stadium was the following Sunday against the New York Giants.

When the league compiled the stats from the opening weekend, Morton was the top-rated passer. That could have made it tough for Landry to switch to Staubach.

"No," Landry insisted. "Not when you're using a two-quarterback system. It isn't hard."

Staubach had made the trip to Buffalo because he would've had to play had Morton gotten hurt. He took the side trip to Niagara Falls and spent much of his spare time reading the novel *Deliverance*. Perhaps the challenges faced by those fictional characters gave him a new perspective on his own battle.

—★—

The Cowboys spent the second Sunday of the season in Philadelphia for the opening of the Eagles' new home, Veterans Stadium.

On their second snap, Staubach dropped back to pass. Ditka cut toward the middle of the field, and Staubach threw right where Ditka was headed. But a defender knocked Ditka off his route and the ball landed in the arms of Philadelphia's Bill Bradley.

Left tackle Ralph Neely and Eagles defensive end Mel Tom went from grappling to watching the return. Then Tom realized Staubach was no longer a quarterback—technically, he was part of the defense trying to tackle Bradley. So Tom grabbed Staubach's arm, spun him around, and clubbed Staubach on the side of his head, dropping him to the artificial turf.

Over the years, the plastic-on-concrete at the Vet would claim many victims; Michael Irvin's career ended there in 1999. On the first series of the first game played there, Staubach became the first casualty, lying motionless on the field.

Staubach suffered a concussion. He tried going back out the next time Dallas had the ball, but coaches didn't let him. He couldn't even remember any of the plays.

Bob Lilly and the defense took care of the rest.

Dallas intercepted seven passes, six from starter Pete Liske. It sure was nice of him to point his left index finger toward wherever he was throwing.

"I mean, he sort of alerted you," Waters said.

Adderley had three of the interceptions, and was looking for the end zone each time. He came in tied for the NFL's career lead in interceptions returned for touchdowns with seven and really wanted to claim the record for himself on this day because he was playing in his hometown, with his mother in the crowd. Alas, he only got as close as the five-yard line.

Lilly, however, found his way to the end zone. In the second quarter, with Dallas up only 7–0, Larry Cole slapped the ball out of Liske's hand. Lilly picked it up at the seven-yard line and scored easily.

Lilly spent much of his afternoon in the Philadelphia backfield. The Eagles had made the mistake of asking rookie Henry Allison to keep Lilly out, and the veteran toyed with the kid. On one play, Lilly moved so quickly after the ball was snapped that he knocked Allison to the ground before he'd even got into his blocking stance. Lilly then tromped over him to tackle the running back for a loss.

"He'd just jump over my head and disappear," Allison said afterward, shaking his head.

It was that kind of afternoon for all the Doomsday guys. Philadelphia averaged only 1.7 yards per carry, and 3.6 yards per pass. At halftime, the Cowboys had caught the same number of Liske's passes as the Eagles had. Adderley finished with more yards than any Philadelphia receiver.

Thus, Staubach was hardly missed.

Thanks to all those interceptions, the offense had touchdown drives that covered only 5, 28, 35, and 55 yards. Morton also marched them 83 yards for a score. For the day, he completed 15 of 22 passes for 188 yards and two touchdowns. It might have been more had Landry let him finish the game.

Landry went to Reeves and said, "Danny, I think I need for you to go in at quarterback. I don't want to take a chance of Craig getting hurt."

Reeves laughed at the backhanded way Landry sent him out for his NFL debut as a quarterback. He threw three passes and completed two for 24 yards.

"I wanted to go for the bomb," Reeves said.

The final score was 42–7. It would've been a shutout except that Landry tried a 48-yard field goal with about two minutes left and Al Nelson returned the miss 101 yards. On the runback, Philadelphia's Rich Harris punched Neely in the mouth, kneed him in the groin, and grabbed his jersey. D. D. Lewis came to Neely's defense, then Neely went after another one of the Eagles. Neely asked another official what he was going to do about it all.

"Aw, shut up," Neely was told. "They needed a touchdown."

This game proved more about Philadelphia than it did about Dallas. Still, the Cowboys came away having scored 91 points in two games, all with Morton at quarterback. He was completing 68 percent of his passes. Once Staubach's head cleared, he could see that he was in trouble.

"If I keep going the way I am, I'll solve that two-quarterback problem," he said.

Then Staubach smiled and said, "At least I know I'm in New Orleans."

When the Cowboys watched the game film, they couldn't believe how viciously Tom attacked Staubach. Staubach still calls it the worst cheap shot he ever took. "Today, he'd be suspended," Staubach said.

Ditka had been Tom's teammate for two years and considered it out of character.

"Unbelievable. Just unbelievable," Ditka said. "I just can't understand why he'd do a thing like that."

Neely vowed to forgive but not forget. Landry refused to comment for fear that he'd say something punishable by the league.

The film also showed that referee Bob Frederick was standing nearby when it happened. He didn't eject Tom or even throw a flag, adding to the Cowboys' ire.

"They've got to fine him when they see what happened," Staubach said. "Then they ought to give the money to me."

# First Fissures

TOM LANDRY WAS A good Christian man—calm, patient, tolerant of others.

George Allen tested those traits.

When he coached the Los Angeles Rams, Allen either spied on the Cowboys or spread the perception he was doing so. It was just a little something extra for Landry to think about while trying to outsmart Allen's ferocious defense. The ploy apparently worked because Allen went into the 1971 season undefeated against Landry, having won all three matchups.

Now the stakes were higher. Allen switched from the Rams to the Washington Redskins, one of Dallas' division rivals. No, *the* division rival. The conflict between the franchises started before the Cowboys were founded. The hatred was mutual, from ownership to players to fans.

Landry and Allen both built their teams around defense, but the similarities between the two ended there.

Allen let his emotions flow, and his players felt close to him because of it. In Los Angeles, he lobbied publicly to get them raises; when he was canned early in his tenure with the Rams, the support of his players helped get his job restored. Since joining the Redskins, Allen opened up an East Coast version of the Rams. Five of Washington's new starters had played for Allen before. It was all part of his "future is now" philosophy. He dumped draft pick after draft pick to acquire older, more reliable players. Allen opened the season without a single rookie on the 40-man roster, something no team had done for as long as such records had been kept by the NFL.

"His father gave him a six-week-old puppy when he was four, and he traded it away for two twelve-year-old cats," Redskins president Edward Bennett Williams said.

Washington was coming out of its "Deadskins" phase, several decades in which the club was hardly competitive. Vince Lombardi changed things when he took over in 1969, but he died of cancer before the 1970 season. The Redskins went 6–8 under an interim coach, prompting the hiring of Allen and his reshaping of the roster.

It sure was working. The Redskins were 2–0, just like the Cowboys. And as they prepared to visit Dallas, the week began with word that Allen was up to his old tricks. The latest stunt involved Steve Goepel, a quarterback from Colgate who'd been a twelfth-round pick by the Cowboys.

After Dallas cut Goepel, the Redskins were the only team that called him. Allen figured a kid from Colgate was smart enough to have absorbed things during his time inside enemy territory, so he invited Goepel to Washington. Billed as a tryout, it really was an interrogation. He asked about the Cowboys' audible system. What were their favorite formations near the goal line? And so forth. Realizing what was going on, Goepel said he thought he was there to play football. Allen—whom everyone knew disdained rookies, much less twelfth-round picks cut by another team— claimed he was just testing the quarterback's football acumen.

The league had put in antispying rules in 1968 following the accusations the Cowboys made against Allen. This didn't constitute a violation, but it certainly gave the Cowboys something else to think about.

"They could get some information from him, a general feel of what we try to do offensively," Landry said. "All information is helpful. You might confirm what you believe is happening. But George Allen, for instance, knows us pretty well."

On Tuesday, as the Cowboys went out to play some touch football, Herb Adderley joked, "Let George take a look at *that*." (It also was raining, forcing another delay for the opening of Texas Stadium. It was now set for October 24 against New England.)

On Wednesday, Landry moved practice to the Cotton Bowl. Better safe than sorry.

The Redskins were supposed to be struggling on offense because Sonny Jurgensen broke his shoulder during the exhibition season. But Billy Kilmer—the bounty from one of Allen's first trades—stepped in and led Washington to wins over the St. Louis Cardinals and New York Giants, a pair of NFC East foes. Loading up on division wins is the best way to win the division, and it was important in the tiebreaking formula, should it come to that. So the Redskins certainly were doing everything right so far this season.

—★—

The Friday before the Eagles game, Craig Morton's little pal Bill Miller checked out of Santa Rosa Medical Center for a weekend at home. That night, Morton called to catch up with him, two weeks after their hospital visit. Morton promised to send him a jersey and to continue calling each week.

On Sunday, Billy watched Morton and the Cowboys stomp the Eagles. Later that night, he wasn't feeling well. He had blood tests taken Monday. By Tuesday night, the leukemia he'd beaten back for so long could no longer be controlled.

He died the next day.

When the Millers returned to their home in New Braunfels, a package was waiting in the mailbox. From Morton.

—★—

If Allen's spies were watching Dallas' touch football game on Tuesday, they certainly would've noticed Duane Thomas. He even scored a touchdown.

He also tore the web between his middle finger and ring finger catching a pass from Staubach. It took several stitches to stop the bleeding.

"You okay?" lineman John Niland said.

"Are you a fucking doctor?" Thomas said, scowling.

Thomas had no use for reporters either.

"I don't want to talk about anything. Didn't you ever feel like not wanting to talk?" he said.

Asked simply when he would be playing, Thomas allowed, "Old Father Time will tell."

Landry said the club had until the following Wednesday to either activate Thomas, put him on the taxi squad, or waive him.

"We'll probably keep him," Landry said. "Our job now is trying to get him in the groove. I'd estimate it'd take him a couple of weeks to get into the real action. He's missed quite a bit."

The Cowboys weren't in much of a rush.

Calvin Hill had the second-most yards rushing in the NFC, and Walt Garrison was doing well, too, as a runner and receiver.

The league-wide statistics showed that the Cowboys had gained the most yards in the NFL through two games. However, the Redskins had given up the fewest yards, making for an interesting matchup Sunday.

To no one's surprise, Landry was sticking with Morton—and Roger Staubach.

Morton would start against the Redskins, but the two would continue taking turns running the first unit at practice. Despite Staubach's absences and Morton's success, the two-quarterback system was still in place.

A few days before playing Washington, Landry received a telegram.

The (New) Redskins are coming to play . . . baby!
Sincerely,
Two million-plus Redskins fans

On Sunday, those fans had reason to go wild right away when Charlie Harraway cut away from Chuck Howley, escaped Mel Renfro, and kept going for a 57-yard touchdown run. They went bonkers again in the second quarter when Kilmer threw deep and Roy Jefferson pulled it in between Herb Adderley and Charlie Waters, turning it into a 50-yard touchdown and a 14–3 lead.

The Redskins were about to score again when Dave Edwards intercepted a pass at the 6. Morton drove the Cowboys all the way to the other 6, only to stumble while trying to hand off to Hill, causing a fumble that was recovered by the Redskins. Morton led three other drives deep into Redskins territory, and each time came away with only a short field goal.

Washington led 14–9 at halftime, and Kilmer had barely loosened up. He'd taken only 17 snaps, compared to 47 by Morton. Quick drives that produce touchdowns sure beat slow ones that produce field goals.

This would've been a perfect time to see what Staubach could do. But Landry stuck with Morton. It wasn't until there was 12:23 left, and Dallas was trailing 20-9, that Landry gave Staubach a chance.

Right away, he saw Gloster Richardson open deep for a touchdown, but the defense was closing in before Staubach could throw. So he scrambled and wound up taking a 29-yard loss.

"A field goal wasn't any use to us then, anyway," Staubach said.

He marched the Cowboys to a touchdown on his next drive, going 69 yards in nine plays. The Redskins were giving up passes over the middle, so he and Mike Ditka helped themselves. Hill finished the drive with a 1-yard touchdown that got Dallas within 20–16 with 3:08 left. Now it was up to the defense to get the ball back.

That meant stopping the run, and the Cowboys hadn't done that all game. Doomsday's chance for redemption came right at the two-minute warning, with Washington facing third-and-3. A stop would force a punt and give Staubach another try. A first down would let the Redskins run out the clock.

Kilmer handed off to Tommy Mason, and he busted through for six yards. That was it. The Cowboys fell to 2-1 and the Redskins were 3-0 for the first time since 1943.

Washington players whooped and hollered in the locker room as if they'd won a playoff game. They presented Allen with the game ball, and he declared, "I've got to find a way to cut it up into forty pieces."

Allen was determined to get the most out of this victory.

He said the Redskins did nothing special to get ready for Dallas; they just didn't make many mistakes. He said he couldn't recall ever losing to the Cowboys. He added that he hoped this victory would "make up for the Senators coming to Texas," referring to Washington's baseball team announcing a few days earlier that it was moving to the Dallas suburb of Arlington.

Landry complimented the Redskins on being "good right now." He noted that it remains to be seen whether their aging lineup would hold up later in the season. He also wondered what was going on in his locker room.

Did the Cowboys think they could just show up and win? Did they think every week would be as easy as Philadelphia, instead of remembering how close things had been at Buffalo? They sure played like it, with the defense allowing two long touchdowns in the first half and a total of 200 yards rushing, and the offense failing to turn long drives into touchdowns.

"It wasn't defense, offense, quarterback, or anything," Landry said. "It was the team."

With his left hand held together by two fresh stitches, Bob Lilly agreed. He hoped his teammates understood their egos cost them this game as much as anything Washington did. The Redskins weren't four points better than the Cowboys, but they were today because they played harder and smarter.

"I've known for quite a while we have a lot of room for improvement. Maybe some of the guys haven't realized this, but I've known it," Lilly said. "We just haven't been tested since last year and haven't been playing that well. We've won them all, but we haven't played all that well. I think we needed a test like Washington. They made hard-nose football a reality for us."

—★—

The worst part for players came Tuesday. The film session.

As always, Landry showed each play to the entire team, running it once so they could see the outcome, then rewinding it again and again to focus on specific players. A single play could be shown 12 times—pure agony for anyone who knew a busted play was his fault, pure boredom for anyone not involved. Some guys would have sweat rings that met in the middle of their gray, team-issued T-shirts. Others swallowed barbiturates to keep them sedated. The whole viewing routinely took three to four hours.

The projector got a workout showing a play from the second quarter: a run by Hill on third-and-goal from the 2, with Dallas trailing 14–3.

"We failed to make it because we missed three blocks," Landry said. "That tends to stop you."

Seeing the play live, Landry had been so disgusted that he sent out Mike Clark for a nine-yard field goal instead of going for it on fourth down. That drew the loudest boos of the day.

Most of this viewing was spent watching the defense.

Landry's scheme required players to follow a script—being "coordinated," in his vernacular. If things went as planned, two or three players would be in position to stop every play. Guys could violate the system to try making a tackle or an interception, but it better work. Against Washington, there had been too much freelancing that didn't work.

"One man would make a mistake in his area and they'd go for ten, eleven, twelve yards," defensive line coach Ernie Stautner said. "Then we'd get panicky, and somebody would try to compensate for somebody else. They'd just hit us at the right place at the right time."

Landry guaranteed at least a few things would be different the next game. He changed the lineup.

"I hope this shocks us into what we need to do," Landry said.

The changes:

- Staubach would start. Morton blew his chance to seize the job by failing to finish those deep drives against Washington. A touchdown or two probably would've kept Staubach on the bench in the second half and a win certainly would've made it tougher for Landry to stick with his two-quarterback system.

  *Landry: "The quarterback change is nothing. I just decided that we'll go with Roger."*
- Cliff Harris was replacing Charlie Waters at free safety.

  *"I'm not real disappointed in Waters' play. But the responsibility of the free safety is stopping the big play, and we've had four against us in three games that have gone for over fifty yards."*
- Billy Truax was taking over at tight end, putting Mike Ditka on the bench, and Lance Alworth was taking over for Gloster Richardson at receiver. Truax missed the first two weeks because of fluid in his knee and Alworth made his debut against Washington, playing through ongoing pain in his ribs.

  *"We've been lacking some end blocking, especially to the outside and off-tackle. We feel at this time the changes may help."*

- Duane Thomas was activated.

  *"Thomas is in good shape. It's amazing how much he retains. He missed very few assignments. We'll work him at fullback and halfback, but how we'll play him I don't know. . . . Calvin Hill's running has been tremendous. He's been making most of his yards without any blocking. If he gets some, no telling what he'll do."*

Up next were the New York Giants.

Landry's old team finished second to Dallas in the NFC East last season and came in 2–1, just like the Cowboys. Another similarity: their only loss came against Washington.

But the Giants were a weird club—their two wins were by a total of three points; their loss was by 27. It was a continuation of their weird summer.

During training camp on the campus of C. W. Post College, rookie Joe Zigulich quit midway through the first practice, declaring, "I'm tired of pro ball;" he never returned. Another day featured a fire in the second-floor dining room. Several players jumped out a window; lineman Charlie Harper flubbed the landing and broke an ankle. The school sent the team a bill for broken window screens. Then there was the time running back Ron Johnson missed a game because of a chess injury. Not chest, chess. He and tight end Bob Tucker played for 14 hours straight at the team hotel, and when Johnson got up, he had leg cramps. Johnson was coming off the first 1,000-yard season in club history, so his absence was significant.

This would be Dallas' only appearance of the season on *Monday Night Football*, and it was the final game to be played at the Cotton Bowl. While it was fitting that the finale came during the State Fair, there wasn't much nostalgia over this being the seventy-eighth and final regular-season game at the old place.

New York fumbled the opening kickoff, then Dallas fumbled it back on the first snap. The ball kept rolling around all night.

A forgettable first half ended with Dallas leading 13–6. As the teams headed for the locker rooms, Landry decided to continue shuffling his lineup. He swapped out two-thirds of the backfield, putting Morton in place of Staubach and Thomas in place of Garrison at fullback.

Staubach wasn't dazzling the first two quarters, but he was doing fine, especially considering it was the most he'd played in a month, since the final exhibition game. He completed 8 of 17 passes for 106 yards and a touchdown. He didn't throw any interceptions, and he never took off running. He did lose two fumbles, one coming five yards from the end zone while scrambling late in the first quarter, but Dallas had scored three times and had yet to trail. He was playing at least as good as Morton had when he got to start the second half the week before.

In his first live action since the Super Bowl, Thomas hadn't missed a beat. Playing only special teams in the first half, he crushed his old West Texas State teammate Rocky Thompson pretty good on several returns. Landry wanted to see what else he could do, especially since Garrison had another of the fumbles.

On the first play of the third quarter, Thomas blocked for Hill and toppled Fred Dryer, the Giants' star defensive end and future leading man on television. Thomas hit Dryer so hard that his helmet was the first thing to hit the ground, paving the way for a nine-yard gain.

Hill ran for five more yards on the next snap, then went for 11—and got clobbered. With Hill's left leg in the air and his right leg firmly planted, Giants safety Spider Lockhart came from the side and knocked Hill's right knee the wrong way. So Thomas took over at halfback, and Dan Reeves came in to play fullback.

It was as if the game up to this point had been trial-and-error for the Cowboys to get the right combination of players. Finally, they found it.

Thomas dashed around left tackle for 13 yards on his first carry. His next carry went for 6 yards, and then 9. The way Thomas was being cheered, you'd have thought his time away had been spent with the Peace Corps.

"It's amazing how fans begin appreciating you again after you pull 20 yards in two carries," Don Meredith told the national audience.

Thomas finished with 60 yards on just nine carries. Others ran more often, but nobody on either team gained more yards. He put to shame the notion that players needed training camp and exhibition games to get their timing down. Maybe everyone should spend their summers sulking and lashing out at the organization.

"He said he wasn't tired, and that's the amazing part about the whole deal—he wasn't," Reeves said. "I was dying out there, when he was just a little winded."

Reeves knew Thomas was mentally ready to play.

Around around 1:00 a.m. the night before, Thomas had called Reeves' room at the team hotel and asked if he could visit.

"I want to go over my assignments," Thomas told Reeves.

"Come on down," Reeves said.

Thomas dropped his angry persona and was back to being the affable kid who'd gotten along with Reeves the previous year. Their conversation, though, was all football.

Thomas wanted to know not only his duties, but everyone's role on every play. It's the way he was taught to study back in high school and he'd always done it, even when he saw that others didn't. This thirst for understanding the plays was among the things Landry appreciated most about him. Of course, there was a major benefit to it, too. By knowing where receivers would be blocking, Thomas would know which way to cut once he got through the line. Things like that could turn a small gain into a medium gain, medium gains into long touchdowns.

Still, it was a lot of information to absorb at once after 10 months away from it. So during the second half against the Giants, Thomas and Reeves developed a routine. If Thomas looked at Reeves after huddle, then Reeves would remind Thomas of his role on that play. No glance meant he knew what to do.

Morton spent the second half admiring Thomas' runs. He threw only five passes, completing three. He pretty much decided the game in the third quarter when he threw deep to Bob Hayes. There were three defenders in the area, but none could catch the former holder of the world record in the 100-meter dash. The touchdown covered 48 yards and put Dallas ahead 20-6.

The Cowboys kept the Giants under control by slowing Fran Tarkenton.

Landry made the rare move of swapping out his defensive linemen every few plays to make sure Dallas always had fresh legs chasing Tarkenton. Backup end Pat Toomay replaced George Andrie and Larry Cole, and backup tackle Bill Gregory relieved Lilly and Jethro Pugh. Tarkenton was able to move the ball all game, but New York didn't score a touchdown until late in the fourth quarter.

Dallas won despite fumbling seven times, losing five. It helped that New York lost five. The Giants also hurt themselves with receiver Rich Houston dropping a touchdown pass, then stumbling and falling out of bounds on another sure touchdown.

"If we'd have been playing any team that wasn't making errors, they'd have beaten us," Landry said.

Landry said he pulled Staubach because he was "rusty." He overthrew Hayes on one likely touchdown and underthrew him on another.

"He was keying well and finding his receivers, but the ball just kept sailing on him," Landry said.

The problem wasn't only that Staubach threw poorly. It was how often he threw, period. He had been under orders to call more running plays, like Morton did. However, Staubach was so eager to prove himself as a passer that he kept calling his own number. It was understandable; now, he also understood the repercussions. The ground rules for quarterbacks were the same as for those defensive players who took chances against the Redskins—if you freelance, it better work.

Landry went to discuss it all with Staubach after the game, but the quarterback cut him off.

"Coach, just don't say anything," Staubach said. "You'll never understand me. What you did by pulling me out of the game was uncalled for. You'll just never understand me."

—★—

The last two games provided insight into Landry's "feel" for handling his quarterbacks.

Staubach was on a short leash and Morton a long one. Landry didn't see anything wrong with giving it a tug every once in a while, either. He hoped the threat of a tug would help keep them sharp.

"As long as I have two quarterbacks, this is the way I plan to use them," he said. "When one isn't doing well, I'm going to see if the other has a hotter hand."

Landry showed his ongoing commitment to quarterback leapfrog by announcing Morton would start the next game, against New Orleans, and Staubach the following game, against New England. The announcement also was meant to be a confidence-booster for Staubach.

"I want him to know I have no different feeling about him as a number one," Landry said.

With the season a month old and no quarterback decision in sight, the shuffling was becoming a growing concern.

Sure, the Cowboys were 3–1, but their only really good performance came against a really bad team. Landry said the club has been doing well "in spurts," never getting everything going at the same time. Could the Morton-Staubach uncertainty be the source of the inconsistency?

"If I thought so, I might do something about it," Landry said. "I feel what we're doing is the best way."

In 1971, there were no sports-talk radio shows, much less entire stations devoted to it, and no Internet. The tone-setters were still the newspapers, and the Cowboys had four papers covering them on a daily basis—the *Dallas Times-Herald*, *Dallas Morning News*, *Fort Worth Star-Telegram*, and *Fort Worth Press*. The paid observers were loading up against Landry's handling of the quarterbacks. Beat writers turned into columnists, giving their thoughts under headlines such as "Two Plus Two Equals Who?" and "A Guessing Game."

Steve Perkins of the *Times-Herald* asked Landry whether Morton would be benched if he completed 21 straight passes against the Saints.

"Probably," Landry said. "We've got a two-quarterback system."

About 15 minutes later, Landry sent publicity director Curt Mosher into the press room with an update. If Morton went 21-for-21, he would start the following week.

Bob St. John of the *Morning News* conducted an anonymous locker-room poll. On the record, everyone said there was little difference between the quarterbacks, that they hardly even noticed who was in there, and that both could lead the club to a championship. Off the record, two guys told St. John they preferred Morton or the dual system—in other words, anything but Staubach.

"I think Roger's going to be an outstanding quarterback, but Morton calls a better game," one of the players said. "Roger tends to throw too much. With the blocking and running we have, I don't see how anybody can stop us from running."

The truth was, most offensive players felt that way. They liked knowing what they were going to get from Morton. They liked that he didn't take many chances.

The defensive guys, however, knew how much they hated facing an unpredictable quaterback, especially a guy who could throw and run like Staubach.

—★—

As if having two quarterbacks wasn't enough of a dilemma, Thomas' performance meant Landry had to figure out a plan for his three running backs.

"We'll use them interchangeably," he said. "We think it's important to play quality like we have when the opportunity presents itself."

Hill's injury wasn't as bad as everyone feared, and it bought the Cowboys some time. Landry announced that Hill would miss two weeks, with Thomas starting both games at halfback. He said Hill would remain the starter once he was healthy. Well, probably.

"I can't be sure, but I anticipate this," Landry said.

Hill had been told his injury was only a bruise and figured he wouldn't miss any games. He was looking forward to playing the Saints. He had one of his best games there two years ago, as a rookie, when his father-in-law was president of the Saints and Sinners, the team's rabid fan club.

When a reporter broke the news to Hill about Landry declaring him out for two weeks, Hill threw down a shoe and said, "I'm not going to go through what I went through last year. I'll be back."

His bid to play all 14 games was done. The bigger problem was the chance of Thomas stealing his job again.

"I don't see my not playing," Hill said. "But then, I didn't see my not playing last year."

This news even prompted a few words from Thomas.

Asked about playing the Giants, he said, "It felt like a football game."

How could he be so good after such a long layoff?

"I was just practicing," he said.

Ready to take over at halfback?

"I'm not even thinking about that now," he said. "All I'm thinking about is going home."

The Cowboys had a chance to straighten themselves out by playing the Saints, the team picked to host the Super Bowl because owners across the league were so sure they wouldn't be contenders.

Led by rookie quarterback Archie Manning, New Orleans had something to look forward to once he matured. Not now, though. The Saints were 1–2–1 and coming off their worst game, a 21-point loss to the Chicago Bears. Facing Dick Butkus and the rest of that defense was a harsh reminder for Manning of the difference between the NFL and college ball.

"He has learned just enough to be confused," Saints general manager Vic Schwenk said. "He has forgotten that this is basically a simple game."

The Saints had never beaten the Cowboys in five matchups, six counting this preseason. But they generally played Dallas tough.

"We seem to motivate them that way," Landry said. "The Saints are a young club, and young clubs are usually inconsistent. They may play real well one week and not so well one week or the next."

The Cowboys were favored by two touchdowns. Even a close game would feel like a loss. Plenty of fans were hoping Dallas would get a big, early lead so they could switch channels and watch Game Seven of the World Series, Steve Blass and the Pittsburgh Pirates against Mike Cuellar and the Baltimore Orioles.

# Uh-oh

THERE'S NOTHING LIKE A SATURDAY NIGHT in New Orleans. Even with a curfew, there's fun to be had and great food to be eaten. For Chuck Howley and George Andrie, the restaurant of choice was Kolb's, a German place on St. Charles Street.

As they finished their meal, their dirty dishes and silverware were cleared away by a kid who recognized them. He also was a Saints fan, and a mouthy one.

"The Cowboys are a bunch of bums," the busboy said, "including you two!"

Howley and Andrie told the kid to get away. The waiter saw what was happening and rushed over to smooth things out. As everyone went their separate ways, Howley looked at the busboy and said, "I'm not saying what's going to happen tomorrow, but I guarantee you this, kid—we'll see you back here in January. And I want to hear what song you're singing then."

Other than Mardi Gras, nothing drew a crowd in New Orleans like the Cowboys.

Dallas lured the Saints' first sellout, in 1967, and their biggest crowd ever, in 1968. With 83,088 tickets sold for this game, the Cowboys were now the guests of honor at four of the five biggest crowds in club history.

Right from the start, everyone got what they expected. The Cowboys quickly drove to the nine-yard line and Craig Morton threw into the end zone to start the blowout.

Except that Morton didn't see safety Hugo Hollas. And what was supposed to be a Dallas touchdown became an interception, the first of many mistakes the Cowboys would make.

Anyone watching who didn't know better would've thought the guys with fleur-de-lis on their helmets were the reigning NFC champs.

- Dallas' Richmond Flowers tackled punt returner Al Dodd before the ball even came down. That gift of 15 yards was followed by Manning throwing a 29-yard touchdown pass for a 7–0 lead.
- Morton threw another interception, this one getting returned 60 yards. That led to a field goal and a 10–0 deficit for Dallas.
- Tom Landry asked Mike Clark to try a 50-yard field goal; he was 1-of-10 from 50 or more yards in his career and hadn't even tried one that long in two years. Even if Landry figured a miss would be no worse than a punt, he had to factor in that his special teams already had given up a touchdown on the return of a missed field goal this season. Clark indeed missed, and the Saints returned it 77 yards; it would've been more, but Dodd wore out. Manning ran the final 13 yards for a touchdown and a 17-0 halftime lead.

A quarterback change seemed like an obvious way for the Cowboys to start over in the second half. There was little doubt that if Roger Staubach played the way Morton had, he would have been pulled.

But Landry stuck with Morton until the middle of the third quarter. By then, he was 10 of 24 with two interceptions and zero scoring drives against a defense that rarely shuts anyone out for very long, much less a team of Dallas' caliber.

"I didn't change sooner because I didn't think it was that much Craig's fault," Landry said. "He was under a lot of pressure. Our blocking was breaking down, and he was getting hit a lot."

Left tackle Ralph Neely was beaten so badly at the end of one play that he grabbed a guy by the jersey and pulled him down. It was worth a holding penalty to keep him from getting a clean shot on Morton. Of course, the quarterback could've helped himself by not making the play last so long.

"Damn it, Morton, get rid of the damn football," Neely screamed in the huddle. Then he drew another holding penalty and was benched.

Once Staubach was in, he provided a spark all right. Two drives, two touchdown passes. Suddenly, it was a game again: New Orleans 17, Dallas 14, with most of the fourth quarter remaining.

The Cowboys were about to get the ball back near midfield, giving Staubach a great chance to make it three straight touchdowns and the lead. A field goal would've been fine, too, because it would've tied the game.

Charlie Waters was back to catch a punt, then saw it was coming up short. As he ran forward to catch it, Landry screamed, "Let it go! Let it go!" He wanted Waters to play it safe and let the ball hit the ground; wherever it stopped, so be it, Dallas would have great field position regardless.

But Waters couldn't hear him over all those fans.

The ball arrived in Waters' hands at the same time teammate John Fitzgerald did. The collision cost the Cowboys the ball and a great opportunity. With about two minutes left, Cliff Harris went back for a punt that would've given Staubach less time and more yards to cover, but a chance nonetheless. Harris fumbled it away. New Orleans recovered close to the goal line, and Manning ran it in for another touchdown, sealing a final score of 24–14.

This was only the fifteenth win in Saints' history, and easily the greatest. It also was a candidate for the Cowboys' most humiliating loss. It wasn't just that they fell to the Saints. It was that they didn't deserve to win. They lost three fumbles and threw three interceptions. The special teams had all the breakdowns already mentioned, plus a penalty for roughing the punter that gave New Orleans a first down. The offensive line opened few holes for the running backs and allowed five sacks (known as "traps" in the jargon of the day). The Doomsday crew allowed only six completions while forcing seven punts, but they had trouble stopping Manning when he ran.

Manning was on the move when he threw for the first touchdown, and he avoided six guys on the next touchdown run. He also used his feet to turn some crucial third downs into first downs. A week that began with him worried about losing his job ended with him earning the NFL offensive player of the week award.

"It wasn't a good game offensively for us," Manning said. "Emotionally, it was great."

The Cowboys headed home like many weekend visitors to New Orleans—mentally and physically drained, wondering what the hell happened and what they could do about it.

The flight back to Love Field was mercifully brief. Everyone grabbed their things and headed home. Except Landry.

Braniff Airways couldn't find his luggage.

"The end," he said, "of a perfect day."

The 1971 Cowboys accomplished a bizarre form of progress. They needed only five games for their season to become a crisis—much quicker than the nine games they needed in 1970.

It was as if they'd learned the wrong lesson from the travails of 1970. Instead of remembering they were at their best when playing for each other, they seemed to remember more that they were able to goof around until nearly Thanksgiving and still reach the Super Bowl.

Losing to Washington should've shaken players more than it did. The fact most guys dismissed it as a blip, telling themselves everything would be okay, should have been a sign something was wrong with this club.

Losing to New Orleans made it impossible to ignore.

The locker-room psychologists went into analysis mode. All sorts of theories emerged.

Staubach and Andrie thought guys were guilty of looking ahead—thinking about what Washington was doing, who the Cowboys would play in the playoffs, and maybe even what the temperature would be in New Orleans on Super Bowl Sunday. Everything, it seemed, but the team they had to beat next. "Last year," Andrie said, "we got there, but we were never looking at the Super Bowl along the way."

Herb Adderley and Bob Lilly saw something similar but different. It was a lack of focus, all right, but not necessarily because guys were looking toward the Super Bowl. Their daydreams were about money, women, and everything else that comes with being a celebrity.

"What we have to remember is that for each and every one of us, our major occupation is football," Adderley said. "If we're not thinking one hundred percent football, we're cheating ourselves and our teammates."

Lilly put it more succinctly: "We have some prima donnas on this ball club."

Neely's analysis was almost a mash-up of those other themes. He saw a bunch of guys who made mistakes because they lacked the proper focus, then were more concerned with how those mistakes affected their image than they were about how those mistakes hurt the team. His premise was based on the widespread fear of the Tuesday film sessions, gatherings he also lambasted as "shitty and childish."

"When you make a mistake during a game—and, remember, this is *during* a game—there are two things you think of. One is you say to yourself, 'Oh, God. That's going to look good Tuesday during the films.' The second thing you think of is, 'What are the press and the public going to think about this?'" Neely said. "The players have to play for themselves and remember that there's only one thing involved—winning the football game. If you have to take lumps on Tuesday, take it as an individual or as a team, and try to forget it. Of course, this is easier said than done. When you've got somebody on your butt, it's hard to ignore it. But this isn't a young ball club any more. It's not old, either, but we've been playing long enough we shouldn't have to worry ourselves about what coaches have to say on Tuesday."

Landry chimed in, too. In what was described as a "tough-talking press conference," he said the problems weren't the two-quarterback system or anything else to do with Xs and Os. It was poor attitudes and a lack of desire.

Xs and Os, he could fix. Attitudes and desire, he wouldn't even try.

"If there was just a breakdown in, say, the blocking, I could make a change and correct that. But when the whole team is breaking down; it is the whole team that has to change," Landry said. "I'm talking about mental intensity. We've been waiting for somebody to give us something. . . . If it's not obvious to the team that it's time to get going, there's not much hope for you. . . . If anything's going to convince you, it better be [losing to] New Orleans. If you don't get the message there, then you're deaf."

—★—

There was still a game to prepare for, this time against the New England Patriots and their hotshot young quarterback, Jim Plunkett.

Plunkett had been the top overall pick in the 1971 draft, taken a spot ahead of Manning. Plunkett and the Patriots already had won two of their first four games, matching their total from 1970. However, New England came in smarting following a 41–3 loss to Miami.

Landry had said Staubach would start against the Patriots unless Morton went something like 21-for-21 against the Saints. Since that certainly didn't happen, Staubach would get his turn.

Thomas woke up Wednesday with a stiff back and didn't practice. He was still expected to start. After his preseason stint in New England, it seemed unlikely he would miss a chance to show the Patriots what they were missing.

As much as the Cowboys needed to worry only about the Patriots, they did have to keep the Redskins in a mind a little. Washington was up to 5–0, putting Dallas two games behind in the division.

What the Cowboys really needed was to make a fresh start. Conveniently enough, they were getting the chance to do exactly that by moving into a new home: Texas Stadium, a state-of-the-art marvel built just for them, a tribute to the powerhouse they'd become and a symbol of the greatness they were counting on sustaining for years to come.

18

# Texas Stadium Is Open
# for Business

A S MUCH AS CLINT MURCHISON JR. loved an elaborate prank, he
found joy in subtle jabs, too.

Like the first football game at Texas Stadium being a college game
between Texas Southern University and Bishop College—or, from his
perspective, schools from Houston and Dallas. Murchison's vision for this
place started in the Astrodome, which billed itself as The Eighth Wonder
of the World, so he wanted folks from Houston to go home talking about
what he considered the Ninth Wonder. While the schedule just happened
to work out that way, Murchison surely had something to do with the
selection of the first song played at that game: "What Kind of Fool Am I?"
The tune is a bit somber for football, but the message was aimed at all the
naysayers—from his own father to city leaders in Dallas and well beyond.

It *was* foolish, though. Moving to the suburbs, away from his fan base.
Leaving a giant hole in the roof. Making people buy a 40-year bond with
a minimal return just for the right to buy season tickets. Demanding a
$50,000 bond for a luxury suite at a time when the average house in the
United States cost $25,000. Believing so many people would want these
luxury suites that he built an entire deck of them.

Yet Murchison recognized how much people were willing to spend
on sports. They might squawk about rising prices and traffic jams, about

Texas Stadium feeling like a stiff dress shoe after years of that comfy old sneaker known as the Cotton Bowl. But they were going to put up with it all to watch their favorite team in their favorite sport. And if they wouldn't, somebody else would.

The bond sales proved him correct.

By the first game, the Cowboys were sold out of the $1,000 seats between the 30-yard lines—all 8,000 of them. That was a quick $8 million. The club made another $4 million by selling suites—80 at $50,000 apiece. About half went to companies, half to regular ol', deep-pocketed fans.

And don't forget the season tickets that had to be purchased to make the bonds worth a damn. They cost $10 per seat, per game. The first year a bond owner doesn't buy a season ticket, he or she no longer owns the bond.

Suite owners had to buy a dozen season tickets. At least their tickets included access to the Stadium Club.

Single-game sales also were being offered. They cost $7 and $5 and were for a specific seat; no more open seating like at the Cotton Bowl. By comparison, a typical movie ticket in 1971 cost $1.50.

—★—

Architects, engineers, and everyone else involved in the building of Texas Stadium was told to keep two things in mind: How would the open roof affect things? And how would it look on television?

Because the roof was the stadium's centerpiece, Murchison had to make sure the concept would work. Obviously it would keep rain and snow from falling on fans. The bigger concern was the sun.

To simulate the angle and intensity of the sun's rays at different times of day and different times of year—say, noon in early September and 4:30 p.m. on Thanksgiving—Murchison had an engineer build a "sun machine." The device featured a light bulb attached to a sliding crossbar over a mock stadium. Charts of the sun's position showed where to aim the light, and it was up to architects to troubleshoot any potential problems.

"One of the primary considerations is to shade the sideline customers," Tex Schramm said.

Although there was talk of finding a temporary way to close the roof, it was never going to happen. Murchison was so adamant about not paying for heating and cooling that he had the roof designed so that it would be nearly impossible to support the weight needed for anything to cover the hole.

Club officials also did their homework on artificial turf, settling on 3M's "Tartan Turf" after about 18 months of research and testing.

Stadium general manager Bert Rose described the weave of the Tartan brand as being "more like a rug than blades of grass." He had those rugs laid in 15-foot strips, instead of the usual 5 feet, and stretched from sideline to sideline. With yard stripes painted right over the seams, the field looked like one giant patch from the stands—and on television.

Another reason for picking Tartan was that its lush green color was supposed to last longer than the competition. This was crucial for both aspects of the mandate—looking good and handling the exposure to the elements through the open roof.

"We were particularly impressed, however, with Tartan's impact cushion since this bears directly on the physical well-being of the players," Rose said. "We are convinced that the base, or pad, is the finest available."

In 1971, the dangers of artificial turf were being taken about as seriously as the dangers of cigarette smoking, which is to say there was only lip service. Sure, there was an inherent sense that it was a bad idea—*a violent game basically being played on a driveway, with only a sheet of plastic and a layer of rubber for cushioning*—but there was so much money to be made, and so many conveniences to be enjoyed, that everyone accepted it. If anything, research was being done to promote the benefits. This wasn't only the Cowboys; it was anyone building a new field with plastic grass or folks tearing out the natural turf to put in the fake stuff.

The rug cost about $350,000. That was chicken feed compared to the $1.2 million Murchison spent on an electronic scoreboard.

The screen was big: 140 feet wide and 17.5 feet high. And it was high-tech, circa 1971, filled with light bulbs synchronized by computers. Creators called it a one-of-a-kind system, with a sibling being built for the 1972 Summer Olympics in Munich.

At the touch of a button, operators could display one line of six, 17-foot high letters, perfect for single words like "Howdy," "Nifty," and "Oops." Or they could create five lines with 24 characters per line to show statistics and scores of other games. They also could cue up 30-second, animated, flashing films—cannons firing and flags waving to celebrate touchdowns, a huge arm pulling down a quarterback to celebrate sacks.

Five people ran the system during a game. They also could program messages as they went along.

"To make the messages interesting and effective requires the imagination of a number of people," Rose said. "Everybody has a hand in it. We sat around all summer thinking of things that would be amusing to our fans."

Since every eyeball in the house would be drawn to the screen, advertising boards were placed around it. At first, though, the two prime spots carried logos of the Cowboys and the NFL.

Cotton Bowl lovers had plenty of complaints, mainly about the ambience. It wasn't the same. By pricing out the low-budget fan, the Cowboys were losing the most passionate supporters—average Joes and Janes who could spring for tickets and a few beers but couldn't dream of paying for a bond, much less everything else on top of it, even with the financing options being offered.

Those who could afford it got their money's worth.

Even if they now had to pay a 15-cent toll to drive to Irving, arriving to paved parking lots all around the stadium made it better than Fair Park.

Inside, there were dozens of restrooms and nearly as many concession stands. The lights were bright, the speakers loud and clear.

The game-day workforce was more than 1,000 strong, including the 119 lovely young ladies known as Texettes. Dressed in white cowboy hats, white miniskirts, and white boots, they smiled and offered to escort guests to their seats. Going upstairs? Let's take the elevator. Right after you, ma'am.

Once fans located their section, row, and seat, they plopped into blue, theater-style chairs with armrests and plenty of leg room, a big upgrade from the Cotton Bowl's cramped, wooden bleachers.

All that was pauper style compared to the $50,000 Circle Suites.

These 16-foot by 16-foot boxes were marketed as a "personalized penthouse at Texas Stadium, similar to a second residence, like a lake home or a ranch." Buyers were encouraged to customize them—and were required to use specific contractors. One person got an outside bid for $6,000; the approved provider stuck them with a $17,000 tab. As Murchison knew all along, folks might gripe, but they still paid for it.

Competition broke out to see who could have the most elaborate and distinct suite.

Business mogul Edwin Cox went with a Southwestern theme, lots of red, yellow, and green, with animal skins and weathered paneling. The National Bank of Commerce evoked an English pub, all the way down to red glassware.

Oilman Frederic Wagner and builder James L. Williams shared a box that evoked the elegance of Louis XIV French court, awash in Cowboys blue—the wall panels, the velvet-covered chairs, and the velvet swag drapes. The ceiling was recessed, with French crystal chandeliers dangling. Ooh la la.

Four Square Properties sprung for a double-sized suite. The company decked it out with brown suede sofas atop blue-green tweed carpet atop parquet floors. The wall behind the bar was decorated with alternating squares of mirrors and suede.

Then there was the foursome whose biggest expense was Cowboys jerseys customized with their names. They hung the shirts on the wall, set up a dozen blue and white canvas directors' chairs, and had just as much fun as any of the big spenders.

One more luxury was available in each booth: closed-circuit television. That gave them access to instant replays, just like the viewers at home—except that, in 1971, no one in Dallas could watch a home game because of the NFL's rules that blacked out local games. The rule allowing local telecasts for games that sell out 72 hours in advance didn't begin until 1973.

Television sets were placed in the press box, too, one for every two seats. Leather seats, by the way. Strolling through the press box during the opener, Murchison said, "It's a nice little place to play a ball game, wouldn't you say?"

# A Grand Debut

FANS WERE ENCOURAGED TO arrive early for the first Cowboys game at Texas Stadium.

Come on in, take a look around. Buy some souvenirs and refreshments. Then find your seats in time to catch the warm-up acts—the Apache Belles from Tyler Junior College in East Texas, the 200-piece band from Monahans High School out in West Texas, and a 40-man barbershop chorus from North Dallas, all followed by Tommy Loy blasting the national anthem on his trumpet just as he had before every Cowboys game at the Cotton Bowl since Thanksgiving 1966.

The pre-game entertainment was guaranteed to be good. There was no telling how the football would be.

It was Roger Staubach's turn to start and his best chance yet to prove he deserved the job. This was only days after the anonymous survey of players showed more guys favored Craig Morton, and Staubach knew Landry was leaning toward the incumbent.

"I can't afford a bad performance, that's for sure," Staubach said. "If I don't do well, I'm in trouble."

Landry made one big decision regarding the quarterbacks: From now on, he would be calling the plays, sending them in via tight ends Billy Truax and Mike Ditka. Landry did it some against New Orleans and liked how it went.

Staubach didn't like it as a matter of principle. Part of the duty of playing quarterback is deciding what happens next. However, play calling was one of the areas Landry favored Morton over Staubach. So if this wiped that out, Staubach was all for it.

"I'll give Roger all the help I can," Landry said.

From the start, the Cowboys looked worthy of their exquisite stadium.

On the third play, Staubach threw to Bob Hayes for a 20-yard gain and a first down. Then Landry called Dive G Take, a handoff to Duane Thomas around the right end. Guard Blaine Nye and tackle Rayfield Wright held up their men, allowing Thomas to scoot around the corner. As he headed up the field, Thomas saw a safety coming toward him, so he cut back across the field. Receiver Lance Alworth flattened the safety, then Hayes ran interference for Thomas the rest of the way.

The touchdown covered 56 yards and put the Cowboys ahead just 2 minutes, 16 seconds after kickoff. Thomas had to love getting away from coach John Mazur and the Patriots once again—this time, on his own terms.

As the final seconds of the first quarter ticked away, Dallas led 10–7 and was preparing to kick a field goal. But time ran out and Landry thought about it some more as the teams switched ends of the field. He decided to send out Staubach to try converting a fourth-and-1 from the 20. Walt Garrison bashed through the line and made it nearly to the end zone. Staubach carried it in on the next play, and the game was never in doubt again. They Cowboys refused to make the same mistake as last week, in New Orleans, when they gave an inferior team some early confidence.

Dallas pulled away just before halftime.

Staubach and Hayes connected for two touchdowns passes in three minutes. The first was the kind of play Landry was looking for from Staubach as proof his third-year man was working from experience and not just raw ability. The play was designed to go to Hayes, but the corner-back forced him inside when he was supposed to go outside. Staubach stayed with him, though, waiting for Hayes to break free. Once he got loose, Staubach hit him for a 35-yard score.

New England's possession between the two Staubach-to-Hayes TDs was downright comical. After reaching the Dallas 38, Doomsday started pushing the Patriots back. A series of sacks and penalties left New England facing fourth-and-63 from its own 9-yard line.

Dallas led 34–7 at the break, then 37–7 after three quarters. That's when Landry told Staubach he'd done enough and let Morton handle the rest. The final score was 44–21.

The Cowboys came away thrilled with their performance and what it might mean for the rest of the season. Maybe New Orleans was their bottoming-out point and this was the start of their recovery.

"We were pulling for each other out there," Lee Roy Jordan said. "You could hear the offense cheering the defense on. That's the sort of thing we had last season. You know, not everybody needs a pat on the back. But some people it helps. And big plays inspire more big plays."

Landry wore a new double-breasted jacket in honor of the new stadium. Or maybe it was for the team's new attitude. He sensed all week that things were going to be better because of the way practices went.

"And I could tell in the locker room before kickoff they were going to play tough," he said.

A few hours later, more good news came from Kansas City. The Redskins had allowed a 17–6 halftime lead to fizzle into a 27–20 loss, Washington's first of the season. So now the Cowboys were only one game back in the division.

Things were starting to break right for Staubach too.

After missing the opener with an injury, getting KO'd from his first start after one pass, and getting benched in his only extended outing, this performance gave Landry plenty of reasons to believe in him—especially with Landry himself calling the plays. Staubach completed 13 of 21 passes for 197 yards and the two touchdowns to Hayes. He also remained poised in the pocket, running only twice—2 yards for a touchdown and 13 yards for a first down.

Now all Staubach could do was wait and see whether it was enough.

"I don't think I hurt myself," he said. "But I'm still leery." From the Patriots locker room, former Cowboys linebacker Steve Kiner had nothing but praise for Staubach. He said aloud what many Dallas defensive players were saying privately.

"Staubach is one hell of a football player," Kiner said. "He's very capable and a strong leader. The more experience he gets, the more recognition he's going to receive this year. If I was the coach, I'd go with him all the way."

Back in the Dallas locker room, Murchison came around with a couple of friends in tow—Lieutenant Governor Ben Barnes and former President Lyndon Baines Johnson. LBJ watched the game from Murchison's booth, along with his wife, Lady Bird, and another former first lady, Mamie Eisenhower.

Murchison introduced LBJ and Barnes to several players. When the entourage got to Morton, Murchison announced, "The president said he wanted to see you play, so I sent word up to Tex Schramm to tell Tom to put you in during the fourth quarter."

"Yeah?" Morton said, smiling. "You weren't leading the boos, were you?"

—★—

While the Cowboys learned a little about each other against the Patriots, everyone learned a lot about Texas Stadium.

Murchison discovered that his "sun machine" was a piece of junk. Sunshine blinded people on the east side of the stadium. Players struggled to see the ball as they went in and out of the shadows cast across the field.

"That makes me mad," Murchison said. "The sun is not supposed to do that."

NBC announcer Jay Randolph kept apologizing to viewers for the poor quality of the images caused by all those unexpected shadows. Thus, both mandates were violated—the part about the roof not being a factor and about looking good on television.

"You could have nine cameras and still not eliminate this problem for television," Randolph said.

Air didn't circulate inside the building very well either. It was 62 degrees at kickoff and felt hot and stuffy inside. Reviews of the Tartan Turf ranged from Walt Garrison calling it "better than I thought it would be" to New England's Larry Carwell calling it "the worst turf I've ever seen or played upon."

"I used to think it was bad in the Astrodome, but this has to be the hardest anywhere, and I include Minnesota where it is like a paved road," Carwell said.

Too slick was another common complaint. Some guys struggled to figure out what type of shoes gripped the turf best for them. Bob Lilly experimented with two different kinds of cleats for a while. He ended up choosing soccer-style and thought they did just fine. Rayfield Wright went with the same soccer-style cleats he used at the Cotton Bowl and didn't like it.

"Personally, I like the turf at the Cotton Bowl better, but I guess we'll adjust to this one," Ditka said. "Funny, but no one asked me when they were selecting a turf for Texas Stadium."

The scoreboard programmers needed a little breaking in, too.

It took playing a game for them to realize they weren't set up to show the information needed every play: the down and distance, what yard line the ball is on, and how many timeouts are left. It would be easy to solve, but it was surprising that nobody thought of this before.

At least the parking lots worked out fine. Traffic wasn't as bad as anticipated, either.

"Of course, there were some problems because people didn't know where to go, but these things are to be expected and will work themselves out," Schramm said. "Generally speaking, though, I'm well pleased with everything. The crowd noise was not bad—actually, not as bad as we had anticipated. Everyone seemed to really like the facilities."

But success wasn't determined by the opinions of the front office, players, or TV types. It was up to the paying customers; what did *they* think?

A surge in bond sales and renewed interest in the remaining luxury suites told the Cowboys all they needed to know.

# The Shuttle & More Trouble

THE MORNING AFTER BEATING New England, about half the team headed east to Sulphur Springs for their annual visit to the ranch owned by loyal fan Walter Helm. He just loved having all the guys come out for a day of dove hunting, fishing, and whatever else they wanted to do on his 13,000-acre spread.

Mike Clark won the dove hunting competition, bagging the limit in less than an hour and a half. Fellow kicker Toni Fritsch never had a chance; a city boy from Vienna, he shot at anything with wings, not knowing a dove from a meadowlark. His training-camp English teacher Don Talbert pulled one of his favorite pranks on Fritsch: shooting into the air so the buckshot would spray all over Fritsch. Talbert did the same to Dave Edwards, and the linebacker snarled, "You goddamned varmint!" Thus, Talbert came away from this trip known as "Varmint."

Bob Lilly, Cliff Harris, Charlie Waters, D. D. Lewis, Pat Toomay, and Blaine Nye were among those who brought their motorcycles. Riding dirt bikes had become the thing to do on Mondays for a group of players. Forget flopping on the sofa or a leisurely round of golf. For these guys, down time was the wind in their face, powerful beasts at their control, adrenalin surging from the action, with the hint of danger that comes with each dust-spewing turn and gravity-defying jump.

—★—

Tom Landry stood before the team at their Tuesday meeting going over the usual things. He talked about the upcoming game against the Bears in Chicago and about how he'd be changing quarterbacks every play.

That's right. Instead of alternating starts, Craig Morton and Roger Staubach would alternate snaps. Instead of tight ends bringing the plays from Landry, the quarterback would take it straight from the coach to the huddle.

It was called the "quarterback shuttle," and Landry had done it several times before—in the early days, when Eddie LeBaron was bringing along Don Meredith; in '65 when he was deciding whether Morton or fellow rookie Jerry Rhome should replace Meredith; and again with Morton and Rhome in '67, when Meredith was hurt.

Landry decided on this plan after seeing how well Dallas played while he called the plays and Staubach ran them against New England. It made him ready to trust Staubach more than ever, but he wasn't ready to give up on Morton.

Staubach and Morton stared at each other in disbelief, then rolled their eyes.

"What the heck is this?" Morton thought.

Staubach never agreed with the decision. Over time, he came to believe it was Landry's way of declaring that schemes win games, not players.

"Coach Landry was a phenomenal preparation coach, Xs and Os," Staubach said. "He could do everything on paper, like the industrial engineer he studied to become. He didn't take into consideration other aspects, especially at the quarterback position, things like leadership, what it meant to the team to have one leader. He just said, 'Here's a play, execute it. You're a quarterback.' He saw everybody as mechanical."

Landry announced his decision at the Wednesday news conference. He had to explain his reasoning as many ways as he could.

"I think it's the best way to go against the Bears," he said. "They show you a lot of changes on defense and move around a lot. We think it's the best way to attack them. It makes us more flexible."

Landry was reminded that the previous times he tried the shuttle, at least one quarterback was too young to know what he was doing, and that wasn't an issue now. Landry said it all came back to him calling the plays. He said that was the major change he'd decided to make since losing to the Saints, and going with the shuttle was the next logical step in his mind. Since he was calling the plays, he might as well give them directly to the quarterback.

He had all sorts of reasons why this was a good idea.

There was no chance of misinterpretation. The coach and quarterback could discuss options and adjustments based on what they'd seen from the defense. As the quarterback jogged to the huddle, he could be thinking ahead, going over coverages and coming up with audibles.

All seemed plausible. But if this was such a great way of doing things, why didn't more teams try it? Why didn't Landry do it more? Why didn't he try it sooner this season?

"You go by what you think best. I have no reservations. We'll do better this way than any other, in my opinion," Landry said. "I have told the quarterbacks about this, but I didn't ask them what they thought about it. The team may not agree with it completely, either. You can't get forty men to agree on anything unless you are winning and heading for the Super Bowl. My job, however, is to think for them on major changes like this. That's what I'm paid for."

For all the shuttling the quarterbacks had been doing, Dallas had the top passing offense in the NFC. Staubach now had enough attempts to qualify among the individual leaders, and he landed at No. 1 in the conference. Morton was fifth.

But it was Morton's turn to start. Staubach would open the game standing right next to Landry, getting ready to trot in with the next play.

—★—

The only people supporting the shuttle were Landry and the Chicago Bears.

"That's a good move on their part," Chicago coach Tom Dooley said with a smile.

"I'm glad they're experimenting *this* week," safety Ron Smith said.

"They'll probably get tired running on and off the field," Bears linebacker Doug Buffone said. "Maybe they'll even run into each other."

Retired Cowboys running back Don Perkins had been in the lineup for all previous incarnations of the shuttle. He was in Dallas for a regional March of Dimes meeting when Landry announced he was dusting it off, and Perkins added his credible voice to the chorus of critics. "It takes something out of the unified effort of the team," he said. "It's like 10 men working together and a messenger. There is more cohesion with 11 people staying intact."

A "messenger." Interchangeable parts. Such terms devalue what's supposed to be the most important job on the field, maybe the most challenging in all of pro sports. Knowing a coach feels this way has to sap a quarterback's confidence. Going in and out also prevents them from getting into a rhythm. Then there's the impact the revolving door has on the rest of the players. There's a different feel on handoffs to running backs and on spirals to receivers. The line is affected by different cadences in the snap count and by different ways of blocking—like knowing to never give up on a play when Staubach is back there because he's liable to be scrambling from sideline to sideline to goal line and back. Switching from one quarterback style to another midgame is tough enough. Switching back and forth all afternoon could be inviting trouble.

"When you're on offense in the shuttle, you better remember who's calling the snap," Perkins warned. "It can be a little tricky."

—★—

The Bears came into the game 4–2, just behind the Vikings in the NFC Central. Their lineup featured two of the four most productive receivers in the conference.

They also were dealing with injuries. Star running back Gale Sayers was out, as were their top two quarterbacks. Third-stringer Bobby Douglass was coming off a win in his first start, a victory over the the Lions in a game that nobody involved with would ever forget, for the most unthinkable reason—a player died.

In the final minutes of a close game, Lions receiver Chuck Hughes collapsed after a pass thrown to another player fell incomplete. People thought he was faking, maybe stalling to stop the clock, until Bears linebacker Dick Butkus realized he wasn't and frantically called for help.

Doctors tried reviving Hughes on the field, giving him mouth-to-mouth breathing and chest compressions. He eventually was carried off, and the game finished with near silence throughout Tiger Stadium.

Hughes died because a clot in an already hardened artery cut off the blood flow in his heart. It's still the only time an NFL player died on the field during a game. He was 28.

—★—

On Halloween afternoon in Chicago, the shuttle got off to a great start as the Morton-Staubach tandem drove 68 yards for a 7–0 lead. Duane Thomas scored the touchdown, providing shades of the previous week's victory over the Patriots.

Nothing else would be that easy.

The Bears were ahead 10–7 by the end of the first quarter, and the Cowboys would never lead again. It was crazy. The Cowboys gained 287 yards more than the Bears, limited the Bears to only seven first downs, and still lost 23–19.

The problems went beyond the quarterback shuttle.

Thomas fumbled on a hit that aggravated his back injury. Cornell Green was returning an interception when he was hit by Bob Lilly, causing him to fumble the ball back to the Bears. The most excruciating mistake was Cliff Harris fumbling a punt with 1:14 left.

The Cowboys wasted plenty of scoring chances, like getting only a field goal out of a drive that started at Chicago's 8-yard line following a fumble recovery by George Andrie. That field goal wasn't even a gimme, as Mike Clark had missed from 25, 30, and 42 yards. Tricky winds were part of the problem, but so was his tendency to connect with the bottom of the ball, popping kicks up instead of knocking them hard and deep.

"You just hope to get those out of your system," Clark said.

Chicago's Mac Percival had no trouble with the conditions. He made field goals of 44, 38, and 35 yards, without a miss. And, to think, it was the Cowboys who had discovered Percival in their 1967 Kicking Karavan.

Long returns on kickoff and punts set up all of Chicago's points. Penalties helped the Bears, too.

"They weren't going to get field position unless we gave it to them," Landry said. "It would have been so easy to win. That's what makes you sick."

Morton and Staubach combined to throw 47 passes, one short of the club record. They produced 344 yards, the most since early in 1969. They put together plenty of long drives. But you had to wonder whether the lack of rhythm caused by the quarterback shuttle was a factor in so many of those drives stalling.

The only times they didn't alternate every play was a two-minute drill before halftime and again over the final seven minutes. Morton had all those snaps.

"I left Morton in during those times because we knew we were going to have to throw and he was reading the Chicago defenses well," Landry said.

To Staubach, this meant Landry either didn't trust him much or he trusted Morton more. The bottom line was the same.

"I'm back to where I was the year before," Staubach thought. "Craig is going to be the quarterback."

The loss dropped the Cowboys to 4–3. Preseason predictions of 7–0 over the easy part of their schedule would've been worth a chuckle except for the stomach-churning reality that now they were heading into the tough half of the season.

Washington won, putting Dallas two games behind in the division again. Next up for the Cowboys was a trip to St. Louis, the team that kicked them when they were down last November to the tune of 38–0.

"I said last week that we'd taken a step, but not a giant step, that we'd have to play better. Well, we stubbed our toe," Landry said. "We're in the same position as two weeks ago, only with two less games to play. We're not out of it, but we have a tough road now. I guess we are going to find out now what we are made of."

By sticking with Morton down the stretch, Landry made it clear who he trusted with the game on the line. Staubach came away fearing it was 1970 all over again.

—★—

On every flight home, Landry held a news conference and otherwise mostly stayed with his wife, Alicia. So everyone took note of him huddling with his assistant coaches much of this flight.

Halfway through the season, there was a lot to discuss, major problems to solve.

Landry was getting closer to picking one quarterback. He also was considering ways to improve the kicking game, from the coverage squads to the kicker. It was getting tough to send Clark out there without knowing what to expect. He'd made nine field goals and missed nine.

It would've been so much easier to salvage the season if the Cowboys had one glaring weakness. But they had a lot of little things wrong. Some of the symptoms were showing on the stat sheet—14 lost fumbles after giving up 12 all of last season; 11 interceptions compared to 16 the entire previous year. Penalties were up, too.

Their wins weren't impressive either. The teams they'd beaten were a combined 6–18 against everyone else.

"We haven't beaten anyone who had any momentum," Landry said.

When the plane landed and everyone caught up with their families, Chuck Howley went to find Marianne Staubach.

Howley and her husband were roommates on the road and at the hotel the night before home games. Marianne packed a freshly made batch of chocolate chip cookies whenever Roger was going to start. Because he didn't start against Chicago, New Orleans, or Washington, she hadn't made cookies—and the Cowboys lost all those games.

"Bake cookies!" Howley jokingly told her, as if snacks were the linchpin to the season.

—★—

The next day, the dirt bike crew met at their usual hangout, the series of weaving paths by Lake Grapevine. Lilly, Harris, Waters, Edwards, Mike Ditka, and Dan Reeves were all there, plus a newcomer, Ralph Neely.

Thinking he was bigger and badder than everyone else, Neely bought a bigger, badder bike. This made it tougher to control, and he spent as much time picking himself and the bike off the ground as he did riding.

By the time everyone else was tuckered out, Neely still wanted to ride. Harris offered to go along for one last spin.

Harris suggested riding up an incline to a plateau with a nice view. They would check it out, then head home to get ready for a team party, the annual Las Vegas Night thrown by the team's wives club.

Harris rode up first, stopped, and waited for Neely. The novice took off and got about halfway up before falling over. The guy known as "Rotten," because nothing was ever worth a damn, was now outraged that his piece of shit bike couldn't climb a stupid hill.

Neely threw it into second gear on his next attempt and made it to the top with ease. Except he didn't slow down as he approached the plateau. That turned the incline into a natural launching ramp, sending him about 20 feet in the air. He kept the bike under control for the landing, but didn't use the foot pegs to cushion the impact. He put his feet down on the ground as if he was slowing a 10-speed bicycle, sending the full force of the landing into his legs. He broke the right one in three places.

The guys hauled Neely to Ditka's truck and dumped him in back with all their muddy bikes. They sped off to Baylor Hospital. Every bump added to Neely's excruciating pain, but nobody cared. All that mattered was getting their story straight.

Landry didn't know how many guys were riding dirt bikes, and they preferred he not find out. They agreed to say they'd been riding horses. And that a snake bit Neely's horse. And that the horse was so spooked, it threw him off. They also decided Reeves had to tell Landry, figuring his status as a player-coach made it more of his burden.

The bikers made it to the casino party just as the big medical news was making the rounds. Only, it wasn't about Neely.

George Andrie had been at home that afternoon when he felt some chest pains. He decided to go to the hospital, but didn't make it. The pain returned and was more intense, so he stopped at a gas station and had someone there call for an ambulance. His problem ended up only being a bad case of indigestion. The fright—so soon after the Lions receiver died of a heart attack—proved to be all the cover needed for Reeves to tell Landry the truth about Neely's injury. Landry didn't ban the guys from riding, but he did tell the whole team how stupid he thought it was.

Tony Liscio was among the guests at the party. Liscio had been the starting left tackle from 1966 until midway through the 1970 season, when Neely took his place. He was traded to San Diego over the summer in the deal for Lance Alworth, then traded again to Miami. He retired instead and was selling commercial real estate in Dallas. Edwards told him to get in shape, the Cowboys needed him. Then they had a drink and laughed.

Staubach was at the party, too. Ray Renfro, the assistant coach in charge of the passing offense, pulled him aside for a chat.

"Don't tell anybody," Renfro said. "You are going to be the starting quarterback."

Renfro said the coaching staff was asked to vote on it, and Staubach was their choice. Of course, Landry had the only vote that mattered, and Staubach wasn't going to say a word until he heard it from him.

Well, except for telling his wife. He framed it as the big chance he'd been waiting for, the make-or-break opportunity.

"I am going to finish the season," he told her, "or it's going to finish my career."

★

SECTION IV

---

# Righting
# the Ship

# The Turning Point

ROGER STAUBACH WENT TO work Tuesday expecting the best news of his NFL career. He didn't get it.

Craig Morton ran the first team at the informal, touch-football practice, as he had all season.

Maybe Ray Renfro had gotten bad information. Maybe Tom Landry had changed his mind, had remembered that Staubach was a third-year quarterback.

Something else happened, though. A players-only meeting called by Lee Roy Jordan.

Jordan had reached his boiling point. He felt like the Cowboys were just a collection of guys going through the motions together. They needed to become a team. At 4–3, unsure at quarterback and having just lost Neely, there was no time to waste. Salvaging the season would have to start now.

Jordan thought the biggest problem was that they weren't practicing hard enough. It was time to step it up a notch. They had to sharpen their focus Wednesdays, Thursdays, and Fridays if they were going to improve on Sundays.

"The defense needs to challenge the offense, the offense needs to challenge the defense," Jordan said. "We need to get our level of competition high enough so that when we get into the game, we don't have to reach another gear—we're already there. Sometimes we think we're going full speed, but we're not. You don't know it until the guy across the line from you knocks you on your butt."

Personal agendas had to be put aside, too. No matter their support or frustration over the quarterbacks, Duane Thomas, or anything else, everyone needed to understand that they were in this together. They got themselves into this mess, now it was up to them to get out of it.

The message spread quickly. The most respected guys from each cluster of the club—black or white, young or old, offense or defense—all spoke up, building on the themes of hard work and team unity, making sure it resonated with everyone.

The harder they worked, the more they would care. It didn't matter who scored a touchdown or made a tackle. As long as the team succeeded, they all could take pride in it. Receivers talked about making more downfield blocks on running plays, or on catches by other receivers—the exact kind of team-first thinking they needed.

It was an easy sell. A year before, Jordan turned around the season with a similar meeting pushing a similar message. The Cowboys went from 5-4 to the Super Bowl.

When Jordan finished, he went to another meeting. With Landry.

The captains decided the juggling of the quarterbacks was behind their herky-jerky season, so they took their complaint to the boss. Jordan did the talking.

"We need one quarterback," Jordan said. "We need to get focused and to all get together in support of one guy."

He didn't say which one; players knew they had no input in that. It was a decision that they wanted.

"I'll take that into consideration," Landry said.

Staubach left team headquarters that afternoon without hearing anything from Landry.

A few hours later, the coach called him at home.

"Roger, I've made a decision," Landry said. "I've decided you are going to be the starting quarterback for the rest of the season."

"Coach, I really appreciate that," Staubach said. "I won't let you down."

That was the extent of their conversation.

There wasn't much more to say.

—★—

Later that night, Landry called Morton.

It was after 10:00 p.m., and Landry sounded surprised that Morton answered. Knowing how much Morton enjoyed the night life, Landry always was surprised when Morton answered.

"Craig, you're home?!" Landry said. "Can you come over?"

"Certainly," Morton said.

By the time he hung up, Morton already knew. Good news could've been delivered over the phone. Landry was more likely to request a face-to-face meeting to deliver bad news.

The drive over was short. So was their conversation once he got there.

"Craig, I've decided to go with Roger," Landry said.

"Can you explain why?" Morton said.

"I've got a feeling," Landry said. "This is what I want to do. Thanks for coming over."

So last year's Super Bowl starter got back into his car and drove home, knowing he was now a backup.

—★—

The crowd for Landry's regular Wednesday luncheon and news conference filled the room. Reporters had no idea about the conversations with the quarterbacks the previous night. All they knew was that Landry seemed to be leaning toward naming a single quarterback for the rest of the season and they wanted to be there for the big announcement.

They wanted to hear Landry justify picking Morton over Staubach.

That's what everyone expected. They knew how loyal Landry was, how much he valued experience. They saw Landry's decision to use Morton the final seven minutes against Chicago as being a clear sign, just like Staubach had.

Landry showed up earlier than usual. He finished eating earlier, too. Then he stood to speak, and everyone snapped to attention. TV cameras zoomed in, radio guys hit record, and the newspaper types dug out something to write on.

Landry opened with the news that Don Talbert would replace Ralph Neely at left tackle and Gloster Richardson would replace Bob Hayes, who had aggravated a pulled muscle against Chicago. Landry also made the mildly surprising announcement that Mike Clark was moving to the taxi squad and Toni Fritsch would make his NFL debut on Sunday in St. Louis.

"I think we've reached the point now where I must make a choice on a quarterback," he said. "If any part of our team right now is concerned over the possibility that we don't have an established number one quarterback working for us—if that upsets them at all, and I'm not sure it does, really— then I must make a choice on the quarterback. We will go with Staubach.

"It's a real shame that you have to make a choice. Both quarterbacks have been outstanding. . . . But I think it is time for Roger to make his move. I feel he can do it. I have confidence he can or I wouldn't be picking him. Don't ask me if he'll go the seven games. Who knows? Whenever you make the choice, you assume he has the opportunity, even for years to come. But who can say he'll be the top guy forever? I assume he has the capability, but he's got to get out and do it."

Landry said he would continue calling the plays, going back to shuttling them in via tight ends.

"I'm convinced this is the way to go," he said. "We are not out of the race. It could turn around in a hurry. I think a change is necessary now. Last year, when we turned it around with a 5–4 record, I didn't think a change was necessary."

Landry called this a staff decision. What he failed to mention was that most of the staff had been supporting Staubach for a while.

Ermal Allen—the assistant coach in charge of analyzing the strengths and weaknesses of foes, as well as turning a critical eye on the Cowboys—had been lobbying for this since the exhibition season.

"Staubach was so far ahead of Morton in every way that we grade them," Allen said. "It wasn't even close."

Dan Reeves was in an awkward spot because of his dual role as an active player and an assistant coach. He and Morton had been friends for a long time, and he knew most of the offense supported their pal. But he also knew Morton was at his best reading defenses and running low-risk plays. Staubach's arm was stronger, and he was more willing to take chances. At 4–3, Dallas couldn't afford to stick with the status quo.

"Our team was looking for a change," Reeves said. "Roger would be a change."

Renfro, the coach overseeing the passing game, supported change for change's sake, comparing it to a golfer who switches putters or balls just to feel like he's changing his luck.

"Landry knows what Craig can do, how far he can take you," Renfro said. "I don't feel Craig has strong confidence in big games. It might be different had we'd won the Super Bowl and he'd had a decent day. He's a sensitive person. When he was put in the New England game and they booed, it just killed him. Stuff like that really hurts him.

"Roger thinks he can throw the ball anywhere. And if he gets good protection and good pass routes, he's going to throw completions. Still, Craig can handle the offense as well as anyone, in my opinion. With his ability, yes, I think he's a championship quarterback. It all goes back to one thing—Roger's gotten us into the end zone more."

—★—

Landry valued his own experience as much as he did a quarterback's, which is why this decision was so tough.

Despite all the griping about the two-quarterback system and the quarterback shuttle, he trusted them because he'd done them before. He knew what to expect. There was a track record. Good or bad, he'd learned from it.

He also had experience making an agonizing choice like this. It was 1965, Morton's rookie year. The Cowboys lost another road game on Halloween, dropping them to 2–5 at the midpoint of a season that began with great promise but was falling apart because of a revolving door at quarterback. Landry was so devastated after the fifth loss that he cried in front of the team, apologizing for having let them down. He spent the next few days thinking about how much pain Don Meredith had played through the previous year. He factored in how much teammates believed in Meredith. He ended up deciding to stick with the veteran over his two promising youngsters, Morton and Jerry Rhome. That faith was rewarded as Dallas went 5–2 over the second half. The 7–7 finish was the Cowboys' first nonlosing season, and it earned them a trip to the postseason for the first time. Trivial as those things might seem now, they were huge accomplishments at the time. They also were a springboard to success. The Cowboys finished first in the NFL's Eastern Conference, and its successor, the NFC East, every season since. Now that streak was in jeopardy. And while his gut told him to go with Staubach, he was still drawn to Morton. The lesson from the '65 example was being rewarded for having faith in the proven veteran. He still valued experience over potential. That explains why Renfro knew on Monday that a change was coming, but Landry needed until Tuesday night before he was certain enough to tell Staubach.

"Sometimes," Landry said Tuesday afternoon, "this job isn't a lot of fun."

—★—

A popular bumper sticker of the era read, "Today is the first day of the rest of your life." That certainly was true for 29-year-old, retired naval officer Roger Staubach when he showed up for practice on Wednesday, November 3, 1971.

While he'd worked with the first team before, it had been like driving someone else's car. Now it was all his. He could adjust the seat and mirrors the way he wanted, program the radio to his favorite channels, whatever he needed to get comfortable.

"If there are a few mistakes made, I'll still be in there. I won't be walking the tightrope any more. That way, I'll come through in the end," Staubach said. "I promised Mr. Landry that I wouldn't let him or the team down—but everything is going to have to be said in performance. I've always felt that when I walked on a field, I would walk off a winner somehow, but that's because I'm surrounded by the type of people [who] give me confidence."

Morton saw the move as being about what Staubach *might* do instead of what everyone *knew* he could do; after all, he was the quarterback who had Dallas within minutes of being Super Bowl champs and that was with a wrecked arm. He hated the decision but accepted it. Having spent years as No. 2 behind Meredith, he knew his duty was to stay ready and to stay out of the way.

"When we turn this thing around, before it is over, I'll have to play," Morton said. "I've been throwing the ball better than any time in my life. I know what I'm doing out there, and I have confidence in my ability—I don't doubt it any more. That's my strength. The whole team has got to realize now we can't wait around for somebody else to help us. The other guys have got to back up the starters. Whether I'm pleased with it or not is immaterial."

—★—

Regardless of what people thought of Staubach's promotion, he'd proven himself capable of being a starting quarterback in the NFL.

Fritsch hadn't proven a damn thing. His promotion was much more of a gamble.

Using Renfro's golf analogy, this was trying an entirely new swing with a new set of clubs on a new course.

"We just felt we needed a change at this time," Landry said. "Toni has kicked well in practice. I think Mike will work out any problems he has."

A few weeks before, Fritsch had become disillusioned with NFL life.

He couldn't make sense of this: The Cowboys had gone to Spain to scout him, to Vienna to woo him, and sent him to California for training, yet after two months in Dallas, he hadn't gotten into a game. The paychecks were nice, but his leg was being wasted. Whatever groove he'd gotten into during the exhibition season—making all his kicks, even from 46 and 51 yards—was lost by now. It didn't seem fair to keep his wife and young son so far from friends and family, so he asked for three plane tickets home. Tex Schramm talked him into staying, encouraging him that his chance would come.

Truth be told, Landry never planned on using Fritsch that season. He figured the former soccer star would need at least a year as an apprentice. He hadn't factored in the boredom and the emotional toll for a 26-year-old husband and father transplanted to a different continent, speaking a different language. None of those things factored into the decision to use Fritsch. This was about getting Clark out of the lineup as much as it was about getting Fritsch in.

"That's the way it is with a placekicker," Clark said. "You're a hero one week and a bum the next."

Placekicking was only part of the problem on special teams. The return squads were struggling, too, giving up long returns and fumbling too many punts.

So Landry shook up the practice routine, making kicking the first and last thing they worked on. He was considering changing the players on the coverage and return squads. Even 35-year-old Chuck Howley, the team's oldest starter, was an option.

"Nobody's too old when you are where we are," Landry said. "You want the best out there. It's foolish to beat a team offensively and defensively and lose the game on the kicking."

—★—

On Saturday night in St. Louis, Staubach studied the game plan in his hotel room. He thought about how he'd handle various situations. He tried to ignore the fact his best lineman, Neely, was gone for the rest of the season; that his top receiver, Hayes, wasn't starting because of an injury; that running back Calvin Hill was still out with a knee injury; that cornerback Herb Adderley was out with an injury and rookie Ike Thomas was making his NFL debut in his place; that the kicking would be done by a 26-year-old Austrian soccer pro who'd never played an NFL game.

No wonder the tension got to him.

He headed downstairs for something to eat. He saw his roommate, Howley, and Lilly having dinner in the hotel lobby. They invited Staubach to join them. It couldn't have been planned any better.

Here were the team's two elder statesmen, the reigning Super Bowl MVP and the guy known as Mr. Cowboy. They were acutely aware that only a few Novembers remained in their careers, only a few more chances for them to become Super Bowl champions. The Cowboys faced long odds against winning it all this season, but nobody lost hope, especially after the late run last season. If this season could be turned around, it would be because of Staubach. Howley, Lilly, and the rest of the defense thought he could do it; hell, they'd wanted Landry to pick Staubach since training camp.

Staubach always believed in himself. He came away from this meal knowing his teammates believed in him, too.

He sensed the optimism in practice the last few days, having heard guys say, "Hey, there's a new second half of the season." He also heard them say they "were excited to see what the hell Roger can do." So Staubach closed his eyes that night with a comforting thought: "The guys are really rooting for me."

—★—

A little before kickoff, Talbert received a telegram from Neely wishing him good luck. The Cowboys would need it. With all the lineup changes, there was no telling what was about to happen.

Staubach came out sharp, completing six of his first seven throws. The one miss was a drop. His first solid series fizzled at the 20, continuing the team's trend of drives that went far, but not far enough. At least this failure let Fritsch get the first kick of his career out of the way. It was a 27-yarder, and he nailed it, putting the Cowboys ahead 3–0.

Fritsch went out again midway through the second quarter to try a 42-yarder. He missed. On the next snap, Cardinals quarterback Jim Hart threw deep to speedy Jim Gilliam. Thomas, the rookie corner-back, had the speed to keep up with Gilliam, but he was preoccupied with simply staying close. Although he heard teammates screaming, "Ball! Ball!" he didn't look up in time and Gilliam caught it for a 51-yard gain. St. Louis ended up scoring a touchdown to take a 10–3 lead into halftime.

Midway through the third quarter, things got nasty.

As Charlie Waters returned a punt, Jordan's shoulder pad found the chin of St. Louis' Terry Miller. About the same time, Cardinals center Irv Goode threw a punch at Cowboys lineman Tody Smith. Jordan's hit was an accident. Goode's was not. He was ejected and the Cowboys got 15 yards tacked onto the end of Waters' return, putting them only 15 yards from the end zone. Again, they failed to score a touchdown, but Fritsch made a 14-yard field goal to get Dallas within 10–6, sparking a new mood on the sideline.

"The fight got everybody worked up," Talbert said. "You could feel the difference from then on."

The next 24 minutes would prove to be the most pivotal stretch of the season, the turning point within the turning-point season in franchise history.

Hart found Jackie Smith for a 26-yard touchdown pass that stretched St. Louis' lead by enough to probably put the game and Dallas' playoff hopes out of reach—but Dan Dierdorf was caught holding on the play, so it didn't count. A few plays later, Jordan wrapped up running back Johnny

Roland, and Pat Toomay pried the ball loose. Howley recovered, and the Cowboys were back in business, still down 10–6.

Had Landry been in the two-quarterback system, he would've switched to Morton by now. Like it or not, he stuck with Staubach.

A penalty pushed the Cowboys to their 10, and they almost had to punt right away. But on third-and-6, Staubach scrambled for a first down, making it by only a few links of the yard markers. His running, even the threat of him running, left the Cardinals off balance. He ran twice more and completed all four passes on a drive that took 15 plays and ran 8:37 off the clock. It ended with Staubach throwing a four-yard touchdown pass to Mike Ditka for a 12–10 lead. The snap was bad on the extra point, but holder Dan Reeves remained in control, scooping it up and running around the left end to make it 13–10.

The Cardinals again burned the rookie Thomas, getting a 37-yard pass that put them in range for a tying field goal. Two plays later, Thomas had a pass come right to him for a sure interception and probably a touchdown, one that would've sealed the win. But he dropped it. St. Louis ended up kicking a 36-yard field goal that knotted the score at 13.

Landry called for a balance of runs and passes to keep the defense guessing. The only constant on this drive was throws to Lance Alworth on third downs. Staubach connected with him on a 9-yarder and an 11-yarder. On third-and-3 from the 19, Staubach overthrew him on a slant.

With 1:58 left in a tie game, Dallas faced a 26-yard field goal attempt.

Out went "Wembley Toni," the guy who scored two goals in the biggest soccer game of his life. But he'd played soccer all his life. This was his first NFL game. He'd missed one kick today, and he didn't even have a chance to kick the last time he was on the field because of the botched snap.

"Hey!" Cardinals linebacker Larry Stallings hollered. "You're gonna choke, man! You're gonna choke!"

"Shut up," Edwards shouted back. "He can't understand you anyway."

Fritsch understood, all right. It just didn't bother him. As soon as the ball left his foot, Fritsch knew it was good. He ran toward Landry with his arms raised and the Cowboys leading 16–13.

There was still one defensive stand left, one more chance for Hart to try going after Thomas.

Dallas went to a prevent defense and St. Louis took advantage, hitting a few short passes. Then Hart threw long for his fastest receiver, Mel Gray.

He sprinted down the sideline and past safety Cornell Green. Not a single Cowboy was between Gray and the end zone, and nobody was fast enough to catch him from behind. But he dropped the pass. Jethro Pugh sealed the victory by sacking Hart on fourth down.

In the first start of the Roger Staubach Era, in the first game of Toni Fritsch's career, the Cowboys scored 10 points in the fourth quarter to pull out a win they absolutely had to have. The team that couldn't recover in the fourth quarter against Washington, New Orleans, and Chicago found a way this time, and everyone was involved—offense, defense, and special teams. Dallas didn't turn the ball over and got a crucial turnover.

"This is the first game we've played since last year where everybody is hustling and fighting and wanting it," Landry said. "It takes more than one game to bring you back, but it is a start."

The transformation from a group of guys to a team had begun. Adderley could see it happening—players going around congratulating and thanking each other, regardless of position, rank, or race.

"They starting saying 'we' and 'us' instead of 'I' and 'me,'" Adderley said. "That's what it takes."

The star of the postgame celebration was Fritsch. Everyone gathered around him in the locker room and sang:

*"Hurrah for Toni! Hurrah at last!*
*"Hurrah for Toni! He's a horse's ass!"*

"There will be dancing in the streets of Vienna tonight," Cowboys owner Clint Murchison Jr. said.

Fritsch came away with cuts on his right ear and right arm courtesy of some St. Louis head-hunters who'd gone after him on kickoffs. He also came away with the game ball, although he didn't know why.

"I think they want me to go home and practice because I miss one kick," he said.

Then he was told that it was an honor, and the gesture clicked—"man of the match," as it's known in soccer.

"I was not with fear, but I am telling myself all the game, 'Toni, you must, you must,'" he said. "You cannot learn this in a practice, it has to be in a game. When I have more feeling for the game, I won't miss."

This was the first of 15 fourth-quarter rallies in Staubach's career, the first of his 23 game-winning drives. Thus, the legend of "Captain Comeback" began in his very first game as the No. 1 starter.

Afterward, however, he was irked that 372 yards of offense produced a single touchdown.

"It takes a lot to satisfy me," Staubach said. "We're a more explosive team than we showed today."

They also were closer to first place in the division. The Redskins and Eagles tied, so Washington held at six wins while Dallas was up to five.

# Paybacks & Momentum

ROGER STAUBACH PREPARED FOR his next start with a reminder of how close he came to never becoming the starting quarterback of the Dallas Cowboys.

Mel Tom and the Philadelphia Eagles were coming to Texas Stadium. Back in September, a cheap shot by Tom ended Staubach's season debut after two plays. Craig Morton took over and led Dallas to a lopsided win. Had he beaten the Redskins the next week, Tom Landry easily could have named Morton the starter for the rest of the season.

NFL Commissioner Pete Rozelle fined Tom $1,000 for the brutal hit. Tom appealed, and the hearing was held in New York on the Tuesday before the rematch, with Lee Roy Jordan there on behalf of the Cowboys. Rozelle listened to Tom blather about trying to block the quarterback "the best I could," while admitting Staubach "was just standing there." The game film was all the evidence Rozelle needed.

"Mail me a check," the commissioner told Tom.

Coincidentally, the big topic this week was whether Staubach was putting himself at risk of getting walloped by running too much.

He took off seven times against the Cardinals. However, two were crucial third-down plays that he converted, and two more came at the end of each half.

What bothered Landry most was seeing Staubach run in the middle of the field, essentially daring everyone to come and get him. Landry also didn't like what Staubach did when defenders arrived. Instead of sliding, he lowered a shoulder and plowed forward, intent on grabbing all the yards, feet, or inches he could. Landry recalled one play where Staubach "looked like he was trying to be a fullback."

Staubach admitted he took off at the first sign of trouble. If his intended receiver was covered, it was easier to look for room to run than to see if he could throw to his second or third options. Landry chalked it up to Staubach being overly concerned about avoiding mistakes in his first start since being promoted.

"I think he'll settle down more this week," Landry said. "He's certainly a tough runner, but it's not his business to run."

Perhaps to remind Staubach of what can happen, Landry added, "I sure hope Craig will be ready when he's called upon."

Staubach had become more patient in the pocket. Over each of his first two seasons, he ran once for every three passes he threw. So far this season, it was once for every five passes. Landry acknowledged that the threat of Staubach running helps his passing. Defensive linemen can't be as aggressive coming after him for fear of him stepping aside and zipping through the area they've vacated.

"He's like a little snake," St. Louis defensive tackle Bob Rowe said. "As a scrambler, he has to be one of the best. All he needs is a little daylight, and he's gone."

Besides, from Landry's perspective, it could've been worse. At least Staubach wasn't riding a dirt bike on his day off.

The Eagles came to Texas Stadium on a roll, going 2–0–1 since Ed Khayat became their coach. He'd banned long hair and facial hair and seemed to have a rule against allowing touchdowns. The defense had given up just three in three games while becoming a turnover machine: seven interceptions, 10 fumbles.

"You get a bunch of cats with nothing to lose, and they can really give you a hard time," Herb Adderley said. "They'll try anything to beat you."

As much as the victory over the Cardinals gave fans reason to believe, so had the game against the Patriots, and that proved to be false hope.

Dallas still had to string together wins—something the team hadn't done since September—to earn anyone's faith.

In search of momentum, here are some of the things that happened in the game against Philadelphia:

- Toni Fritsch missed two field goals.
- Walt Garrison fumbled 17 yards from a touchdown.
- Bob Hayes dropped a wide-open, 51-yard pass at the goal line.
- Dallas was penalized 10 times for 115 yards, mostly because injuries scrambled the offensive line.
- That jumbled line left Staubach running for his life in the second half, leading to what he called "the sorriest passing exhibition I've ever put on."

The Cowboys also led 20–0 until giving up a touchdown in the final minutes. Yes, despite committing a multitude of crimes that usually lead to defeat, the Cowboys won again.

"We had a good effort at first," Landry said. "But as the game went on, it got rather sloppy."

Doomsday made this one possible.

The Eagles used two quarterbacks, and Bob Lilly and Jethro Pugh pestered each into throwing an interception. Dallas also forced three fumbles. The defense gave Staubach good field position so often that he needed only one good drive of his own.

"The Cowboys' front four is something else," said Rick Arrington, Philadelphia's starting quarterback. "Nobody is going to run against them with great success unless you can keep them guessing."

Staubach was solid in the first half, even throwing a 22-yard pass to Hayes deep in Eagles territory just before getting pummeled by his nemesis, Tom. But then his line began to erode.

Left tackle Don Talbert sprained an ankle, bringing in Forrest Gregg. Then Gregg pulled a hamstring, and a game of musical chairs began.

Rather than take their lumps with one guy out of position at left tackle, the Cowboys tried a series of incremental moves. Rayfield Wright switched ends of the line, going from right tackle to left tackle. Blaine Nye replaced Wright by moving one spot to his right, from guard to tackle. Backup center John Fitzgerald came off the bench to replace Nye at right guard.

Left guard John Niland and center Dave Manders were the only guys who stayed put. The protection was a mess. Staubach was sacked several times and hit so often that he came away with bruises on his back and blood on his knees and elbows.

Landry dismissed Staubach's shoddy second half because he was bailing water from a leaky boat. If anything, Landry liked the way Staubach handled himself under those circumstances.

"He was just trying to get out of the way of people," Landry said. "As it ended up, his running was about the only thing we had going for us for a while."

"Coach Landry didn't really say that, did he?" Staubach said when the quote was relayed to him.

This was the second game at Texas Stadium, and it didn't sell out, drawing about 5,000 fewer fans than the opener. They booed Tom during pre-game introductions, but he claimed it wasn't as bad as he expected. The Cowboys avoided any retaliatory cheap shots on him because they knew officials would be looking for it, and it wasn't worth a penalty, fine, or suspension. Not with the outlook starting to brighten up.

The best part of the afternoon was spent watching the $1.2 million scoreboard. The updates from the Washington–Chicago game were more riveting than anything happening here.

The Redskins kicked five field goals to build and hold a slim lead. The Bears went ahead 16–15 with 11 minutes left, drawing the biggest cheer of the day from Cowboys fans. Another roar went up when that became the final score.

Dallas and Washington now had six wins each, with the Cowboys headed to the nation's capital the following Sunday. A battle for first place in the NFC East was exactly the test this team needed to find out whether the last two weeks were the start of something special or just another tease.

"We know what we've got to do now," Hayes said. "The man don't have to tell us."

"It's the game we want," Chuck Howley said.

Landry's prediction about the Redskins was right. Age was catching up to them. Their old guys were getting hurt.

As Dallas prepared to meet Washington again, the Redskins were without receiver Charley Taylor, running back Larry Brown, and tight end Jerry Smith. Washington was in a 1–2–1 funk, scoring just one touchdown over the last two games.

Landry also might have gotten a kick out of his old pal George Allen being the one facing a dilemma at quarterback.

Billy Kilmer had led the Redskins all season because Sonny Jurgensen was hurt. Now Jurgensen was healthy. Allen used him in the final few minutes against the Bears, and he played well. Landry figured Allen would start Jurgensen. Even President Nixon—a staunch Redskins fan and a longtime pal of Allen—was excited that Jurgensen was back.

But Allen announced that Kilmer had taken him this far and would remain the starter.

Landry was glad to hear it. His defense was giving up big passing plays, and Jurgensen was more likely than Kilmer to heave the ball long and on-target. Dallas ranked second-to-last in the conference against the pass, and Landry let everyone know this worried him.

His most pressing concern, though, was the offensive line.

All the switching around against the Eagles was a patch for that afternoon, not the way to go the rest of the season. There wasn't enough time left to get three guys comfortable at new spots. They needed one guy to plug in at left tackle. The problem was that they didn't have anyone else they could trust. Bob Asher and Ralph Neely were out. Now Talbert and Gregg were hurt. The only lineman on the taxi squad was rookie Rodney Wallace, and he wasn't ready for such a promotion. The trade deadline had passed, too.

So Landry turned to a guy he knew in the commercial real estate business.

Tony Liscio was at his office when Landry's secretary called to say the coach wanted to speak with him. His mind went blank.

At the team party the night Neely was hurt, Dave Edwards had told Liscio to start getting in shape. He laughed. This past weekend, Liscio was driving back from homecoming weekend at Tulsa University with his old college teammate Joel Walenta, and they were listening to the Cowboys–Eagles game. When Talbert went down, Walenta said, "Better get home, Tony. They're going to call you." Liscio laughed again.

He really thought it was ludicrous. He hadn't run an inch since leaving the Chargers. He wasn't even sure he could completely straighten his legs. However, he did know the playbook.

"Let me think about it for a day or two," Liscio told Landry.

"I'll give you thirty minutes," Landry said. "I have to make a decision at left tackle."

Liscio called his wife.

"What do you think?" he said.

"Go ahead and try," she said.

Liscio had been a third-round pick by Vince Lombardi and Green Bay in 1963. Miscast as a defensive lineman, he never made the team. Dallas signed him, moved him to offense, and he quickly became a starter.

A knee injury cost him some games in 1964, then a staph infection wiped out his 1965 season. A ruptured disc in his back slowed him in 1970. He and Staubach were the only players who suited up for Super Bowl V but didn't get into the game.

Liscio had been a good teammate as well as a good player. Having been on mostly black teams while growing up in Pennsylvania, he always got along with everyone in the locker room. Landry respected him so much that after trading Liscio to San Diego, the coach offered to go to his house to break the news in person.

Liscio wasn't bitter about being traded. He was proud to have grown up along with the club. He also believed he could still play, so he moved his wife and three kids to San Diego. When the Chargers dealt him to the Dolphins midway through the exhibition season, the thought of moving them again, all the way to Miami, was overwhelming. He decided to save everyone a lot of trouble by retiring and moving back to Dallas.

"I had accepted the fact I was out of football," he said. "I had become a fan. I wasn't missing it all that much, really. It's not a lot of fun playing injured."

Now, after telling Landry he'd give it a try, he was driving to the team's practice field for an informal tryout with offensive line coach Jim Myers. Liscio limbered up, then asked Myers what to do next.

"I've seen all I want to see," Myers said.

The Cowboys still had to get Liscio's rights from San Diego. The Chargers agreed to put him on waivers. Who else would put in a claim for a retired lineman with a history of health problems?

George Allen. That's who.

Allen didn't want Liscio as much as he didn't want Dallas to get him. He figured something was up and wanted to get in the way, especially this week. But because the Redskins had a better record than the Cowboys (6-2-1 trumping 6-3), Washington was behind Dallas in the priority order for making a claim. So the Cowboys got their man. But they still needed to work out a contract.

Tex Schramm wanted Liscio to play under his existing contract of roughly $30,000. That is, a prorated share—5/14ths, less than $11,000. Liscio wanted to be guaranteed $20,000.

Schramm started pacing. He offered a full share of playoff money.

"We ain't going to the playoffs," Liscio thought.

So they struck a deal: Liscio would get his regular deal and a guarantee of $20,000. If the Cowboys made the playoffs, the bonus money would cover some or all of the difference; if the Cowboys missed the playoffs, the team would fork over all of the difference.

On Thursday, the 31-year-old Liscio was in a Dallas uniform, playing football for the first time since the exhibition season and with the Cowboys for the first time since before the Super Bowl.

Liscio was six pounds lighter than his old playing weight. The question was his durability. He could only hope the time away healed his body. The first time Liscio hit a blocking dummy, he hurt a shoulder. Soon, he pulled a hamstring.

"No way I can play Sunday," Liscio told himself.

But the adrenalin was flowing. He was back with the guys. He decided to tough it out.

Still, could he be ready by Sunday?

"It's a mystery to me," Liscio said. "Stamina-wise, I believe I can hold up. But legs are the most important thing to an athlete. I try not to worry about it, just going to act like I've been here all year. If I worry about getting hurt, I won't be able to do the job. I'll do my best, and if I run out of gas or pull something, I'll come out."

At the end of practice, players lined up and ran sprints. Except for Liscio. He turned and went to the locker room, determined to save his legs for the field. Besides, he wanted to get a head start toward the whirlpool— or, as it would soon be called, the USS *Liscio*.

On Friday, Schramm called Liscio into his office. Allen and the Redskins were stirring things up again.

Allen filed a complaint to the NFL office claiming that while studying Dallas' game films from earlier this season, they saw Liscio standing on the sidelines. Thus, the Redskins considered his return some sort of long-planned conspiracy and wanted the commissioner to block it.

"I was never on the sideline," Liscio told Schramm. "What can we do?"

Schramm knew this was gamesmanship, just like Allen's waiver claim. Allen had known he was behind Dallas in the pecking order and was just trying to get under the Cowboys' skin. Now he'd done it again. Schramm drew up a letter to the commissioner, and they both signed it. Rozelle probably got a good laugh out of it.

That same afternoon, the Cowboys faced a more legitimate problem.

Fearing a muddy field in Washington, coaches gunked up a patch of their own practice field to see how Toni Fritsch would handle those conditions. Not very well. He slipped, pulling the hamstring in his right leg, his kicking leg.

Landry told Mike Clark to be ready because he was likely to be activated.

Clark was ready, all right.

Fritsch had been the first real competition Clark faced in his career, and he handled it poorly.

Seeing coaches record every kick from the start of training camp, he began paying more attention to what Fritsch was doing than to his own kicks. His form got out of whack, and his thoughts became messed up, too. The competition continued during midweek practices, and Clark's problems only got worse. Getting benched was exactly what he needed to snap out of it.

"The first couple of days I was off the team were pretty rough," he said. "First time I'd experienced anything like it in nine years in the league, going to the taxi squad. I didn't have a very good attitude. I didn't know how the other guys felt about me. Then I just decided it wasn't the end of the world. I went flying, hunting, got control of my emotions again."

His attitude improved, he did all the things taxi squadders are supposed to do—like being part of the scout team. Their job was to simulate the opposing offense to help the defense get ready for what it was going to face. Clark played end and enjoyed it.

He also stayed on the field after practice to get in extra kicks. Once he proved to himself that he still had it, he stopped worrying.

"For the first time in nine years, I grew me some fingernails," Clark said. "I'm kicking right now better than I've ever kicked."

—★—

As Staubach prepared for his third straight start since being declared the No. 1 quarterback, Jordan noticed a change in the offense.

"The confidence," Jordan said. "The one-ness they're developing."

The offense was better on Sundays because they were more in sync the rest of the week. By no longer running both Staubach's and Morton's plays, practices were more efficient and more effective. Staubach was always working with the first stringers, getting down the nuances of every quarterback-receiver relationship, such as who likes passes high and who likes them wide, how much arc or zip do they prefer.

Staubach also was impressing everyone with the way he took charge.

The winning drive in St. Louis was the first test he passed. The way he dealt with the dismantled offensive line against Philadelphia went a long way with teammates, too. He adapted and made it work without making a big deal out of it. That's leadership. And, to Staubach, it was second nature. Whether it was an innate quality or something developed over all those years in military training, he was comfortable being the one everyone relied on.

Guys also let him know they were comfortable being led by him. They did so in a jock sort of way—teasing and taunting him. Giving him a hard time sent the message, "You are our guy. We're going to listen to you, but we're also going to push you to do better."

"They were playing hard for me because they knew I could help them win," Staubach said. "I knew certain players liked Craig more than me, but they adapted to me. They were giving me one hundred percent, too. There sure weren't any issues. They believed in me. If they didn't, I would've been toast."

—★—

Folks in D.C. hadn't been this excited for a game since Sammy Baugh was slingin' the ball around and the buck stopped at the desk of Harry S. Truman.

Scalpers were getting $60 for good seats, $35 for bad ones. Money also helped fuel the motivation for Redskins players—as in, the playoff bonuses they could soon be collecting.

"They stand between us having zero and twenty-five thousand dollars, or at least on the way to having twenty-five thousand dollars," offensive lineman John Wilbur said. "It's like becoming a year younger or retiring a year earlier. I don't know how anybody else feels, but I need the money."

Allen tried stoking his players' emotions by posting a newspaper clip that noted Washington had never swept the season series against Dallas.

"An additional challenge," he said.

The easiest way for a road team to take a crowd out of a game is by scoring early, and that's exactly what the Cowboys did.

Staubach led a long, slow march from Dallas' own 14-yard line. Facing third-and-6 from the Washington 29, Bob Hayes and Lance Alworth both lined up on the left and ran routes toward the middle of the field. Staubach was supposed to throw to Alworth, but he noticed that when the receivers turned in, the entire defense followed them. The entire left side of the field was vacant.

"So I took off," Staubach said.

Someone grabbed his foot on the way out of the pocket, but Staubach stepped out of it. It was the only resistance he faced on the way to the end zone. The play would endure as the longest rushing touchdown of his career and the most important play of this game.

Given a 7–0 lead to protect, Doomsday didn't let Washington get any closer.

Fans booed Kilmer by the second quarter and cheered Jurgensen just for warming up. The crowd got its wish when Jurgensen went in during the third quarter, only to see his first pass caught by Cliff Harris. Jordan picked off one of his final passes. The front four provided plenty of pressure, too, with Larry Cole getting two sacks.

Yet the strength of the Dallas defense was stopping the run. After giving up 200 yards on the ground in the last matchup, the Cowboys limited the Redskins to 65. The longest gain by a running back was 9 yards.

"They hit a lot of percentage passes on us," Landry said. "But unless you're able to run the ball, too, this isn't going to be enough."

The Cowboys didn't reach the end zone after the opening possession, but Staubach kept the ball moving.

Drives of 44, 54, and 72 yards ended with field goal tries. Clark missed a 43-yarder into a stiff wind, made a 26-yarder, and missed a 31-yarder with the wind at his back. He added a 48-yarder with the wind in the fourth quarter, making the final score 13–0. For all the improvements he thought he'd made, he was still nailing only 50 percent of his kicks.

Liscio did just fine. He went to the stadium early with trainer Don Cochren and got his right leg taped "from toe to crotch." He was tight all the way until pre-game exercises. Emotion took over, and he decided he was ready. He missed only one play, and his removal was a mistake. Liscio was trying to get an official to throw a flag, and Landry thought he was signaling the sideline for a replacement. He came away from the game sore but thrilled.

Dallas players leaped and hollered with joy as they left the field. The first 10 games were behind them, and while they didn't all turn out the way they'd hoped, the bottom line was quite nice: The Cowboys were headed home alone atop the NFC East. The Redskins had grabbed first place when they won in Dallas seven weeks ago, and now the Cowboys had grabbed it back. This was their third straight victory and their first all season against a team with a winning record.

They didn't just win, either. They shut out their top rival at their place in a high-stakes game. Sure, the Redskins weren't at full strength, but the Cowboys considered this proof enough that they were for real. This was the declaration that they were making another late-season roll. The defense was as good as ever, and there was no telling how good this offense could be. With Liscio plugging the hole at left tackle, Staubach was back to doing his thing passing and running. His dual threat brought a new dimension and he wasn't making many mistakes, alleviating Landry's concern about his lack of experience. Staubach had yet to throw an interception since becoming the No. 1 quarterback.

"I'm getting the same feeling I had last year," linebacker Chuck Howley said.

"The feeling of confidence," left guard John Niland said.

Fans sensed it, too. More than a thousand were waiting at Love Field.

"We can't let up," Staubach said. "We can't start looking at the standings as we've done before. We just have to mind our own store."

He also had to mind a bruise on his throwing shoulder. He wouldn't have long to heal because the NFC West–leading Rams were coming to Texas Stadium on Thursday for the annual Thanksgiving game.

—★—

On a chilly Tuesday night, about 1,500 fans showed up at the Plymouth Park Shopping Center a few miles from Texas Stadium for a pep rally organized by the team's cheerleaders—the Cow Belles and Beaux.

Tex Schramm had yet to launch the phenomenon of the Dallas Cowboys Cheerleaders. That would come in 1972. This was the final season of cheers being led by a group of local teenage boys and girls from area high schools.

The winner of a Tom Landry look-alike contest wore a fedora and overcoat. He was a student at the Baptist seminary, Landry-esque in its own way. Part of the big finish was the presentation of a plaque to team owner Clint Murchison Jr. honoring "The Heart of the Cowboys Fan."

Suddenly, everyone wanted to celebrate. The current and former mayors of Irving joined in holding a giant pair of scissors for a ribbon-cutting of Texas Stadium before the Thanksgiving game. So what if two Cowboys games and four college games had been played there? Miss Dallas and Miss Irving took part in the ceremony, and CBS broadcast it to the country.

This was the sixth straight year the Cowboys played on Thanksgiving. It was a terrific platform to help the country get to know the team and the players as they were all coming of age. Being 4–0–1 on the holiday certainly helped their image.

There were all sorts of good story lines for this matchup.

Both teams had just moved into first place by beating their rival. Lance Rentzel was coming back to Texas as the Rams' leading receiver. Dallas hadn't beaten Los Angeles since 1962, but all those losses came when Allen coached the Rams. Now Landry would be matching wits with Tommy Prothro, who was in his first season in the pros after nice runs at Oregon State and UCLA.

There was a touch of drama, too: Would Staubach play?

That bruised shoulder turned out to be a pinched nerve in his neck, leaving Staubach feeling as if he was walking around with a knife stuck in there. He couldn't throw at all Monday or Tuesday. He tossed the ball some on Wednesday but still felt plenty sore.

In pre-game warmups, Staubach looked stiff. His motion wasn't smooth. Landry watched every throw looking for clues his quarterback could play. As far as Landry was concerned, Staubach didn't have to feel good, just good enough.

Staubach had to chuckle about how quickly things had turned around. A few weeks ago, Landry found excuses *not* to play him. Now the coach was looking for any evidence that he could. He found it, too.

By the time Staubach went out, the scoreboard made him feel a little better. Dallas was up 7–0 because Ike Thomas returned the opening kickoff 89 yards for a touchdown.

"I just ran under it and kept going," said Thomas, who had never in his life returned a kickoff for a touchdown. He was so excited he nearly spiked the ball before crossing the goal line.

That play set the tone for the afternoon. The Cowboys nearly did a lot of things wrong, but kept saving themselves with big plays. They fell behind 14–7, but tied it on a 51-yard touchdown heave from Staubach to Hayes. They went ahead with a 21-yard touchdown pass to Lance Alworth, his first score of the season.

"Now I feel like a Cowboy," he said.

The Rams helped with all sorts of mistakes: a fumble by Rentzel on a reverse . . . an overthrow on an otherwise perfectly executed fake field goal . . . running back Les Josephson ducking to avoid a pass thrown to him because he thought it was meant for someone else; the ball bounced off Charlie Waters' chest and into Howley's hands. Prothro also made the curious choice of punting on third down.

In the fourth quarter, with the game tied at 21, Staubach aggravated his shoulder injury on a run to the Los Angeles five-yard line. His arm went numb, so he took himself out. Craig Morton trotted in and pitched the ball to Duane Thomas going left. Thomas shoved a cornerback out of the way with an angry stiff-arm and scored what turned out to be the final points of the game. Dallas won 28–21.

"Beating two division leaders in five days is a pretty good week's work," Rayfield Wright said.

The Cowboys' winning streak was up to four straight. Only three games remained, all against teams with losing records.

"If we don't flub it," Landry said, "we are in great shape."

Liscio was, too. He'd gone from a long layoff to holding his own against two tough defensive ends, Washington's Verlon Biggs and Coy Bacon of the Rams. He also came away with a new opinion of the Cowboys, and of his chance to collect that playoff bonus.

"When we were a young team, we'd play teams that would hardly get any penalties or have any turnovers and we'd say, 'They get all the breaks,'" Liscio said. "Halfway through the Rams game, we were getting all the breaks. That's when I realized, we don't make any dadgum mistakes."

# Problem Solving

WHEN TOM LANDRY WELCOMED Duane Thomas back for the 1971 season, he willingly created two sets of standards—rules for Thomas and rules for everyone else.

Landry knew it wasn't fair. He might not have liked it, but he decided the team needed Thomas to win a championship.

"I knew Duane could help," Landry said. "When Duane isn't running well, he's still running better than most people."

Saying Thomas had rules hardly seems accurate. He was pretty much allowed to do whatever he wanted. He also was allowed *not* to do whatever he didn't want.

Dress code on the road? Thomas avoided the $50 fine by wearing a jacket with a tie slung around his neck.

He took a whole row to himself on flights, sitting in the middle of three seats as if daring anyone to join him. He pulled a yellow toboggan cap down low and either slept or stared. Stewardesses learned to avoid him.

The team didn't even bother trying to give him a roommate. He was the only player with a room to himself.

He treated some teammates like enemies.

"What do you say, brother?" Calvin Hill said, greeting Thomas one morning.

"I ain't your brother," Thomas shot back.

Mike Ditka had a ritual of wishing everyone good luck before a game, even Thomas. Thomas always ignored it. One Tuesday, Thomas went to Ditka and said, "Hey man, don't ever hit me on the back before a game. It breaks my concentration."

"Hey, Duane," Ditka replied. "Go fuck yourself."

Thomas decided the daily roll call was a waste of time. He pointed out this inefficiency by refusing to acknowledge his name when it was called.

"You see me," he said. "You know I'm here."

Dan Reeves was in charge of calling roll at the full squad meetings. Thomas' defiance made this morning ritual a miserable experience for Reeves. It became so bad that he persuaded Landry to drop it. The new plan was for position coaches to make sure everyone was at their breakout meetings. As Thomas' position coach, Reeves could hardly enjoy those gatherings, either.

"It was tense, like walking on eggshells," Reeves said. "You never knew what to do. You're trying to get your group ready, and he wouldn't speak to anybody."

When players were introduced before home games, they ran through a line of girls in miniskirts shaking pompoms and gathered with their teammates on the field. Not Thomas. He would cut through the girls and go straight to the bench.

During games, Thomas copied Jim Brown's shtick of getting up slowly and ambling to the huddle. Team doctor Marvin Knight stopped asking if Thomas was okay because he wouldn't get an answer.

The biggest indignities came at practice.

Thomas would only work with the first-team offense. He refused to do anything with the scout team, even though everyone was expected to do so. While Thomas stood and watched, the running back rotation turned over more often, meaning everyone else took more of a pounding from Bob Lilly, Lee Roy Jordan, and company. One day, Garrison saw Thomas standing off to the side chewing gum. He might as well have been wearing a sign that read, "Untouchable." Garrison couldn't take it anymore.

"What the hell is wrong with Thomas?" Garrison yelled, daring Landry to make Thomas follow the same rules as everyone else.

"It's your turn to run," Landry commanded. "Get in there."

Veterans were irate. If anyone earned privileges, it was Lilly or Jordan, Chuck Howley or Mel Renfro. Landry never even gave them an extra water break. Yet this 24-year-old, second-year guy was getting away with whatever he wanted. Thomas didn't do calisthenics with the others either. He said he didn't think his teammates took it seriously enough, so he went off to do his own routine by himself. Thomas' reluctance for working with the scout team was similar.

"Hey, if they want to work hard, do it right, then I'll do it with them," he told Landry. "But they don't want to, and I won't do it."

Of all the mysteries of this season—why and how things went awry early on, why and how they were getting straightened out, the difficulty Landry had picking a starting quarterback—this was the most difficult to comprehend.

The "plastic man," as Thomas described Landry in his July screed, had turned into the invisible man when it came to dealing with the running back, all for the sake of winning. "We've come to accept him as he is," Landry said.

Bob Hayes gave Thomas the nickname "Othello," for the tragic hero in the Shakespeare work. The press dubbed him "The Sphinx," a riddle too difficult for the masses to solve. Pat Toomay took the analysis deeper, saying Thomas was to the Cowboys "what Russia was for Winston Churchill: the proverbial enigma wrapped in a riddle, doused with Tabasco, and stuffed into a cheese enchilada."

Yet it all came back to one thing.

"He played," Garrison said. "That son of a bitch *played.*"

Said Herb Adderley: "He is total concentration and one hundred–percent athlete every time he goes on the field."

Thomas was such a stunning talent that even the staunchest critics recognized tolerating him was a necessary evil.

"As long as he does his job," Jordan said, "we don't have to be buddy-buddy."

—★—

So, what was Thomas really thinking?

Nearly 40 years later, here's how he describes it: "My first year, 1970, I received my master's degree in football. 'Oh, okay, I can master this game.' Next, in 1971, I was getting my PhD, so I could doctor the situation. That's why I was always challenging everything. I was going by my own instincts.

I was learning how to trust myself. I was into self-development. We all have to find our formula in achieving greatness. We're extrapolating a lot of things as we're going through that course."

He maintains he enjoyed his teammates. He respected them. He just didn't want to be bothered maintaining relationships beyond his daily confidantes, Adderley and Rayfield Wright.

"It was like a challenge," Thomas said. "Are you challenging me? What makes you think you can make me talk? I'm introverted and proud of it."

In the book, *Duane Thomas and the Fall of America's Team*, he wrote that he appreciated Landry more after his brief stay with the Patriots and experiencing their coach's "because I said so" approach. Thomas said he pulled the cap over his face on airplanes because of sinus trouble. As for the disconnect between him and the stewardesses, that stemmed from them finding it strange that he wanted Sweet'n Low in his tea.

"I realized one thing," Thomas wrote. "I was out there on my own. I was the most glorified, the most talked about, the most recognized, and the most miserable. But I got my happiness when I hit that field. That was my world, my home. . . . I was in too deep."

—★—

The knee injury that was supposed to have kept Calvin Hill out for only two weeks had cost him five games. Now, he was ready to return.

So for the first time all season, Hill and Duane Thomas were both healthy and ready to go. What would Landry do now?

The easy answer was to play them both. It became easier still because Walt Garrison had a problem with his right thigh. Trainers called it a charley horse and slapped a pad over it. He'd been playing through it for weeks, but now they decided to take X-rays. They found some calcium buildup, and Garrison was told to rest, whether he thought he needed it or not.

"If they'd told me it was all right, I wouldn't have known the difference," he said.

At Tuesday's practice, Reeves told Thomas he would be getting some work at fullback in place of Garrison.

"No, I'm not playing fullback," Thomas said.

Staubach stepped in, telling Thomas to listen to his coach.

"It's none of your business," Thomas said, throwing a harsh stare at Staubach.

"Yes it is!" the quarterback shot back.

—★—

The new-look backfield of Hill and Thomas was to debut Saturday at Texas Stadium. The game sold out on Tuesday, four days before kickoff, earlier than any home game ever had.

The surge in ticket sales wasn't caused by excitement over the running backs or a growing buzz over the hometown juggernaut-in-the-making. It was all about the first-ever regular-season visit by the best drawing card in the NFL: Joe Namath.

"Broadway Joe" was coming off his first game since missing 19 straight because of injuries. He actually was supposed to have missed 20 straight, but the Jets turned to him the previous Sunday when starter Bob Davis got hurt and, boy, did he deliver.

Namath threw three touchdown passes, turning a game New York was losing 17–0 into a thrilling 24–21 defeat. His last pass was thrown into the end zone for the possible winning touchdown. It was intercepted, but Namath still walked off to a standing ovation.

"I made two or three mistakes out there, mistakes in judgment which ordinarily I wouldn't make," he said. "If I had been game sharp, it wouldn't have happened."

Namath spent part of the week taping the first in a series of television talk shows he'd be hosting. "Tingles went from the tips of my toes to the top of my head," said one of his guests, bowling champion Paula Sperber.

Landry, meanwhile, spent the entire week fretting over his pass defense.

Although cornerbacks Herb Adderley and Mel Renfro were bound for the Hall of Fame, strong safety Cliff Harris was early in a career that would land him in the Ring of Honor and free safety Cornell Green still had several good years left, teams were eager to throw against them. From the perspective of an opposing offense, the odds were better than trying to run against the front seven featuring Lilly and Jordan. The problem was that teams weren't just trying it. They were succeeding.

Through 11 games, Dallas had allowed more yards passing than it did over 14 games in 1970. The Cowboys went into December ranked thirteenth out of thirteen teams against the pass in the NFC and twenty-fifth of 26 across the entire NFL.

"No one back there is playing as well as he should," Landry said. "We have got to shut off the big play. If we don't, it's going to cost us a ball game down the line."

The deep ball being Namath's specialty, this season-long weakness stood out even more this week.

— ★ —

Before the game, Ike Thomas sat in front of his locker and tried to picture himself taking another kickoff for a touchdown.

"Naw," he told himself, "it couldn't happen again."

But it did. Right away. Dallas won the toss, elected to receive, and Thomas caught the kickoff one yard behind the goal line. He was supposed to go up the middle, but he saw a hole open to his left. He scooted through it and was in the clear. The Cowboys had never had anyone return two kickoffs in their career, much less a single season; this rookie just did it on the opening kickoff of consecutive games. "When I crossed the goal line, I thought about last week and nearly spiking it too soon. I figured I'd better run a little farther this time," Thomas said. "Man, I still can't believe two runbacks. It's just like a dream."

The whole game was.

Dallas led 14–0 before Namath threw a pass. After his first completion, he threw an interception that set up another touchdown. The Jets fumbled away the ensuing kickoff, setting up yet another touchdown for the Cowboys. They led 28–0 with 3:14 left in the first quarter, and New York coach Weeb Ewbank told Namath to take a seat. Even "Broadway Joe" wasn't going to rewrite this script, no matter what the stats suggested about the Dallas secondary.

The lead grew to 35–0 and 38–3 at halftime. It was 45–3 when Craig Morton took over. The final was 52–10, the most points by any NFL team all season and the most against the Jets since 1963. The Cowboys could've had more, too, but they let time run out while within five yards of the end zone. (Apparently, Landry's mercy on the Jets didn't register with their linebackers coach, Buddy Ryan. Sixteen years later, as coach of the Philadelphia Eagles, Ryan would take delight in running up the score against Landry's Cowboys, even using a trick play for a rub-it-in touchdown at the end of a lopsided win.)

"The Jets had their hopes up with Joe, but it's hard to get up to our pitch," Landry said.

The secondary stood most proud. They allowed only 19 yards passing on 20 attempts, with Adderley picking off two passes and Renfro snatching another.

"We were keyed up for Namath and also by the little ridicule we took all week for being thirteenth in pass defense," Renfro said. "That hurt."

Then there was the smashing success of the new backfield combo—a combined five touchdowns on 174 yards rushing and 98 receiving.

"I noticed the offense was lacking something out there today," Garrison said. "It was nice to be missed."

The raw numbers were impressive, but the real value of the Hill-Thomas pairing was seeing the defense befuddled by the challenge of trying to stop so many scoring threats on the field at once. Dallas' first two offensive touchdowns were perfect examples.

On the first, Staubach faked a pitch to Thomas going left, then threw to Hill on the right side. New York was blitzing and had cleared that side of the field.

On the second, Staubach faked a handoff, freezing a linebacker, then looked deep at Hayes. A safety had joined the cornerback running with Hayes. None of the Jets noticed that Hill was creeping along the same path as Hayes, about 10 yards behind. Staubach hit Hill for another easy score.

"That cornerback didn't look around until I was a yard deep in the end zone," Hill said.

Those were the first two touchdown catches of Hill's NFL career. He finished the game with four catches for 80 yards. He also ran for 62 yards and another touchdown.

Like it or not, Thomas played fullback. He had to like the results: a season-best 112 yards and a touchdown. He scored another touchdown on a screen pass that he tipped to himself and caught with one hand.

"This," Staubach said, "was the game we've been looking for."

—★—

There was only one thing wrong now. The playoffs were still three weeks away.

The offense was settled everywhere. Staubach was 5–0 since becoming the main man and had thrown 111 straight passes without an interception. The running backs were coming off their incredible debut as a 1–2 punch. Tony Liscio and the line were doing just fine. Lance Alworth caught a touchdown pass in two straight games, forcing defenses to consider him more than a decoy, and Hayes was as healthy and dangerous as ever.

Landry had to feel a little better about his secondary after the way players responded to being challenged before the Jets game. Jethro Pugh had been out since before Thanksgiving, and he was coming back this week to play the Giants at Yankee Stadium.

"We are as good right now as we could have hoped to be," Landry said.

At 9–3, Dallas held only a half-game lead over Washington, but the two remaining games were practically gimmes. Landry's clubs may have been prone to upsets early in the season, and their postseason problems were well documented, but this was the fourth straight year they hadn't lost a regular-season game after Thanksgiving. They obviously knew how to finish strong.

Winning one of their final two games would clinch a wild card. Winning both would clinch the division—and a trip to Minnesota for the playoff opener. Under the rules set up by the merger in 1970, the host teams in the first round were determined by a rotation. This season, the NFC East winner was headed to the home of the NFC Central winner, and the Vikings had clinched it. (Seeding based on record didn't start until 1975.)

Since Minnesota had the best record in the NFL, and awful weather during the playoffs, Cowboys fans debated whether it would be better to settle for the wild card. The benefit would be a trip west to face the winner of the worst division; the downside is that it also would eliminate the chance of hosting the NFC Championship Game.

The immediate concern for the Cowboys was the Giants, who were 4–8 and losers of three straight. Injuries and turnovers were ruining them. Overconfidence posed a greater challenge than the Giants did.

Ike Thomas didn't return a kickoff for a touchdown, but the Cowboys didn't need it. Hayes returned to his role as the king of big plays, scoring on touchdown catches of 46 and 85 yards, once again deciding the game early.

Dallas led 28–0 with 4:17 left until halftime. When it was 35–7 and the Cowboys had all but clinched a playoff berth, New York's band curiously broke into "Joy to the World." Fans disgusted with the football and the selection of music started to leave. Before they reached the exits, New York fumbled a kickoff return, and the Cowboys scored again. The final score was 42–14.

Again, the brilliance wasn't the numbers but how they were compiled.

- Staubach handed off or threw to Hill on five consecutive plays. Convinced the defense was sucked in, he threw deep to Hayes for the 46-yard touchdown.
- Dallas ran eight times the next series. Six were inside the tackles. The times they went outside produced 32 yards and a 3-yard touchdown, both by Thomas.
- The coaches get the credit for the next touchdown, having detected that a linebacker hesitated when a play was headed toward him. Staubach faked a handoff his way, then lobbed it over him to the guy he was supposed to be covering, Hill, for a 10-yard touchdown.
- Then there was the biggie, the 85-yarder to Hayes that was the longest touchdown in the NFL that season. Staubach called it "just a lucky play" because of all that went wrong. He ducked to avoid a linebacker who'd dived at his head, and Hayes caught the ball between two cornerbacks. Those guys collided, leaving him all alone for the final 40 yards.

"What we've been doing is great, and we think we're the best team in football. But saying it doesn't mean anything," Staubach said. "We'll have to prove it in the playoffs."

The Cowboys continued their streak of being the only team to make the playoffs every year of the Super Bowl era. They remained a half game ahead of Washington in the race for the NFC East crown. They also tied a club record with their sixth straight regular-season win.

Hill ran for 89 yards and had another 50 yards receiving. Thomas ran for 94 yards. Each scored twice. Staubach completed 10 of 14 passes, with two of them dropped. Doomsday allowed just one touchdown, late in the first half; New York's other score came off the return of an interception of a pass Morton threw late in the fourth quarter.

"It's the best Dallas team I've seen," said Giants coach Alex Webster, a pretty good source considering he'd played or coached against the Cowboys twice a year since the club began in 1960. "They've got quite a machine, and they've got it rolling."

Few people were still in the stands when the game ended. One of them ran onto the field and unrolled a banner that read, "Ride 'em Cowboys."

There was one more noteworthy part of this game—a bomb threat called in to the press box at halftime.

Nothing was found. Just when everyone was starting to joke about it, a screeching chair caused more than one heart to miss a beat.

When Landry heard about it, he said, "Well, if you got to have a bomb, I guess that's the best place for it."

Told that an explosion might have interrupted the game, Landry refused to change his stance.

"Oh, we'd stop the game," he said, grinning as wide as ever, "for about 30 seconds. And then continue with great enthusiasm."

—★—

Another sign of how smoothly things were going was the list of subjects not being discussed.

Like Staubach's scrambling. He hadn't needed to run a single time the last two games. Landry even said Staubach should've taken off on the 85-yarder to Hayes. After avoiding the linebacker, and with Hayes double-covered on a deep route, running would have been the higher-percentage move.

Kicking was another forgotten topic. Mike Clark was making all his extra points and was rarely needed for any field goals. His kickoffs weren't great, but they were high enough for the coverage squads to limit the returns. The way the offense was scoring, they were getting plenty of practice.

The pass defense had tightened up. Penalties and turnovers were down.

"It's mental attitude and confidence," Landry said.

The finale against St. Louis wasn't worth the price of admission. The Cardinals suspended their leading rusher and had a bunch of other guys out with injuries. They weren't even going to suit up a full 40-man roster. Landry and his staff spent most of the week getting ready to play Minnesota, although that matchup wasn't guaranteed; a Dallas loss and a win by Washington would send the Cowboys out west to play either the Rams or 49ers. They were too confident to consider that.

By their recent standards, the Cowboys squeaked out a win over the Cardinals. Dallas led only 21–6 at halftime. St. Louis got within 24–12 in the fourth quarter, then the Cowboys scored again to make it 31–12. Thomas scored four touchdowns for Dallas, while St. Louis got only four field goals.

"There's no question we had trouble getting ready this week," Staubach said. "But there's no excuse for being that bad. I was just awful. Just awful."

Here's how terrible he was: 10 completions on 16 attempts for 147 yards and a touchdown against a gimmick defense, some sort of 3-2 or 3-5, with a blitzing linebacker on nearly every snap. It was a desperate bid to wreak havoc, and it did cause one problem—Staubach threw an interception, his first since becoming the starting quarterback. His streak ended at 134 straight throws that weren't caught by the opposition.

"The linebacker didn't take the run fake, and I tried to throw it over him to Alworth. But I threw it over Alworth, too, and right into [safety Dale] Hackbart," Staubach said. Then he smiled and added, "It's just as well—all they would have been writing about next week was 'this guy hasn't thrown an interception.'"

Thomas ran 53 yards for his first touchdown and 3 yards for his next. He took a screen pass 34 yards for a score and capped it with another 3-yard run. The four touchdowns tied the club record held by Hayes, Hill, and Reeves.

For all the crap Thomas made everyone else endure, this was his payback: a league-best 11 rushing touchdowns and a league-best 13 total touchdowns, all in just 11 games.

Most importantly, the Cowboys were NFC East champs. Their playoff march would begin next Saturday in Bloomington, Minnesota, against the Vikings.

So, Duane, any thoughts about this game, this season or the postseason?

"Go away, man," he told reporters. "Leave me alone."

# Chemistry

"ROTTEN" RALPH NEELY LEANED on his crutches and studied the left side of the offensive line. He kept watching for some big, mean defensive guy to charge at Roger Staubach from his blind side, to blast through the position Neely was supposed to be playing, so someone would come over and mention how much the Cowboys missed him.

Tony Liscio wasn't letting it happen.

"He's doing better than I'd be doing," Neely said. "You never see his man getting in there, do you? And you know I wouldn't say that, even if I was expected to say it, unless it was true."

Liscio's transition from real-estate salesman to starting left tackle—and the team's most consistent blocker, according to line coach Jim Myers—was the most dramatic example of Dallas' depth and resourcefulness. But there were so many examples.

Staubach, all three running backs, both starting receivers, and Mike Ditka missed games because of injuries. So did Herb Adderley and Jethro Pugh. Toni Fritsch lasted only two weeks as the kicker because he got hurt. Yet Dallas always had a capable replacement.

From Tex Schramm's computer to Gil Brandt's wily ways, the Cowboys' front office stocked the roster, and Landry deployed guys as he thought was best. He didn't always manage the personalities very well, and he let the quarterback controversy drag on way too long. Still, the results showed that he knew what he was doing.

— ★ —

Tex Schramm hated this. The playoffs were here and his team was supposed to be looking ahead, still hungry about what they had left to accomplish. But it also was awards time, and, to Schramm, nothing good could come from that. Guys who got pats on the back might get complacent. Guys who thought they deserved honors and didn't get it might pout.

Besides, the standards for these awards were moving targets. In voting by conference coaches, the Cowboys had eight players picked for the Pro Bowl, the most from any NFL team. But on the all-NFC team put together by the UPI wire service, only Bob Lilly made it.

"I guess we must be killing a lot of people with teamwork," Lilly said.

Staubach won the "My Favorite Cowboy" award voted on by fans. The best part was the reward—a trip for two to Hawaii. He also received a higher honor, the Bert Bell Award as outstanding player in the NFL.

Imagine that: A guy who wasn't even his team's best player at his position at the start of the season ended up being named the best player in all of pro football.

"It's amazing, isn't it, how things have happened," Staubach said.

The Bell Award was given by the Maxwell Football Club in Philadelphia. The organization also gives the Maxwell Trophy to the outstanding college player. Staubach won that in 1963. This made him the first person to pick up both honors, yet another accomplishment.

"Getting the Bert Bell Award is a great thrill. But, really, I don't feel I have personally established myself in the NFL," Staubach said. "I've done some things as an individual, but I'm in the midst of a team that's doing a fantastic job running the ball and playing defense. I know this sounds like rah-rah college stuff—'I owe everything to my teammates,' and so forth. But in my case it happens to be so true. Everything has exploded around me, and I happen to be the quarterback."

Yes and no.

Staubach solidified the most important position on the field. Everything fell into place after that. Yet, for as much as everyone believed in him on Sundays, guys like Lilly, Lee Roy Jordan, and Herb Adderley were the club's driving forces. They took care of the behind-the-scenes leadership so Staubach could concentrate on getting first downs and avoiding turnovers. And he did that quite well. His passer rating of 104.8 led the entire NFL;

it's even more spectacular considering the league average that season was 62.2.

"The Cowboys have been here quite a few times, so if we don't make it, everyone's going to forget what's happened to get us there," Staubach said. "It's not that important if you don't make it all the way."

Just ask Craig Morton.

A year before, he was voted most popular player. Had Landry picked him over Staubach, the Cowboys probably would have made the playoffs anyway. Staubach said as much.

Morton was keeping his thoughts to himself.

"The team comes first. I come second," he said. "There's no way I'm going to say or do anything that might disrupt our team."

—★—

Here's how well things were going for the Cowboys.

During the club record, seven-game winning streak they carried into the playoffs, they trailed in only two games: the nail-biter over the Cardinals that started it and 14–7 in the second quarter against the Rams on Thanksgiving. They were on a run of 14 straight quarters without being behind.

The Cowboys finished the regular season with the top offense in the NFL, gaining the most yards and scoring the most points. Nobody was even close in either category. Talk about balance, Dallas was No. 2 in the NFL in yards passing, No. 3 in yards rushing; the Cowboys led the conference in both categories.

Landry's special assistant Ermal Allen used his own formula to rate every player in the NFL on a scale of 1 to 200. Points were accumulated based on ratings in various categories. Staubach came out "so far ahead of every other quarterback in the National Conference it isn't even funny." Miami's Bob Griese led the AFC, and Staubach topped him, too.

As for the defense, a closer look at the stats show the secondary wasn't as bad as Landry feared.

Teams threw more passes against the Cowboys than any other club, so they were bound to give up plenty of yards. A better way to evaluate them was comparing yards per attempt. Only four teams were stingier.

Dallas gave up the second-fewest yards rushing—and was the best when the numbers were calculated per attempt. The Cowboys also set a club record with 25 fumble recoveries, another league-leading figure.

The dominance traced to the front of the defense, where running plays were stuffed and where the pressure on quarterbacks was unleashed. The driving force of that group was Lilly, who at 32 may have had the greatest season of his career.

"When you're getting ready to play Dallas, you spend about half your time trying to figure out how you're going to handle Lilly," Philadelphia coach Ed Khayat said. "And if you put as many men on him as you should, they have a lot of people who'll eat you alive."

In the Chicago game remembered for the quarterback shuttle, Lilly had 12 unassisted tackles, "and that's almost unheard of, even for a line-backer," Landry said. No matter what the Bears did to try slowing him, it didn't work. They couldn't even draw a flag.

"Lilly escaped the holding so fast, the referee couldn't believe he was being held," defensive line coach Ernie Stautner said. "It's ridiculous what they get away with on Lilly. I've seen them tackle him, ride him back to the passer like they were riding a Brahman bull. Pretty soon, one of them will carry a rope out there and try to hogtie him."

On Thanksgiving, Lilly kept getting past Pro Bowl guard Tom Mack so easily that center Ken Inman screamed, "For Christ's sake, at least slow him down!"

It was as if the anger Lilly unleashed with that flying helmet at the end of Super Bowl V was back in the bottle, bubbling and gurgling like a mad scientist's potion. It fueled him to be the best so he could make his team become the best.

Now the Cowboys were about a month away from finding out if they were.

"Last year and this one, we had our troubles early and then we settled down and just kept winning," Lilly said. "In earlier years, it seems we won big early and then had our troubles later.

"Maybe we've finally got the timing down just right."

★

# Breaking Through

# Another Ice Bowl?

THE COWBOYS WERE HEADED to Minnesota for an outdoor playoff game between the teams with the best records in the NFC. Ice Bowl references started right away.

Ice Bowl II, the *Dallas Times-Herald* called it. The paper used that fearsome label atop a weather box that would run on the front page of its sports section every day this week. In Monday's paper, the forecast for Saturday in Bloomington, Minnesota, was a high of 19 degrees, low of 11.

This spurred a debate over the best way to prepare for such conditions. Should the Cowboys stick with their usual plan of flying in the day before and taking a look around? Or should they get there a few days sooner to start getting acclimated, maybe even spend the whole week there?

This was no idle chitchat about the weather. There was some serious history behind it—the original Ice Bowl.

On December 30, 1967, the Cowboys got to Green Bay the day before the NFL Championship Game. Temperatures were tolerable. They dropped that night and kept dropping. Players awoke to the hotel operator telling them it was 7:30 a.m. and 13 degrees below zero. Yes, she repeated to those who asked, which was almost everyone, 13 *below*. George Andrie showed roommate Bob Lilly just how cold that was by splashing a glass of water against the window and watching it freeze on contact.

It was cruel being outside for three straight hours in such conditions, much less slamming bodies into each other. Dan Reeves cut his lip, but didn't know it until he stood next to a heater on the sideline; the blood had to become warm enough before it would drip. Several players to this day lack feeling in their fingers and toes. So it was practically impossible to have the precision needed to run and throw. Green Bay handled it slightly better than Dallas, winning on a quarterback sneak in the final minute. This remains the great "what if?" in franchise history. Under better conditions, could the upstart Cowboys have toppled the reigning Super Bowl champion Packers and reached Super Bowl II? Would they have won that game and been branded champions, rather than building a reputation as the team that couldn't win the big one? Would it have been the start of a run of championships? Then again, it's possible the sustained success since then was spurred by this team's hunger for its first title.

Twelve of Dallas' starters from that fateful day would be starting against the Vikings, with more on the bench. Plus, starter Herb Adderley and backup Forrest Gregg were with Green Bay back then.

If the Cowboys faced such conditions again, would it help having so many guys who'd been through it? Or was that experience so awful that they'd be mentally whipped before kickoff?

"I'll bet you," linebacker Dave Edwards said, "if we go out there Saturday and it *is* 20-below again, a bunch of us will get together and decide, 'Well, it may be cold, but it isn't as cold as it was last time.'"

In the debate over a day-before arrival versus several days of acclimation, tight end Billy Truax brought the experience of having spent an entire week in Minnesota prior to a first-round playoff game following the 1969 season, when he was with the Los Angeles Rams. They practiced on a high school field, but only after the snow was scraped off it each day. The Rams lost.

"We were ahead 17-7 at the half and just let the game get away from us," he said. "The weather had absolutely nothing to do with it."

Landry's longtime friend Dick Nolan, coach of the 49ers, beat the Vikings in Minnesota in the opening round of the previous year's playoffs. San Francisco went in the day before. That was good enough for Landry. He believed the less time spent in cold weather, the better. They would fly in Friday and do everything they usually do.

"If we have to work out in a snowbank, we'll work out," Landry said. "Handling Minnesota is a tough enough job as it is without worrying about that."

As the week went on, the forecast improved. It was supposed to warm up all the way to the mid-30s.

Still, precautions were being taken. The Cowboys loaded up on a cream applied to exposed areas to help prevent hypothermia; that was another trick the 49ers used in their victory over the Vikings last year. It couldn't hurt.

The Dallas Black Hawks hockey club offered to help too. They invited the Cowboys to practice on their ice.

—★—

The Cowboys and Vikings had an interesting history. It wasn't a rivalry like siblings might have. It was more like neighbors who used each other as a measuring stick.

Both clubs were voted into the league on January 28, 1960. The Cowboys started playing right away because founder Clint Murchison Jr. was anxious to and because the American Football League was starting in Dallas that season. The Vikings were supposed to be original members of the AFL until being offered a spot in the more established league. Their reward was getting a year to prepare. They also were given the top overall pick in the 1961 draft. The Cowboys also had to wait until 1961 to make their first pick because the 1960 draft had been held before they joined the league.

The one-year head start helped Dallas beat Minnesota the first five times they met. But the Vikings got to the Super Bowl before the Cowboys did, making Super Bowl IV. In 1970, Minnesota beat Dallas for the first time, and in a big way: 54–13.

The Vikings were a powerhouse now. This was the fourth straight season they won their division, going 43–14 in that span. Yet they had the same number of championships as Dallas: zero.

Much had changed since the teams last played. That brought up another dilemma—should Landry show that game film as part of the preparation for this game?

He came into the week saying he wouldn't. It was from 14 months ago, too long ago to learn anything except how much better Minnesota was than Dallas that day. There seemed no point to stirring up bad memories.

He changed his mind. In his typical, detached style, Landry said it was to study "what they were doing against us, how we were being attacked and defended." But there was a bit of psychology, too.

His club had won seven straight games and hardly had been challenged since Thanksgiving. It might remind them it's not always that easy, that the last time they played this team on this field they were the ones hardly putting up a challenge.

—★—

Having studied the Vikings for most of the final week of the regular season, Landry had a pretty good feel for them.

They reminded him of the 1970 Cowboys, only a bit more extreme with their strengths and weaknesses.

The defense was truly superb, allowing just 14 touchdowns in 14 games. The offense was truly lousy, ranking next-to-last in passing and near the bottom in total yards and scoring. Landry surmised that Minnesota's talented defensive players forced themselves to be even better because of how much the club relied on them.

The Vikings had a revolving door at quarterback. But instead of cycling between quality players like Dallas did, Minnesota went through three guys who were mediocre on their best days: Gary Cuozzo, Bob Lee, and Norm Snead. Bud Grant gave each two starts in the exhibition season and kept juggling. He changed starters five times during the regular season and considered it no big deal. Like Landry once did with Vida Blue, Grant brought up the fact baseball managers switch pitchers all the time.

"You know, the quarterback isn't God Almighty," Grant said. "He's just one of 40 players."

Grant waited until Friday to announce he was going with Lee.

Lee had the strongest arm of the trio—leg, too, as he was the club's punter. He also was the least experienced, in only his third year, like Staubach. Lee had thrown more interceptions than touchdown passes this season, but so had Snead and Cuozzo.

Settling on one quarterback certainly had done wonders for Dallas. But now Staubach's inexperience was an issue again.

He was the only Cowboys starter without any meaningful playoff action. All he'd done was throw five passes at the end of a lopsided loss to

Cleveland in 1969. Then there was his history against Minnesota. In that 1970 blowout loss, Staubach threw three interceptions. At least he had a good excuse for that mess—a staph infection in his passing elbow.

—★—

A battle like this, between the No. 1 offense and the No. 1defense, is often decided in the trenches.

When the offensive line gives the quarterback time to work, they can usually score. But a defensive line that can disrupt that timing changes everything.

Minnesota's front four of Carl Eller, Alan Page, Greg Larsen, and Jim Marshall were known as the "Purple People Eaters." As great as they were, the Cowboys' linemen had an advantage. They practiced every day against the Doomsday Defense.

"Fear? I fear no man," said Rayfield Wright, who was to line up against Eller. "Whatever it takes to win, that's what we'll do."

Most weeks, John Niland zoned in on his matchup a little more each day, slowly tuning out his wife and the rest of the world. This week, taking on Page, he was obsessed from the start.

Niland knew Page from previous matchups and from being Pro Bowl teammates. He liked him, respected him, and knew he could hold his own against him. But Page had just become the first defensive player named NFL MVP, by UPI. This scared Niland. Pissed him off, too; if any defensive player deserved it, it was Lilly.

Page was one of the few pass rushers who weighed less than Niland, so Niland decided to lose a few pounds. The plan was to eat healthy. But with his emotions churning, he hardly ate and struggled to keep anything down. Yet he did drop about five pounds. Johnny Night Life felt like Johnny Twinkle Toes, and that mental edge was his real goal.

Niland also had the best practice tool—Lilly. They'd been going head-to-head every day since Niland arrived six years ago. They also had a deal. Regardless of how hard they were supposed to be going, if one of them declared, "Full potatoes" they would play like it was a Sunday. It helped Niland become a Pro Bowler every year from 1968 to 1973, and it made him sharp for this game.

"No human being is perfect, and Alan is like anyone else," Niland said. "He has certain things that are negative. Not many, don't get me wrong, but some. Because he is human, he will make mistakes. I'll try to take advantage of them."

—★—

The charter flight to Minnesota left around 9:30 a.m. Friday. They checked into the hotel, then went to the stadium for a workout.

Dan Reeves was the first one suited up and out on the field. The tarp was still down, and there was nobody around to remove it.

"That's it," Reeves said. "We win. They didn't show."

The Cowboys came up with a Plan B. They got back onto their bus and drove 20 miles to the University of Minnesota. After practice, it was back to the hotel for a meeting and dinner, followed by the usual 11:00 p.m. curfew.

It was 10 degrees that night. Forecasters were now calling for a kickoff temperature in the mid-20s.

"The day before the Green Bay game, the forecast was for 20," Landry said. "It turned out to be 20 the other way."

—★—

This time the kickoff temperature turned out to be 30 degrees and rising. The only snow inside Metropolitan Stadium was in giant piles shoved off the playing field. The turf was fine, maybe even a bit soft. The wind was more like a gentle breeze.

So much for "Vikings weather."

"When I got up this morning and saw what it was like, well, I was a very happy man," Landry said.

The Cowboys felt so good that Staubach, Bob Hayes, and others wore short sleeves in pre-game warm-ups. Looking across the field, they snickered at how many Vikings were wearing sweatshirts.

Things just kept going Dallas' way, from winning the coin toss to the defense snatching the ball away on Minnesota's first posses-sion. At least, the officials thought so, and they had the only opinion that mattered.

Fullback Dave Osborn carried the ball three yards, running toward the Minnesota bench, when Larry Cole tackled him and Jethro Pugh came away with the ball. Osborn said he heard a whistle blow the play dead, so he let go of the ball. Grant was nearby and heard the whistle, too. He even went onto the field to argue that point when it was ruled Dallas' ball. It was notable because of how nondemonstrative he usually was. The Cowboys turned this gift into a 26-yard field goal by Mike Clark and a 3–0 lead.

The Vikings were in good position to go ahead when Jim Lindsey jumped on a punt at the Dallas eight-yard line. He clearly saw it go off the foot of Ike Thomas, who had fallen to the ground. Again, officials didn't see things the same way. They said it never touched Thomas, which meant Lindsey only downed the punt. Minutes later, Lindsey was jawing with officials again, in nearly the same spot. They claimed he trapped a third-down pass that would've given Minnesota the ball about 10 yards from the end zone. Instead, Fred Cox kicked a 27-yard field goal to tie it at 3.

Something finally went wrong for Dallas on Minnesota's next series. Lee threw deep to Bob Grim and Cornell Green nearly intercepted it, but wound up tipping the ball to Grim for a 49-yard gain. The two-minute warning sounded, and the Vikings gathered on the sideline plotting for the go-ahead score. Two plays later, Lee Roy Jordan and Chuck Howley blitzed. With Jordan closing in, Lee lofted a pass to Lindsey. Lee didn't put much on it because he thought Howley had fallen.

"Actually," Howley said, "I ducked."

He popped up in time for the interception, returning it nearly all the way back to where Minnesota had been before the bomb to Grim. The Cowboys again had to settle for a field goal, with Clark kicking a 44-yarder that probably wouldn't have been good from 45. Dallas was back in front 6–3.

Clint Jones took the ensuing kickoff and would've had the first touchdown of the game if not for an outstanding tackle by Mel Renfro at the Dallas 35. The offense couldn't get any closer, so out came Cox for a 42-yarder. Nope; he pushed it wide to the right.

The Cowboys led at halftime, but not comfortably. And the Vikings got the ball first.

On their second play, Lee faked a short pass to Grim, and Renfro fell for it. Grim took off down the field ready to catch another deep ball. But Lee miscalculated the defense again. Thinking nobody would be back there, he threw a high, arching pass for Grim to run under. The extra time that took was long enough for Cliff Harris to get to the ball first. He intercepted it at the 43 and returned it to the 13-yard line.

Staubach faked a pitch to Calvin Hill, then handed the ball to Duane Thomas. Niland took out Page, and Thomas walked into the end zone with the crucial first touchdown. Only 89 seconds into the second half, Dallas led 13–3. It grew to 20–3 midway through the quarter when Staubach threw a nine-yard touchdown pass to Hayes.

Grant turned to Cuozzo in the fourth quarter, and he fit right in, throwing an interception to Jordan deep in Dallas territory. Cuozzo put together a touchdown drive later in the quarter, but it hardly mattered. The Cowboys won 20–12 and were headed back to Texas Stadium, one win from returning to the Super Bowl.

Landry called it the best defensive performance of the season. It certainly was the most satisfying day for the Doomsday guys who'd heard all week that they were good, but the Vikings were better.

"They had better statistics, but that doesn't prove anything to me," Jordan said. "I still felt we were the best defense around. The way to prove it was out on the field today."

Minnesota's defense held Dallas to a season-low 183 yards. There rarely were any holes for Thomas and Hill, and most of Staubach's completions came on short passes. It's what the Purple People Eaters *didn't* do that made the difference. No fumbles, no interceptions, not enough pressure to make Staubach crack in his first playoff start.

Hayes walked through the Cowboys' locker room singing, "Nobody's gonna stop us now, no nobody's gonna stop us from here on out."

"I mean it," Hayes said. "I don't want to downgrade everybody else in the playoffs, but this was really the team we had to beat."

This victory solidified Dallas as the team to beat. The reigning NFC champs had the most wins of anyone left in the playoffs and were headed home to play San Francisco, the team they beat in last year's NFC Championship Game.

The Cowboys' winning streak was up to eight in a row, yet they maintained the vibe of a team that hadn't accomplished anything yet. Because, in their minds, they hadn't.

"When you've been to the Super Bowl and lost, there is nothing to top it but going back to the Super Bowl and winning," Landry said. "That's where the excitement is now. . . . You learn a little something each time. It just comes from building up playoff experience, like playing in the cold at Green Bay in the 1967 championship game. We learned something from that, so it can't happen to us for the first time again."

The Cowboys still carried the label of being the team that couldn't win the big one, but most guys felt "hadn't" was a better way of putting it. Games like this showed they could do it. Winning on the road against an 11–3 team that boasts the NFL's best defense in temperatures around freezing may not have been *the* big one, but it was big all right. They'd gone to Minnesota and beaten the Vikings at their own game, forcing five turnovers while committing none. Staubach got 13 points off those turnovers and that was enough. So when a writer asked Staubach about whether he feared the team's reputation would eventually catch up to them, Staubach gave the guy exactly what he wanted to hear.

"Yes, there is some of that," he said. "It's a problem. That's why I know we're not good for more than two more games. That'll be all we can do before folding—just two more."

As the reporter jotted down every word, Staubach smiled at those who caught his drift.

"That works out about right, doesn't it?"

# Not Satisfied

STEVEN AND SHIRLEY BOYD were not among the 500 fans at Love Field to greet the team plane home from Minneapolis on Christmas night. But they were among the hundreds who spent that entire night camped out to buy tickets for the NFC Championship Game. What made them stand out is that this was their first full day as husband and wife.

A love of the Cowboys was among the things that led them down the aisle. So they considered this fitting, even somewhat romantic.

"We talked it over and decided that if we went away on a honeymoon we'd miss the chance to buy tickets for the game," Steven Boyd said.

Virginia Velasquez was first in line. Wearing a Roger Staubach jersey, she arrived at 7:00 a.m.—five hours before the Cowboys-Vikings game kicked off and 26 hours before the ticket window opened.

"If they had lost, Christmas would have been ruined anyway," she said.

Such loyalty was a new phenomenon.

The Jets game in December was the first in franchise history to sell out as many as four days in advance, and that was because of Joe Namath. There was still plenty of backlash over the prices at the new stadium and those who felt alienated by the Dallas Cowboys playing in suburban Irving. But, hey, everyone loves a winner, and fans were beginning to believe this club wasn't going to let them down like they had every season since 1966.

Nobody in the club's front office had thought to book the site of coach Tom Landry's news conference for his usual time, allowing someone else to rent the space. So the gathering with reporters was held a day early.

"I guess this shows management doesn't have much confidence," Landry said with a smile.

—★—

In 1954, Landry was in his first year as both a defensive back and assistant coach on the New York Giants when the club spent a fourth-round pick on another defensive back: Dick Nolan, a two-way standout who had helped Maryland win the national championship.

Nolan hit hard, played with passion, and understood Xs and Os. No wonder he and Landry clicked right away. They spent many a night watching game films in Landry's apartment, talking schemes and strategies, plays and players.

When Nolan retired after the 1961 season, Landry hired him to coach Dallas' secondary. One Saturday night at the start of that season, Landry asked Nolan if he was interested in playing again.

"I haven't worked out in months," Nolan said. "I'm 25 pounds over-weight. . . . Okay, when do you want me to start?"

He was in the lineup the next day and the rest of the season. He returned to being only an assistant coach and stayed through the Ice Bowl, leaving to become head coach in San Francisco.

Nolan brought Landry's "coordinated defense" with him to the 49ers. While other teams ran similar versions, it was impossible for an observer to replicate it. The 4–3 formula was so intricate it took someone like Nolan, who had 11 years' experience, to teach it.

Landry and Nolan remained close friends and confidantes, except for this week. Landry called on Monday to congratulate Nolan for beating the Redskins and to say they'll talk again Sunday, after one of them is headed for the Super Bowl.

"I guess it's going to be a matter of being good friends for a long time, but hating each other temporarily this week," Nolan said. "Let's face it—he taught me everything I know."

The week would be a cat-and-mouse game, mentor and student each trying to use their knowledge of the other to gain an advantage. Nolan had the benefit of knowing the Dallas defense as well as anyone. Only Herb Adderley, Cliff Harris, and Larry Cole had joined the starting lineup since he'd left.

The Cowboys beat the 49ers 17–10 in San Francisco in this same round the previous season, so Nolan's inside knowledge had its limits. His first words at the news conference following the 1970 NFC Championshp Game were, "We'll be back." He spent the entire offseason analyzing that game, learning from it. He concluded that the difference was experience. He wanted nothing more than another crack at Dallas. Now, he was getting it.

Landry had some ideas about things Nolan might try, so he began plotting counter strategies.

"I'll make him think I'm going to change a whole lot," Landry said. "What I'll change, I won't say. But I'll change more because of their knowledge of our defense."

—★—

Fans were stoked from the start—booing the 49ers when they came out, then cheering so loudly when Staubach appeared that you couldn't hear him being introduced. Velasquez was no doubt wearing her No. 12 jersey again and among the screamers.

Former President Lyndon B. Johnson and wife Lady Bird were back, joined this time by Texas Longhorns coach Darrell Royal, a day after his team lost to Penn State in the Cotton Bowl.

Minutes before kickoff, Adderley was getting loose on the Dallas sideline and casually looked across the field. He noticed 49ers quarterback John Brodie staring right at him.

"He nodded at me, which told me he was coming at me," Adderley said. "I nodded back, which told him if he hung the ball I was going to get it."

The first quarter was a punt-fest, with neither team able to string together first downs. Early in the second quarter, the 49ers were facing second-and-8 from their 14-yard line when Brodie faked a screen to his right, dropped back, and looked to throw down the field. Lilly was coming toward him, so Brodie had to do something—either take a sack or throw it away. Then he remembered running back Ken Willard was hanging out to his left as a last resort, so Brodie turned and threw his way.

The ball never got to Willard. George Andrie was blitzing and couldn't help but catch it.

"Hit me right in the chest," he said.

Playing in the 151st game of his career, Andrie made just his second interception. He caught it at the nine-yard line, so close to a touchdown that he could see the red-painted turf in the San Francisco end zone. He crossed the six, the four, the two . . . and got tackled by Brodie.

Teammates weren't surprised Andrie made a big play in a big game. That was his specialty. He scored a touchdown on a fumble return in the Ice Bowl and recorded a safety in the last year's NFC Championship Game.

"It never occurred to me *he'd* pop up," Willard said. "I was watching [Chuck Howley], and when I saw him fall down, I figured everything was okay. Some surprise!"

Two plays later, Calvin Hill leaped over the center for the touchdown. He still couldn't break that habit of leaving his feet. Walking back to the bench, he told Duane Thomas, "I think my knee is going again."

That was it for the first-half scoring. Dallas went into the break leading only 7–0, a slim margin considering Doomsday had allowed just one first down. Adderley and the secondary had pestered Brodie into completing only two of nine passes. Andrie's seven-yard interception covered more ground than either of the two receptions by San Francisco players.

Nolan made some nice adjustments during halftime because the offense started moving. They got a 28-yard field goal midway through the third quarter, then tried a 47-yarder on their next series. It would've cut the lead to a single point but went wide left. Under the rules of the day, the Cowboys took over at their 20.

Staubach had been merely okay up to this point. He hadn't made any mistakes, but he also hadn't made any great plays or sustained any drives. He was keeping the Cowboys in the game but wasn't winning it for them.

At the start of the next drive, he almost lost it for Dallas.

Facing third-and-7 from his own 23, Staubach dropped back to throw and kept dropping back, zigzagging to avoid several swarming defenders. He crossed the five-yard line and was still headed toward the goal line, an incredible risk with only a 7–3 lead. A turnover would've been horrendous and a sack would've given the 49ers great field position. Defensive end Cedrick Hardman was thinking the same thing when he lunged toward Staubach. He went in high, though, and Staubach went low to avoid the tackle, then headed toward the line of scrimmage. Tony Liscio and Dave Manders threw great blocks, giving Staubach room to roam. He kept the play alive long enough to find Dan Reeves.

Linebacker Dave Wilcox was nearby, too, yet stuck in no-man's land. If he stayed on Reeves, Staubach would run for a first down. If he went to Staubach, the quarterback could flip the ball to Reeves for a first down. In the blip of time he had to decide, Wilcox went for Staubach, only to watch the ball sail over him and right to Reeves.

"Somebody said the play took twenty-two seconds," Reeves said. "It seemed like eighteen of it was when I was waiting for the ball to ever get to me."

The play went for 17 yards. Staubach faced three more third downs on the drive and converted them all—a 22-yard pass to Billy Truax, a 5-yarder to Mike Ditka, and a pitch to Thomas going left for a 2-yard touchdown that made it 14–3 early in the fourth quarter. The long, slow drive gave Doomsday plenty of time to rest and left Brodie needing two touchdowns on an afternoon when he was struggling to get first downs.

The stars of the defense took turns closing out the victory. Howley knocked down a pass on fourth down, then Lee Roy Jordan came away with an interception on San Francisco's next snap. The offense did its share down the stretch, too, especially Walt Garrison.

He'd become a forgotten man in recent weeks because of the success of the Hill-Thomas tandem. But, as Hill predicted, his knee gave out two carries after his touchdown, so Landry turned to Garrison. He delivered despite an ankle injury that would've sidelined most players.

"It was obvious that he was just about to die," Landry said. "But he was that determined to play."

Garrison found five or six yards when none were there. He just kept twisting, prying, poking, refusing to go down. "Like a bull," Staubach said. It was the most impressive 52 yards on 14 carries you'll ever see, with appreciative linemen helping him up after each tackle.

"You could feel the excitement on the sidelines when Walt started running hard," Jordan said.

Cliff Harris intercepted a pass in front of the goal line with one second left. Staubach took a knee, and the Cowboys were headed back to the Super Bowl, joining the 1966–67 Packers as the only teams to reach the Super Bowl in consecutive seasons.

Green Bay won both times. Dallas lost its first trip. That sense of unfinished business kept a lid on the celebration, despite LBJ and Royal offering their congratulations.

"I've never been in a locker room that took a big win like that so easy," Landry said. "But I've never been with a team that lost the Super Bowl the year before, either. They've felt all year that this is where they belonged."

"We just had to get back," Reeves said. "Once you've been in it and lost—no matter how you lost, that isn't remembered by anyone—then nothing else can satisfy but going back and winning. It was a long road back. We knew it wasn't going to be easy. No one gives you anything in this game. We earned the right to go to New Orleans. I don't think I have to tell you that after all of this, we are going to be ready on January 16th."

# Getting Ready in Dallas

BACK WHEN NFL OWNERS were voting on where to put the Super Bowl, the AFC bosses rejected Texas Stadium because they feared giving the Dallas Cowboys a home game. The NFC powerbrokers got even by rejecting the alternative site pushed by the other conference.

Good thing, too, or else they would've given the Miami Dolphins a home game.

The Dolphins were the surprise winners of the AFC, having beaten the more-experienced Kansas City Chiefs in double overtime, then knocking out the reigning champion Baltimore Colts in the AFC title game.

The Miami-Baltimore game started after Dallas beat San Francisco. The Cowboys and their fans watched, rooting for the Colts and a chance to get even in the Super Bowl. They saw the Dolphins crush them 21–0 and came away wondering whether this upstart club was as dangerous as they looked.

The 1971 Dolphins were a lot like the 1966 Cowboys, a young franchise on the rise through a combination of great young players, solid veterans, and a savvy coach, Don Shula.

"They are somewhat of a mystery to me," Tom Landry said. "We haven't played them, and I've only seen them play twice on television. . . . I saw the second half of their game against Baltimore, and it was obvious they were a team very well prepared. Whatever Miami tried to do, it did well. I don't think we have an edge because of our Super

Bowl experience. Shula offsets any edge we have. He has been down there before."

The Dolphins also had friends in high places.

Around 1:30 a.m. on Monday, Miami coach Don Shula was watching a replay of the AFC Championship when his phone rang. Told it was President Richard Nixon calling, Shula thought it was a prank and almost hung up.

"I started scrutinizing the voice," Shula said. "In only a few seconds I knew it was the president."

Nixon was an unabashed fan of the Redskins, which meant his second favorite team was whoever played the Cowboys. But he claimed territorial rights on being a Dolphins fan by noting he had a vacation home in Key Biscayne, Florida.

The call lasted about 10 minutes, with Nixon offering more than just his regards. He wanted specifics from the Baltimore game, and he offered this warning: "Dallas has a pretty fair coach in Tom Landry."

He gave Shula some play-calling advice, too.

"Run the slant to [Paul] Warfield," Nixon said. "You know the one."

In the first of two weeks to hype this game, the president's involvement became a juicy story line. Political commentators told him to butt out, and football aficionados analyzed the play itself.

As for staunch Republican Landry, it was playful fodder.

"There's no reason for me to feel neglected," Landry said. "We had Lyndon Johnson in our dressing room. Besides, the president is like anybody else—he's got to have his team."

But this was an election year. Would Nixon still have his vote?

"I'm going to wait and see this time," Landry said, smirking. "I'm going to worry him a little."

Lee Roy Jordan thought about the challenge of the Super Bowl, this winner-take-all game that determines a team's reputation.

Win it and you are forever branded a champion. Lose and you're a choker. Don't even get there and nobody cares about you.

He weighed it all and shrugged.

"Not much bigger than the ones we've been playing," he said.

Had the Cowboys lost any of the games shortly after they were 4–3, their season could have been over. There's no telling what a single loss in any of Staubach's first few starts would have done.

But everything came together. Like glue drying, it was iffy at first, then kept getting stronger.

Leave it to Duane Thomas to test that bond. He didn't show up for work on Thursday.

Within hours, Buddy Diliberto of WVUE-TV in New Orleans reported that Thomas was skipping the Super Bowl. He said he got the word "from reliable sources within pro football;" it actually came from a conversation in Houston between a former Cowboys player, an assistant coach on the Oilers, and a third person who was Diliberto's tipster.

As sketchy as it seemed, anything was possible with Thomas. And the plot supposedly was hatched by Jim Brown as part of their ploy to negotiate a better contract. Brown had befriended Thomas the previous summer, and had spoken to Cowboys officials in an attempt to solve Thomas' contract dispute.

The Cowboys couldn't shoot it down because they had no idea what was going on. They couldn't find Thomas to ask him. They sent one person to his home, another to his favorite hangouts, all to no avail.

"But I still can't believe there's anything to the story," Tex Schramm said. "A stunt like that would have everybody in the country down on him—and Brown, too. Battling the organization is one thing, but letting down your teammates is another."

The Cowboys had a meeting at 9:30 a.m. Friday. Thomas walked in at 9:29.

When that session ended, Thomas and Landry went into the coaches' dressing area for about 40 minutes. Thomas walked out, saw *Dallas Times-Herald* reporter Steve Perkins, and said, "Don't fuck with me." Landry stayed behind to call Schramm.

Nearly a half hour later, Landry told Perkins that Thomas offered nothing more than "personal reasons" for his absence. As for Brown's involvement and the idea of skipping the Super Bowl, Thomas told his coach, "No comment."

"He just wouldn't talk at all about it," Landry said. "Football really isn't that important in his life, I guess. He told me, 'My job is football and I will do my job.' He just doesn't think anything else enters into that. He didn't specifically say, 'I will play in the Super Bowl,' but you have to assume that he will because he's here. I know this isn't enlightening you very much, but I am not enlightened much, either."

Now the Cowboys had to worry about more than the Dolphins. They had to consider how much to trust Thomas.

Landry had to decide how much of his game plan to build around his most gifted running back without being certain he would suit up. And, if he did, how hard was he going to try? He'd been mediocre so far in the playoffs. Great defenses were thought to be the reason. Now, even that was being questioned.

Teammates could only shake their heads. Imagine how Walt Garrison felt. On Sunday, Garrison told reporters he'd lined up wrong—not Thomas—on the play that resulted in Thomas' touchdown. Everyone had seen Thomas try lining up on the right side of the backfield, only to shift to the left when he realized Garrison was there. But in the locker room, Garrison took the blame. Once Staubach let it slip that "Duane went to the wrong place. I waited for him to get to the left," reporters went back to Garrison to ask why he made himself the fall guy.

"Thomas gets enough ridicule without me adding to it," Garrison said.

Now Thomas brought it on himself. Again.

And Landry was letting Thomas get away with it. Again.

There was no choice. Thomas had been welcomed back to help Dallas win the Super Bowl. With that the only game remaining, it wouldn't make sense to keep him out of it.

The Cowboys worked out in Dallas on Wednesday, Thursday, and Friday. Rayfield Wright missed them all because of a sprained big toe, and Calvin Hill sat out to rest his knee.

On Saturday, there was a brief workout, then some down time. The charter wasn't leaving until 5:00 p.m. Sunday.

"We have been mixing up the practices this week with a little bit of everything—trying this and that," Landry said. "We haven't set our game plan yet. We'll put that in next week in New Orleans."

The timetable was one of the lessons learned from Super Bowl V.

The previous January, Landry used the week in Dallas as a typical game-preparation week. They went over the game plan midweek and were ready to go by Sunday. However, the game wasn't until the following Sunday. The thinking was they'd spend the week leading up to the game fulfilling all their obligations while merely refining what they'd already put in place. Instead, by game day, they'd passed their expiration date. They played like a stale team.

Herb Adderley, the only person to play in three of the first five Super Bowls, liked the way the Cowboys handled this week before the week before.

"The overall attitude of the entire squad is beautiful," Adderley said. "This is the way we used to go into the Super Bowl with the Packers—have fun, stay loose, but be serious in practice. We're having real good practices, everybody being down when we're on the field, but staying relaxed, too. We're going down to New Orleans with a businesslike attitude. Being in a Super Bowl for the first time, like Miami is, has to affect some of their people. It's impossible to go into a big game like this and not feel something inside. Shula has been there before and he can try to explain it to them, but it's something you have to experience, the atmosphere of being down there all week, the whole week of pressure leading up to game time. You have to go through it to understand what it is."

For all the talk of Shula's Super Bowl experience, it wasn't a very good one. He coached the Baltimore Colts in Super Bowl III, when they were upset by Joe Namath and the New York Jets.

Shula left for Miami a year later, so he was gone when the Colts beat the Cowboys.

The Dolphins won only three games the year before Shula arrived. He brought in a new playbook and a new work ethic, sometimes pushing them through four workouts a day in training camp. It worked. The Dolphins won 10 games and made the playoffs his first season. Now, in his second year, they were in the Super Bowl.

Miami had only one starter on defense older than 26—middle line-backer Nick Buoniconti, who was a whopping 31 years old and in his tenth NFL season. The majority of starters were in their second or third years. What the unit lacked in experience was made up for in ability. They gave up 14 points or less in 13 of their 16 games.

The offense was put together a lot like Dallas: a powerful tandem at running back (Larry Csonka and Jim Kiick), a proven breakaway threat at receiver (Warfield), and an efficient, effective quarterback (Bob Griese).

Only one player on offense was in his 30s; most were 20-something.

"Emotionally, I think the Dolphins probably are in about the same fix we were a few years ago," John Niland said. "I'm sure they're a lot better team than we were then. But, looking back on it, I'd like to think our experience is going to be a tremendous asset."

"I think a younger player might choke. We did it a lot of times, I know," Chuck Howley said. "We made a lot of mistakes in a lot of big games, which cost us the games. I think we're much more mature and much more experienced now, and I think this is our edge on Miami. They might have an edge in youth, but youth in this game doesn't impress me. I'll go for experience any day."

—★—

On Sunday afternoon, a week before the Super Bowl, fans gathered at Love Field to send the Cowboys off in style. Players smiled and waved, vowing to return with a big, shiny trophy.

As Landry boarded the plane, a member of the public relations staff handed him a telegram. It read:

MY PRAYERS AND MY PRESENCE WILL BE WITH YOU IN
NEW ORLEANS, ALTHOUGH I DO NOT PLAN TO SEND
IN ANY PLAYS. LYNDON B. JOHNSON.

Landry smiled and said, "At least we have one president on our side."

# Getting Ready in New Orleans

THE FLIGHT TO NEW Orleans took a little over an hour. The bus ride to the hotel took only a few minutes.

They weren't staying anywhere near Bourbon Street. They were in the town of Kenner, a few football fields from the airport's flight-control tower. The Hilton Inn they would be calling home for the week was a $10, 30-minute cab ride from all the action.

As payback for keeping them so far away, Tom Landry didn't set a curfew for Sunday, Monday, and Tuesday nights. Players could go wherever they wanted, whenever they wanted.

"That'll give them three nights to get the French Quarter out of their system," Landry said. "By Wednesday, I hope they'll be sick of it."

He tapered their free time the rest of the week. They had to be in by midnight Wednesday, Thursday, and Friday; by 11 p.m. on Saturday, their usual cutoff the night before a game.

The Hilton Inn was no five-star resort. Its most distinguishing feature was a soundtrack of airplanes taking off and landing. Five years earlier, a Delta plane on a training flight hit the hotel. Several guests were among the 19 people killed. The Dolphins, meanwhile, were staying at the Fontainebleau Hotel, a swank place about three miles from all the hot spots. That hotel's distinguishing feature was a pair of dolphins named

Jimbo and Tinkerbelle imported for the week from Gulfport, Mississippi.

"We're stuck out here in this shitty hotel in this shitty town," Chuck Howley said. "We'll all be so mad by Sunday that I think we'll go out there and rip somebody apart."

Anger spilled way too soon.

That very first night, in the French Quarter, Margene Adkins splashed a drink in Walt Garrison's face. The next day, in the locker room at the Saints' practice facility, Adkins continued the quarrel by landing a sucker punch on Garrison. Teammates separated them quickly, but word got back to Landry.

He chastised Garrison in private ("I know you drink and Margene doesn't, so it was probably your fault"), and he told the whole club: "If something like this happens again—or anything else occurs which might disgrace this team—I'll fine those involved five thousand dollars."

Landry wasn't about to let anything or anyone mess this up.

—★—

As Staubach started unpacking, Howley asked an important question.

"You've got the chocolate chip cookies, don't you?" Howley said.

"Oh, no!" Staubach said. "Geez, they're not in here. Marianne forgot."

Howley fell for it. By the time he was predicting this would be the end of Dallas' winning streak, Staubach stopped teasing and pulled the cookies out of his suitcase.

—★—

Monday was Media Day, when every player is available to be interviewed by the hundreds of newspaper, radio, and television reporters covering the game. The more prominent the player, the bigger the setup. Small-timers were lumped together.

Reporters surrounded Duane Thomas, curious whether the "Sphinx" would break his silence. Maybe he'd drop another classic line like at last year's Super Bowl, when he said, "How can it be the ultimate game if they play it next year, too?" Or maybe he'd go on a rant against management like he did in the summer. There were so many questions to be asked, too, from his absence last week to whether he planned on playing to seeking an explanation for everything else he had and hadn't done this season.

"Leave me alone," Thomas told the first wave of reporters. "I don't want to talk to anybody."

Reporters came and went, moving on to someone who would talk once they realized this was futile. A few stuck it out, just in case. The Sphinx wasn't cracking. His only other words the entire session were, "What time is it?"

"Five after 11," he was told.

That was the extent of the conversation.

Years later, he explained his performance that day: "You people were studying me, and I was studying you."

Athletes sometimes think that not talking prevents stories from being written about them. Wrong. A compelling enough figure, like Thomas, remains compelling to readers. Silence simply prevents his side of the story from being told. Writers instead use the insight of others or their own viewpoint, which can be tainted by their anger over being spurned. It's a vicious cycle that can be tempered by even a few innocuous words.

"Thomas isn't what most newspapers make the readers think he is," said Dolphins running back Eugene "Mercury" Morris, Thomas' college teammate. "I can understand the things that happened in his life that have made him that way, personal things that people don't know about."

Dallas players stuck up for their teammate, too.

"A man may smile at you and be a hypocrite. Another may growl and really be the more honest of the two," Calvin Hill said. "I'll tell you one thing: This guy is one fine football player. I only wish I could block as well for him as he does for me."

Dave Manders said nothing Thomas had done bothered him.

"I think that's true for the majority of the team," he said.

Nothing? They didn't mind getting the silent treatment? Seeing him skirt the rules they had to follow was okay? Him skipping practice a week before the Super Bowl was no big deal?

"He could have been hurt, been to the doctor," Manders said. "I don't think too many people even knew he was gone. A professional athlete is paid to perform on the field. There's no question that Duane is putting out one hundred percent. Some people did question that he wasn't running well against the 49ers. The holes just weren't there."

The afternoon of Media Day, the Cowboys lined up for a team photo. The photographer asked Thomas to move six inches and he scooted over.

"You moved eight inches," Lance Alworth teased. "You moved two inches too far."

Thomas smiled. It was the first time in months some teammates had seen him do so. Alworth was among those Thomas got along with. Alworth wasn't all that happy in his role, either, so they were kindred spirits—guys who felt they were pawns in Landry's chess match against the opposing coach.

"Whatever his problem is, I think it's his business," Alworth said.

Thomas wasn't among the eight Cowboys picked for the Pro Bowl. But, this week, he became No. 9 because of an injury. Would he go?

"He nodded," Landry said. "I assume that meant yes."

Asked if he ever wondered what Thomas was thinking, Landry said, "If I worry about that, I'd go crazy."

Instead, Landry worried about Miami's defense, a group that allowed the third-fewest points in the league this season and came into the Super Bowl having gone nearly six quarters without allowing a point, quite a feat this time of year.

"I can't recall their names, but they are a matter of great concern to us," Landry said. With that line, he inspired the unit's enduring nickname, the "No-Name Defense."

One name Landry knew was Nick Buoniconti, the middle linebacker who meant as much to Miami's defense as Bob Lilly or Lee Roy Jordan did for Dallas, if not Lilly *and* Jordan.

Buoniconti was an interesting fellow. He got his law degree while playing for the New England Patriots and now worked for a Miami firm. He also had a radio show five mornings a week and owned a restaurant near the Orange Bowl.

At 5-foot-11, he was too small to play middle linebacker for Landry. But he was a perfect fit for Don Shula.

Buoniconti was a coordinator on the field. He put everyone in place before the snap. Once he determined where the ball was going, he took off for it and everyone else followed. It was simple but successful.

So was the countermove to stop it.

Landry recognized that neutralizing Buoniconti would throw off the entire defense. Thus, Landry decided that on every play, Dallas would knock him down or confuse him, either by getting in his way so he couldn't see plays develop or with misdirection, starting plays one direction and ending up going another.

In practices, Dan Reeves pretended to be Buoniconti on the scout team. That meant every offensive lineman on the Cowboys targeted him in every drill.

"I got the heck beat out of me that first week in Dallas," Reeves said. "So I knew how important our guys thought it was to stop Nick Buoniconti."

Among the offensive linemen trying to thwart Buoniconti would be left tackle Tony Liscio—who'd been traded to the Dolphins in September, but retired instead. Funny how things work out.

—★—

Landry certainly knew the names of running backs Larry Csonka and Jim Kiick. Or, as they enjoyed being called, Butch & Sundance.

With their 1-2 punch, the Dolphins not only ran for the most yards in the NFL this season, they also were the most efficient, gaining 5 yards per attempt. Twice this season, each gained 100 yards in the same game. They also knew how to hold onto the ball, having lost a single fumble in 429 carries over the regular season and playoffs. The lone flub? Kiick did it three months ago, in a game Miami won 41–3.

"As big as Csonka is and tough as Kiick is, I don't think anybody wanted to hit them hard enough to make them fumble," Cornell Green said.

Having those 18-wheelers grinding out yards sure made things easier for Miami's quarterback, Bob Griese. He didn't have the most powerful arm, but he also didn't have to take many chances. Being smart, accurate, and nimble was enough to keep the Dolphins moving.

So the key to stopping Miami was slowing the running backs on first and second downs, forcing Griese to beat you on third-and-long. Simple as that sounds, Dallas had the defense to do it. Doomsday was the best in the league at stopping the run, and Landry had two weeks to figure things out.

It didn't take Landry long at all.

He discovered that the Dolphins gave away their intentions before every snap. The cue was the wide receiver. If he was truly wide, it was a passing play. On running plays, he was seven yards closer to the line, ready to be a weak-side blocker. Csonka especially liked to cut back behind blocks from Warfield.

"When he does that, we'll be in the backfield before he can throw the block," Jordan said.

The Dolphins were concerned most about Bob Lilly. They couldn't stop talking about him.

"Well, when you watch as many films as we have, he sort of stands out," Kiick said.

"It doesn't matter whether you run at him or away from him, he always seems to be disrupting the play," Csonka said.

Griese joked that Bob Kuechenberg—the left guard who would be matched against Lilly—had been awfully nice to the center all week, knowing he was going to need his help. Baltimore coach Don McCafferty was quoted in a *Life* magazine article recommending that a running back should help, too.

"He is a player without weaknesses. He has certain tendencies, but no set patterns like others have," Kuechenberg said. "I'll be satisfied if you don't hear his name or mine Sunday."

—★—

Staubach was the most talked about player this week, landing on the cover of *Time* and *Life* magazines. The Cowboys had never made the cover of either, and here he was on both.

"I had more interviews the first two minutes I was here than I had all last year," Staubach said.

It was an irresistible story—the one new starter on a team that came oh-so-close to winning it all last season, and he happens to play the most pivotal position. Since he took over, the Cowboys went from 4–3 to nine straight wins and another chance to win it all. Layer that with his 1963 Heisman Trophy, the delayed start to his pro career so he could fulfill his patriotic duty, and it all seemed too good to be true.

This week only added to the lore.

Staubach spent most nights in Landry's room. While teammates went all over New Orleans sampling the variety of food and drink concoctions, listening to jazz musicians, and investigating other forms of entertainment,

Staubach was watching game films. The sessions might've gone all night if not for Alicia Landry saying, "Tommy, let him get to bed."

His only indulgences that week were a pile of shrimp the first night, seeing *Dirty Harry* with running back Joe Williams another night, and having dinner with his wife and her parents on Friday night.

"New Orleans is a fascinating place to visit for three or four days if you have nothing on your mind," Staubach said. "But Sunday is what it's all about for us. I've got to keep channeled in that direction."

In countless interviews, Staubach maintained he hadn't proven anything yet. "I may be just a passing flash," he said. He also felt that having Landry call plays for him made him less of a quarterback, like a kid whose dad had to cut up his food before he could eat it.

"To be truthful, I'd have to say I'm not too often thinking the same play that he sends in," Staubach said. "I know from field position and the hash marks what two or three plays might be coming. But it's not usually the one I'd select. This is his experience, my inexperience. I guess I'll tell you one thing: If someone is going to call the plays for you, it isn't bad having Tom Landry do it."

—★—

Landry and Shula were members of an exclusive club. They were both 0–1 in a Super Bowl. One of them was going to leave New Orleans as the only coach ever to lose two Super Bowls.

If Landry felt any stress, it didn't show. Rather than tensing up as the game approached, he remained loose, relaxed. Charming, even. Because Landry was no showman, the only conclusion was this revealed his confidence. He knew his team deserved to be here, he knew they were better than the Dolphins, and he knew they had a game plan to prove it.

"We've been looking forward to this since we stepped off the field in Miami last year," he said. "We have a much more determined approach.... We're a little bit impatient. We want to get on with it."

Shula's body language indicated someone less at ease. But he sure tried to sound as if everything was under control.

His first challenge came when his predecessor, George Wilson, begged for credit that the team had blossomed into AFC champions, claiming he handed Shula a "ready-made team."

"Joe Doakes could have coached them," Wilson said. "I was fired when the team was ready to go."

There was more to Wilson's jealousy.

He gave Shula his first job as an NFL coach, in Detroit in 1960. Then Wilson recommended that Baltimore hire Shula as head coach in 1963. So Wilson was understandably furious at being cleared out to make way for his protégé. Further insult was seeing Shula get more out of the Dolphins than he had. Truth was, Miami was no longer loaded with Wilson's leftovers. Only 18 of his players remained; many were the building blocks on offense, but Shula had remade the defense.

Dolphins owner Joe Robbie wasn't known for having a soft touch, but he handled this one deftly. He said Wilson always would be considered part of the club, noting that he gets complimentary season tickets. "And if he wants to see the Super Bowl, he can come as our guest," Robbie said. (Wilson declined the invitation.)

The next time Shula appeared before reporters, he broke the ice by saying, "In case you don't know me, I'm Joe Doakes. You can call me Joe."

He continued: "George Wilson made a very significant contribution to our success. His last year he had a lot of injuries, which is why the team didn't continue to improve its record. But I'm sorry to hear the things he said. I'm very proud of the job we've done at Miami. I've never been one to step forward and take credit. I give it to the players. I don't know what his reasons were for saying what he did, but I'm not going to let it distract me in any way from this game."

Shula also was dealing with the stigma of having blown Super Bowl III, a game that's still considered a colossal upset and universally known for Joe Namath guaranteeing the Jets would win, then backing it up. Shula didn't help his case any by pointing out his Colts were 15–1 going into that game.

"We could have gone down in history as one of the great teams of all time," Shula said.

Shula showed up to the final news conference 10 minutes late. His team's final full workout ran late, but he gave a different reason for the delay and for being in a chatty mood.

"I just had three Scotch and sodas," he said.

He thought he did a better job handling the logistical challenges of a Super Bowl this time around. Three years ago, in Miami, he allowed too many things to take players' minds off football, from having a hotel on the beach to allowing wives and children to come along. This time, families were asked to stay away until Saturday.

"This Super Bowl week has been much better," Shula said. "We've been far more businesslike. We've given the press the time it needs, we've given all the attention to preparation that we should, and the players have had time to themselves to relax and prepare themselves individually for the game. We'll have an easy workout tomorrow, and then I'm taking the team to dinner. I believe it's simpler to keep all the players together tomorrow night rather than have a lot of them puzzled about where to go to dinner and how to get reservations."

Shula believed his team could win.

"But, I'm not guaranteeing anything."

Like going through a haunted house for a second time, playing in a Super Bowl is easier when you know what to expect.

No team appearing in a Super Bowl for a second time had ever lost. The Packers won their first trip and their second. The Kansas City Chiefs and Baltimore Colts set the template the Cowboys were trying to follow, losing their first trip and winning the next time. The only difference was that Dallas made it back the year after the loss.

From the press conferences to the nightlife to the game-day accoutrements, there's nothing like the spectacle of a Super Bowl. There were problems a team could only discover through experience, such as fans overrunning the hotel and late-night calls from friends, family, and strangers seeking tickets. The Cowboys knew better this time. They cut off calls to the rooms at night, and hired extra security around the hotel. There was also the pressure that came with the stakes: walking away either a champion or a big-game loser, collecting a $15,000 bonus or $7,500.

Griese insisted the Super Bowl was no big deal. He called it "just another football game." The Cowboys laughed at his naivety.

"There's just no way, regardless of how hard Griese or anyone else tries to convince themselves of it, that a Super Bowl game can be just another football game," Landry said.

A few weeks after Super Bowl V, Craig Morton had said, "I can't tell you what our game plan was." Whether it was his fault or Landry's, the coach wasn't going to allow that to happen again.

Preparing for the Dolphins, Landry must have felt like he was back in New York in the mid-1950s, up in his apartment going over film with Dick Nolan. He knew he was a step ahead of the competition, and he knew he had guys capable of using this information to their advantage. He'd cracked the Dolphins' code, on offense and defense, and it was simply a matter of pulling it off.

Landry explained to Staubach and Morton every nuance of every play and the reasoning behind it. He went over the plan to thwart Buoniconti on running plays and emphasized throwing short passes to running backs. His research showed the Dolphins played mostly zone coverage, sending their linebackers deep, so they would be vulnerable on dump-off passes. Landry also detected how predictable the Dolphins were when they used backup linebacker Bob Matheson; as long as Staubach recognized Matheson was in and where he lined up, the Cowboys knew what was coming.

Staubach felt so well versed that on Thursday he said, "If anything happened to Coach Landry, I could take over."

From one crisp practice to the next, Landry saw in players' eyes that they knew how good they were. Their confidence was soaring. Not a single person doubted they were going to win. They were too talented, too healthy, too experienced, too well coached.

Everything they'd been through on and off the field for the last year—no, the last six years . . . perhaps even all 11 years in franchise history—was going to culminate in a show of force Sunday afternoon. The team that couldn't win the big one was going to prove it could.

"There's no jinx," Bob Hayes said. "There's no worry we can't win the championship because of what has happened before. The past is finished!"

That's right. This was about the future.

"When we beat Miami on Sunday, it will be the beginning of a dynasty," Chuck Howley said. "It will be a long time before someone knocks Dallas off the pedestal. I believe a Super Bowl victory will trigger a landslide for the Cowboys as the undisputed power in professional football, much like the Green Bay Packers in the 1960s under Vince Lombardi."

Since he first learned of an NFL club starting in Dallas, Tex Schramm dreamed of building a team capable of winning a championship every year. Yet in the parlance of franchise founder Clint Murchison Jr., the Cowboys had dug deep but had yet to strike oil.

"To establish that image, that reputation, you first got to win the Super Bowl," Schramm said. "The Yankees had a certain class about them, and when players joined them, they developed that class. And that's what everybody strives for in an organization. What else is there? But it all starts with winning this game."

The Cowboys were the rising force in a league that was rising in popularity. The seeds for a dynasty were planted. A championship was the fertilizer needed to make it grow.

"A loss in this game would be harder to get over than the one last year, for the players, for the organization, for the fans—everybody," Schramm said. "But once we get over this hump, then we can go ahead, maybe for ten years or so. It feeds on itself. . . .

"Once you start, then it keeps rolling, keeps building up. But first, we've got to win *this* one. It all begins right here."

# Champions at Last

O N GAME DAY, TROUBLE signs were there for anyone negative enough to look for them.

This stadium was the site of Dallas' worst loss of the season. While there was no history against the Dolphins, the city of Miami conjured bad memories for Dallas as the site of last year's Super Bowl.

Then there was the weather—not Ice Bowl cold, but the coldest ever for a Super Bowl, 39 degrees at kickoff.

The superstitious types had their antidote in the Reverend Billy Zeoli.

Zeoli was the man behind the movie *A Man & His Men*, based on Dallas' 1970 season and Landry's faith. He'd also become the regular leader of their game-day devotional. It started in mid-November, before a game the Cowboys won. They invited him back and won again. So they kept inviting him back.

Pre-game festivities were not yet a Hollywood extravaganza. There were performances by 15 college bands and 200 dancing girls, and the release of 20,000 balloons and flocks of pigeons. Al Hirt blew his trumpet, and the U.S. Air Force Academy Chorus sang the national anthem.

Four U.S. Air Force jets were supposed to arrive during the song, but they were a few minutes late. That was an improvement from the fiasco before the last Super Bowl in New Orleans, when a hot-air balloon bounced along the field and smacked into the stands, the gondola crashing into the lower deck, the balloon slapping across the upper deck.

The broadcast of this game was going all over the world. It would be shown in England for the first time, albeit on tape delay, and also in Germany, Korea, Panama, and the Philippines. In New Orleans, the game was blacked out per NFL rules, but for $10 locals could watch a closed-circuit broadcast featuring the Saints' broadcast crew. For fans watching in Dallas, the pre-game show began at 1:00 p.m. for a 1:30 kickoff.

—★—

The Cowboys had the good kind of jitters, the anticipation of a big event.

They knew they were ready. They didn't fear the Dolphins, and they certainly didn't fear losing. They'd lost a Super Bowl before and discovered it wasn't the end of the world.

Herb Adderley was so relaxed that he fell asleep on the bus ride to the stadium.

Tom Landry's pre-game speech was as dry as usual.

"We've got a ball game to play," he said. "You know what to do. Go do it."

Miami fans were easy to spot in the crowd because they were the ones waving white handkerchiefs they'd bought for $1. The cloths were twirling from the start as Miami won the toss and wanted the ball, eager to see what Larry Csonka and Jim Kiick could do against Bob Lilly and the Doomsday Defense.

The Dolphins went to Kiick twice on the first series, punted, then tried Csonka the next time they got the ball. He took a sweep going right and crashed forward for 12 yards. It would be Miami's longest rushing play of the game. It also was the Dolphins' high point of the afternoon.

Because on the next snap, Csonka fumbled.

After 195 clean carries in the regular season and 40 more in the playoffs, Csonka coughed up the ball without even being hit. Bob Griese had stuffed the handoff into Csonka's belly, and he simply didn't get his arms around it.

Chuck Howley recovered, and Roger Staubach put together a solid drive. Facing third-and-goal from the two, the Cowboys had the perfect play to call. It was pass they knew would draw a linebacker and safety to either Duane Thomas or Mike Ditka. All Staubach had to do was wait and see who the Dolphins double-covered, then throw to the other guy.

Both defenders went to Thomas, leaving Ditka wide open. But Staubach goofed. He threw to Thomas anyway. He caught it, but was stopped for no gain. Ditka was still cussing out Staubach when Mike Clark kicked a 9-yard field goal that put Dallas up 3–0. Landry came away satisfied with the 50 yards they gained that drive, not fretting the final two they couldn't get.

"Eventually it's going to come to you if you keep moving it," Landry said.

Preventing the other team from moving it helps, too. And the game's defining play soon followed.

Griese dropped back to pass on third-and-9 from the Miami 38. The Cowboys came after him with their "limbo" rush—Bob Lilly going outside, George Andrie going inside.

Two Dolphins tried slowing Lilly as he approached from Griese's blind side, but he plunged between them. Griese couldn't see that. He was watching Larry Cole charge at him from the other side of the line. It was only when Griese turned to retreat that he realized Lilly was coming, too.

Griese ran toward his end zone, tried to set up to throw again, then turned and ran farther back. Lilly pulled him down at the 9-yard line, a loss of 29 yards.

"I could see him getting panicky, knowing he was so close to the end zone," Lilly said. "He wanted to dump the ball, but he never had a chance."

The Cowboys stretched the lead late in the second quarter on a drive that featured a series of runs all predicated on wiping out Nick Buoniconti. The big play on the drive was a pass to Lance Alworth over the middle that went for 21 yards on third-and-9. He was the target again on first-and-goal from the 7.

Landry called a play Dallas hadn't used on the goal line all season. The idea to try it didn't come from Landry's copious prep work. Alworth recommended it on the sideline after the first scoring drive. He noticed cornerback Curtis Johnson was overplaying him toward the inside, so a pass toward the sideline would be open.

Staubach was supposed to hit Alworth around the four, but only faked the throw. That drew Johnson toward the outside, making the eventual pass a lot more risky.

"I threw the ball as hard as I could, harder than I can remember throwing a ball at that short a distance," Staubach said. "I don't know how he held onto it."

Alworth not only grabbed it, but he also had the presence of mind to tap his toes inbounds before kicking the pylon and stepping out of bounds.

He was just thrilled Johnson didn't catch it.

"The guy barely missed it," Alworth said. "I could see a 99-yard interception or something of that nature."

With 70 seconds left until halftime, and Miami 75 yards from the end zone, Landry went into a prevent defense. It prevented the Dolphins from scoring a touchdown, all right, but it allowed them to gain enough yards to kick a 31-yard field goal in the final seconds.

The halftime show was a salute to Louis Armstrong, the quintessential New Orleans musician who had died the previous summer. The tribute came from an eclectic mix of Ella Fitzgerald, Carol Channing, Hirt, and the U.S. Marine Corps drill team.

While they performed, both coaches adjusted their game plans.

Don Shula recognized Dallas was targeting Buoniconti, so he ordered his linemen to squish together, making it harder for the Cowboys to get to him. Landry expected that, so he told the running backs to start running wide. His coaching masterpiece continued.

For all that was going Dallas' way, the Cowboys led only 10–3—way too close for comfort. At least they were getting the ball to start the second half.

Eight plays later, Dallas was in control for good.

Seven of those plays were runs around the end, an in-your-face mocking of Shula's big change. Walt Garrison loosened things up with some short runs, then Duane Thomas broke off a 23-yarder. Bob Hayes followed with a reverse to the other side for 16 yards.

From the three, Staubach was supposed to roll to his right, but he noticed that backup linebacker Bob Matheson was in the game. And, based on where Matheson lined up, Staubach knew the pressure would be coming from his right. So he changed the play.

Calling his only audible of the game, Staubach rolled left and pitched the ball to Thomas. Safety Dick Anderson read the play and ran right at Thomas. But Thomas saw Anderson coming and avoided him, walking in for a touchdown that stretched the lead to 17–3.

Miami had no answer. Forced to throw to try getting back into the game, Griese saw Kiick open toward the sideline and threw his way. What he didn't see was that Howley had gone to the ground blocking a tight end and was about to get up—right in the path of the ball headed to Kiick.

"The ball was thrown perfect," Howley said. "For me."

Howley intercepted it at midfield and took off for the end zone, with blockers there to escort him. He was headed for an easy touchdown. Until he fell at the nine. It was a lot like Andrie's pivotal play against Minnesota, all the way down to the stumbling finish.

"I guess my feet just couldn't keep up with my legs," Howley said.

Three plays later, Staubach made up for having missed Ditka wide open in the end zone on the early series by hitting him for a touchdown. Staubach only was supposed to look at Ditka to freeze the safety, then turn and throw to Hayes. But there wasn't a defender anywhere near Ditka, so Staubach threw it to him. The seven-yard touchdown pass made it 24–3.

Adderley looked into the stands and noticed Dolphins fans were no longer waving their $1 white hankies.

"I know why," he said. "They're crying in them!"

Miami finally achieved the milestone of cracking the Dallas 20-yard line on the ensuing drive. But the Dolphins hardly had time to savor it. On the next snap, Griese pulled away from center too soon and fumbled. Cole recovered, and the Cowboys would drive to the Miami 20.

Along the way, Thomas had a four-yard run that took Dallas across midfield. It's notable because it turned out to be his final carry for the Cowboys. Ever.

The drive stalled at a fourth-and-1. Dallas lined up for a 27-yard field goal that Landry had no intention of kicking. He called a fake, but not because he wanted to run up the score. All he wanted to do was prevent a disaster.

Landry thought back to the touchdowns Dallas allowed on missed field goals earlier in the year and further back to all the agonizing big-game losses over the franchise's history. Figuring that a botched kick returned for a touchdown would be the only way to jumpstart a Miami rally, Landry told holder Dan Reeves to try running for a first down. Even if he was stopped short, all the Dolphins would get was the ball.

Reeves gained seven yards, and the game was all but over. Dallas' final snap of the season came from the one-yard line. Calvin Hill reverted of his habit of trying to dive over the goal line, and this time it cost him a touchdown in the Super Bowl. He wasn't merely stopped; he fumbled and Miami recovered.

Oh well.

In the biggest game of their lives, the Cowboys were practically perfect. They could certainly live with this fumble.

As time trickled away, Craig Morton went to Landry and said, "What do you think, Coach?"

"I think it's pretty nice," Landry said.

"Congratulations," Morton said, smiling and shaking his hand. "I'm really happy for you."

Fans chanted a countdown of the final five seconds. When the clock stuck 0:00, Lilly, Garrison, Rayfield Wright, and John Niland lifted Landry for a celebratory shoulder ride from the sideline to midfield. Landry's smile was so big, so pure.

Lee Roy Jordan stood off to the side, smiling and breathing easy. Lilly ran into the locker room and leaped with joy.

Their burden was gone. Gone! The Dallas Cowboys were Super Bowl champions, the kings of the NFL.

"I feel like I could jump all the way out of the stadium," Lilly said.

After all the years of waiting, wondering what it was like to be on top, the thrill washed over everyone. Especially the short guy with the buzz cut and glasses.

Clint Murchison Jr. dreamed of this since he first saw the Dallas Texans play in 1952. He started the franchise in 1959, hired the right people to run it and, most of all, was patient. He continued believing in Tex Schramm, Landry, and everyone they believed in through each season-ending loss. After a first-round exit in 1969, Murchison declared the Cowboys would be "the team of the seventies." The past spring, after a Super Bowl loss, he predicted the '71 club would not only be champions but among the greatest clubs of all time. Doggone if he wasn't right. The Cowboys won their last 10 games and buzzed through the playoffs. Their three post-season games went from good to better to best. The offense was so sharp that it had only two meaningless turnovers. The defense was so stiff that it allowed one meaningless touchdown. The destruction of Miami in the

Super Bowl would become more impressive based on what the Dolphins did next—winning every single game the following season and claiming the next two Super Bowl titles.

"This," Murchison said, "is the successful conclusion of our 12-year plan."

Landry was no plastic man now. His coaching brilliance was validated. "The thing that has escaped us," as he called it, was safely in his possession. Forever.

In the locker room, he explained how they did it, the strategies and counterstrategies that broke just right. He talked about wanting "to stay in the game with them for a half, and then win it in the second half," and about sensing determination in his players before kickoff.

"They had a chip-on-the-shoulder attitude, very short-tempered," Landry said. "They were ready."

He laughed when a phone call everyone expected would be from President Nixon turned out to be a message for announcer Pat Summerall. Nixon called soon enough, praising Dallas' offensive line and congratulating the whole team.

"He said he thought it was one of the best performances he'd ever seen and so much like the Vince Lombardi tradition that it was fitting the world championship trophy is named after Lombardi," Landry said.

Landry didn't bring up having snuffed the play to Warfield. Nixon didn't mention it either.

"We won it on good overall performance and heart and desire," Landry said.

The $15,000 reward for each member of the winning team had been so important for so long. Now that it was theirs, it felt more like the bonus it was supposed to be. Winning and being cemented as winners—as players, as a franchise—that's what this was all about.

"They can't say we don't win the big one anymore," Schramm said.

"Nobody can take that away from us," Hayes said.

"God, it's just great," Jordan said. "We've gotten rid of any psychological block—if there ever was one."

"The money may soon be gone, but we'll always have the satisfaction of having won this world championship," Hill said.

"And we'll be back," Schramm said. "This is just a start. We'll be stronger in the next six years."

Reeves was the ringleader of the kind of ritual only big, strong athletes could get away with—tossing their fully clothed bosses in the showers.

"C'mon," Reeves told Schramm, "we've been looking for you."

Murchison got a Super Bowl baptism, too.

"Just to show you how confident I was," Murchison said, "I brought a change of clothes along."

Did he do that last year?

"No comment," he said.

That underscored the difference between this championship and last year's near-miss. Against Baltimore, the Cowboys were glad to be in the Super Bowl and hoped to win. Against Miami, they were only there to win.

Staubach changed everything, the last two and a half months and today. A proud navy man, he had the greatest contribution to steadying the ship. He guided Dallas to enough points to always be ahead, and he made sure drives lasted long enough for the defense to get some rest. His stat sheet in this game was solid: 12 of 19 for 119 yards and two touchdowns, with five rushes for 18 yards.

Thomas was the Cowboys' most dynamic offensive player. He ran 19 times for 95 yards and a touchdown, and caught three passes for 17 more yards. The only reason his numbers weren't more spectacular was because they didn't have to be. Dallas still had Garrison (14 carries, 74 yards) and Hill (seven carries, 25 yards).

Thomas deserved the MVP award and the sports car that went with it. He only had himself to blame for being shunned. *Sport* magazine gave it to Staubach simply because organizers knew he'd be a classy recipient. There was no telling what Thomas might do, or if he'd even speak during the interviews and ceremonies that went along with the honor.

"Holy cow!" Staubach said when told he was named MVP. He shook his head and called it a mistake.

"Don't get me wrong," he said. "I'm not going to give the car back. I have three young daughters, and I can use it. But in this game, quarterbacks appear to be singled out more than any other players and sometimes they get more credit sometimes than the other guys. I was just fortunate to be on a really good team." (True to his family-man form, Staubach arranged to receive a station wagon instead of a sports car.)

Staubach wasn't the rub-it-in type, so he didn't point out to Landry that he'd become the first third-year starter to win a Super Bowl.

Besides, he played more like a 29-year-old than a kid still learning the ropes.

Dallas went 13–0 in games he started this season. He threw only one interception after being named the No. 1 quarterback, none in his 51 post-season passes, and he was still talking about needing to improve.

"I'm going to work harder this offseason than ever before. I'm going to start working out in March. I'm going to study films," Staubach said. "Football fans are a strange breed. They are with me now because we are winners. But next year if I start having some bad games, they'll turn on me just as they would on anyone else. Believe me, I don't take myself too seriously at this stage. I haven't played one full year yet. I can't let down."

As for that loose cannon Thomas, he was as unpredictable as ever.

He'd been one of the first players into the locker room and among the first to shower, seemingly in a rush to leave as usual.

Jim Brown came into the locker room to join him. He had to wait while Thomas was in the shower.

"Hey, Jim Brown! I've always wanted to meet you," Garrison said.

"Walt, you're fantastic," Brown said, much to Garrison's delight.

Brown found Thomas toweling off near the shower.

"Great game," Brown said.

"Thanks," Thomas said.

"What are you doing now—you talkin' or you playin'?" Brown said with a smile.

Thomas laughed. Then he made his way to a raised platform in the middle of the room. NFL Commissioner Pete Rozelle had presented the Lombardi Trophy to Landry and Lilly on this stage and now CBS commentator Tom Brookshier was interviewing all the stars.

Brookshier hardly knew what to ask Thomas. He introduced himself, rambled on about Brown, who was standing behind Thomas, then stumbled to his first question.

"Duane, you do things with great speed, but you never hurry," Brookshier said. "Are you that fast? Are you that quick?"

"Evidently," Thomas said.

Everyone but Thomas laughed. So Brookshier asked Brown to quantify Thomas' speed.

"Well, actually, Duane Thomas is probably the most gifted runner in football today," Brown said. "He's big and he has great speed. It's very obvious that he has fantastic moves. I think that he's probably as smart as any football player playing today. So that combination is fantastic."

"Duane, people don't know you," Brookshier said. "I know this is sort of a tight situation."

"Are you nervous, Tom?" Brown interjected, laughing.

"I'm nervous. I'm getting the interview, I'm nervous!" Brookshier said, laughing, and looking away. Turning back to Thomas, he said, "Do you like football?"

"Yeah, I do," Thomas said. "I do. But that's why I went out for pro ball. That's what I am, a football player."

The awkward conversation continued, with small talk about Thomas' weight.

"It all depends on what I need," Thomas said.

Brown realized what a train wreck this interview was. The whole point of doing it was to get out a message. Since it wasn't coming out in the course of conversation, Brown asked to speak and Brookshier gladly let him.

"Duane feels good today," Brown said. "I think he wanted to win the Super Bowl. He wanted to play football. He wanted to come back and show the American public that he is a good football player. I think that has been accomplished. I think his silence has enabled him to do this. Because there was no controversy involved. There was no conflict with his teammates or his coaches. I think he should be commended for this. But I don't think he wants to say anything more at this particular time."

Thomas left the platform and, for the first time in months, answered questions for the reporters who'd followed him all year. It turned out as awkward as the TV interview.

Are you happy?

"I never said I was sad," Thomas said.

You don't look happy.

"Happiness is inside," he said.

Most of the exhausted, exhilarated players were in no hurry to leave. They'd worked their whole lives for this and wanted to share it with each other, with the guys who'd made it possible.

Six months ago to the day, the Cowboys opened training camp. At the start of November, halfway through the season, they were 4–3 and on the verge of losing hope. Everything they had been through—in recent years, as well as recent months—had been so hard. But the last step had been so easy.

They could wear the label of champions with pride because of the tough road they traveled to earn it. Had it been a smooth ride, there's no way it would have meant as much.

"I'm more satisfied with having won for the benefit of the Howleys and the Lillys," Landry said. "I never had a chance to play on a championship team, and I was afraid that maybe some of these guys would miss it too. That's my greatest satisfaction."

Howley and Lilly arrived in 1961, after Landry's ragtag debut club went 0–11–1. The Cowboys had literally never won a game without them. They were part of championship-caliber teams that couldn't get it done the last five years, always falling victim to one thing or another—a wayward pass or an unlucky cold front, an obstacle of their own making or plain old bad luck. That trophy from Tiffany's being passed around the locker room made it all worthwhile.

"Bygones should be bygones now," Howley said. "We knew we could win the big one. But you get scared when you get there so often and you don't come away with it."

Regardless of how close they had gotten, players fear never getting another chance. That was among the things burning in Lilly's mind when he hurled his helmet at the end of Super Bowl V—*What if I never get this close again?*

Now the championship was his, and Lilly had one more thing to do. It was time to light the victory cigar that went unused a year ago and had spent the year since in his freezer.

Lilly brought it to New Orleans and kept it in his locker throughout the game. Still in his uniform, Lilly peeled it out of the plastic wrapper only to find that it was dried out and falling apart. So?

Holding it together with one hand, he lit it with the other. There was enough life left to blow out some celebratory puffs of smoke. The fuzzy gray lines rose and vanished, just like the team's reputation as underachievers.

Can't win the big one? Next year's champions? Super Bowl bridesmaids? Lilly and the Cowboys didn't have to hear it any more.

Lilly went throughout the locker room sharing the moment with the people who helped make it possible, this group that had just done what no Cowboys team had ever done.

"It's like all your life you've been trying to climb a hill," he said, "and finally—*finally*—you get to the top."

# Afterword: The Legacy

THE 1971 SEASON WAS the turning point in Dallas Cowboys history, the dawn of an amazing transformation.

"Next year's champions" were Super Bowl champions, on their way to becoming "America's Team."

Great timing helped the franchise blossom. The Cowboys established themselves as perennial contenders at the same time the NFL was establishing itself as the nation's favorite sport. For instance, Super Bowl VI wasn't very dramatic, yet it drew the largest television audience of any show in U.S. history. The Cowboys would remain a popular draw on television, with the 1972 arrival of those lovely ladies known as the Dallas Cowboys Cheerleaders also being good for business.

As the years passed and more great Dallas teams followed, the 1971 team became an afterthought. It became taken for granted that the Cowboys were always championship material. Well, they were—they just had a bunch of prominent failures before they actually became champions. That's why the '71 club deserves a special designation just for being reputation-changers, especially considering how drastic of a change it was: the U-turn from being the team that couldn't win the big one to the NFL team most associated with greatness.

"I don't care how many Super Bowls you win, the first one is the most important," Lee Roy Jordan said. "Until you get that first one, you're just another team."

There's also the plain fact that the '71 Cowboys were a great team. Look how well they stack up among all Super Bowl champions:

- The roster featured nine future Hall of Famers: Herb Adderley, Lance Alworth, Mike Ditka, Forrest Gregg, Bob Hayes, Bob Lilly, Mel Renfro, Roger Staubach, and Rayfield Wright. No team in the Super Bowl era boasts more, and the number actually swells to eleven when Tom Landry and Tex Schramm are counted.
- They remain the only team not to allow a touchdown in the Super Bowl. They didn't give one up in the NFC Championship Game, either.
- Over their three-game playoff run, they allowed one touchdown and 18 points. The 1985 Chicago Bears are the only other team to march through the postseason allowing just one touchdown and the only team to surrender fewer points (10).
- Several records the Cowboys set in Super Bowl VI have been surpassed, but remain among the best, such as their 252 yards rushing, time of possession (39 minutes, 12 seconds), and 10 first downs allowed.
- Their lopsided (24–3) victory in the Super Bowl is more impressive considering the team they whipped won every game the next season and the next two Super Bowl titles. Dolphins coach Don Shula said losing to Dallas forced him to sharpen his strategies. Miami players said that loss motivated them throughout their perfect season.
- The Cowboys never trailed over the final six and a half games, which means they were tied or ahead for 26 straight quarters. They were never behind by more than a touchdown over their last 12 games (48 quarters).
- The Cowboys' 10-game winning streak that culminated with the championship was the longest in the NFL since World War II. It has been topped only by the 1972 Dolphins (17 in a row), 2003 New England Patriots (15), 1976 Oakland Raiders (13), 1986 New York Giants and 1984 San Francisco 49ers (12), and 2000 Baltimore Ravens (11).
- Their three losses were by a total of 18 points.

In 2006, NFL Films polled 53 experts to rank the best champions through the first 40 Super Bowls. They put the 1971 Cowboys at No. 15.

In *Dominance: The Best Seasons of Pro Football's Greatest Teams*, author Eddie Epstein used extensive statistical formulas to analyze every team and season through 2001. The calculations showed how much better a team was compared to everyone else that season. His computer spit out the 1971 Cowboys as the ninth-best team of all time.

In 2010, as part of the buildup to the first Super Bowl held in North Texas, organizers asked fans to rank the 100 greatest moments in the first 100 years of football in the region. The 1971 Cowboys topped 'em all.

The camaraderie among the '71 Cowboys also endures, as Pat Toomay discovered in April 2010.

Toomay lives in New Mexico and rarely attends Cowboys alumni events. But he came in for a party prior to the implosion of Texas Stadium. He found himself drawn to a large group of '71 guys. Looking around, he could tell there were more of them together, and having more fun being together, than guys from other eras.

"We flock together," said Jordan, a regular at such get-togethers. "It's like a magnet—whomp!"

The main reason is that so many of those guys were together for so long, through good times and bad.

Nearly all were part of the loss in Super Bowl V. About one-third of the 1971 roster was in Dallas all the way back to the Ice Bowl in 1967 and the NFL Championship loss in '66.

Thus, the '71 title really was a culmination of their hard work, with relative newcomers like Staubach, Calvin Hill, and Duane Thomas providing the final push to reach the top of pro football.

"The years that we lost, or didn't get there, those were battles; in 1971, we finally won the war," Lilly said. "That was the glue. When we finally won the big one, it created a bond that will never be forgotten."

Said Garrison: "I think any time you struggle you become a close-knit group because everybody hates you. You get a title like 'Can't win the big one' and 'Next year's champions' and the only people that like you are the people in there with you. You become a close-knit group because everybody else hates you. I don't think I'll ever play in another Super Bowl. But I'll always be friends with those guys."

# Acknowledgments

THE NIGHT THAT TOM Landry called Roger Staubach to say he'd be the starting quarterback the rest of the season was a big night in my life, too. It was my first birthday. So in putting together this book about events I did not witness, I relied on the memories of those who were there and on the work of the journalists who chronicled the season.

A huge thanks goes out to the players who took the time to share stories of days and games roughly four decades past—although I got the sense they enjoyed it, too. Rayfield Wright was the first player I approached about this project; he smiled wide and said, "I'm always willing to talk about 1971."

Rich Dalrymple and the Dallas Cowboys provided a huge boost by making their archives so readily available. Mike Knoop, Tom Orsborn, and Barry Robinson helped pluck some gems from the archive of the *San Antonio Express-News*. John McFarland provided an extra set of eyeballs when needed, and even made it through Chapter 25 despite being a devoted Vikings fan.

Most of all, this wouldn't have been possible without the patience, tolerance, and understanding of my wife, Lori, and our sons Zac, Jake, and Josh. They knew what it meant if I was sitting at the card table-turned-desk next to the real desk in my office. This was my fifth book, but first narrative. It was a new challenge, and it required more hours than several other books combined.

I hope you enjoyed the final product as much as I enjoyed putting it together.

# Bibliography

## Books

Adler, Brad. *Coaching Matters*. Washington, D.C.: Potomac Books, 2005.

Aron, Jaime. *Dallas Cowboys: The Complete Illustrated History*. Minneapolis: MVP Books, 2010.

Aron, Jaime. *The Best Dallas–Fort Worth Sports Arguments*. Naperville, IL: Sourcebooks, 2007.

Blair, Sam. *Dallas Cowboys: Pro or Con?* New York: Doubleday, 1970.

Burton, Alan. *Dallas Cowboys Quips & Quotes*. Abilene, TX: State House Press, 2006.

Epstein, Eddie. *Dominance: The Best Seasons of Pro Football's Greatest Teams*. Washington, D.C.: Potomac Books, 2003.

Freeman, Denne H., and Jaime Aron. *I Remember Tom Landry*. Champaign, IL: Sports Publishing, 2001.

Garrison, Walt. *Once A Cowboy*. New York: Random House, 1988.

Garrison, Walt, and Mark Stallard. *"Then Landry Said to Staubach . . .": The Best Dallas Cowboys Stories Ever Told*. Chicago: Triumph Books, 2007.

Golenbock, Peter. *Landry's Boys*. Chicago: Triumph Books, 2005.

Harris, Cliff. *Captain Crash and the Dallas Cowboys: From Sideline to Goal Line with Cliff Harris*. Champaign, IL: Sports Publishing L.L.C., 2006.

Hitt, Dick. *Classic Clint: The Laughs and Times of Clint Murchison Jr.* Plano, TX: Wordware, 1992.

Klein, Dave. *Tom and the 'Boys*. New York: Kensington Publishing, 1990.

Landry, Tom, with Gregg Lewis. *Tom Landry: An Autobiography*. Grand Rapids, MI: Zondervan Publishing, 1990.

Lilly, Bob. *A Cowboy's Life*. Chicago: Triumph Books, 2008.

Merchant, Larry . . . . *And Every Day You Take Another Bite*. Garden City, NY: Doubleday & Company, Inc, 1971.

Peary, Danny, ed. *Super Bowl: The Game of Their Lives*. Darby, PA: Diane Publishing Company, 1997.

Perkins, Steve. *The Dallas Cowboys: Winning the Big One*. New York: Grosset & Dunlap, 1972.

Perkins, Steve. *Next Year's Champions: The Story of the Dallas Cowboys*. New York: World Publishing, 1969.

Phillips, Michael. *White Metropolis: Race, Ethnicity, and Religion in Dallas, 1841–2001.* Austin, TX: University of Texas Press, 2006.

Sham, Brad. *Stadium Stories: Dallas Cowboys*. Guilford, CT: Globe Pequot Press, 2003.

St. John, Bob. *The Landry Legend.* Nashville, TN: Word Publishing, 2000.

St. John, Bob. *The Man Inside . . . . Landry.* Waco, TX: Word Books, 1979.

St. John, Bob. *Tex! The Man Who Built the Dallas Cowboys.* Englewood Cliffs, NJ: Prentice Hall, 1988.

St. John, Bob. *We Love You Cowboys.* New York: Sport Magazine Press, 1972.

Staubach, Roger, with Frank Luksa. *Time Enough to Win.* Waco, TX: Word Books, 1980.

Staubach, Roger, with Sam Blair and Bob St. John. *Staubach: First Down, Lifetime to Go.* Waco, TX: Word Books, 1974.

Stowers, Carlton. *The Cowboy Chronicles: A Sportswriter's View of America's Most Celebrated Team.* Austin, TX: Eakin Press, 1984.

Stowers, Carlton. *Journey to Triumph.* Dallas, TX: Taylor Publishing Company, 1982.

Taylor, Jean-Jacques. *Game of My Life: Dallas Cowboys: Memorable Stories from Cowboys Football.* Champaign, IL: Sports Publishing LLC, 2006.

Thomas, Duane, and Paul Zimmerman. *Duane Thomas and the Fall of America's Team.* New York: Warner Books, 1989.

Toomay, Pat. *The Crunch.* New York: W. W. Norton & Co., Inc.: 1975.

Wolfe, Jane. *The Murchisons: The Rise and Fall of a Texas Dynasty.* New York: St. Martin's Press: 1991.

Wright, Rayfield. *Wright Up Front.* Dallas, TX: Emerald Press, 2005.

## Newspapers, Periodicals, and Websites

ESPN.com

NFL.com

*D* magazine archives

Dallas Cowboys media guides

*The Dallas Morning News* archives, 1959–present

*Fort Worth Star-Telegram* online archives

*Los Angeles Times* online archives

*The New York Times* online archives

*Sports Illustrated* archives, 1959–present

*Texas Monthly* archives

*Washington Post* online archives

*Time* online archives

*Pro Quarterback* past issues

Pro-football-reference.com

*Fort Worth Press,* 1971–72

*Dallas Times-Herald,* 1971–72

*Longview News-Journal,* 1971

# Index